D0856265

Vision at Work

The Theory and Practice
of Beit Rabban

The Jewish Education Series:

Barry W. Holtz, *Textual Knowledge: Teaching the Bible in Theory and in Practice* (2003)

Lisa D. Grant, Diane Tickton Schuster, Meredith Woocher, and Steven M. Cohen, *A Journey of Heart and Mind: Transformative Learning in Adulthood* (2004)

Carol K. Ingall, *Down the Up Staircase: Tales of Teaching in Jewish Day Schools* (2006)

Daniel Pekarsky, *Vision at Work: The Theory and Practice of Beit Rabban* (2006)

Vision at Work

The Theory and Practice of Beit Rabban

Daniel Pekarsky

The Jewish Theological Seminary of America

The publication of the Jewish Education Series
is made possible by the generous support
of Mr. Earle Kazis and the Kazis Publication Fund.

Cover image: Education Chart
(Livorno: Moses and Israel Palagi and Solomon Belforte, 1846) (NS) E126.
Courtesy of The Library of The Jewish Theological Seminary.

To Stephanie's parents,
Sylvia and Joe Stone,
and
To the memory of my parents,
Nell and Maurice Pekarsky
With love and gratitude

Contents

Acknowledgements

This project has developed over several years and there are numerous people who have contributed to it at different stages. First and foremost, I want to thank Devora Steinmetz, the founding director of Beit Rabban. Devora invited me into the world of Beit Rabban and granted me full access to it. Equally important, she entered into a sequence of intensive conversations with me concerning the school's development, identity, and challenges and helped me understand its educational outlook in a way that would have otherwise been impossible. When, as a result of my visits to the school, my numerous conversations with Devora, and my review of various written materials (most of them written by her), I developed various drafts of this manuscript, Devora read each one patiently and offered me invaluable feedback. It was critical to the success of this project that I develop an accurate understanding of the philosophical commitments that Devora sought to embody in Beit Rabban, and she worked tirelessly to help me "get it". Simply put: without her active support and input, this project would never have come to fruition. In addition to Devora, I would also like to thank the rest of the Beit Rabban community, including principals who followed Devora, teachers, secretaries, and, of course, the children, all of whom were unfailingly kind and informative during my visits to the school. I want especially to take note of the help of Pearl Mattenson and Ilana Blumberg.

Second, I want to emphasize my great debt to the Mandel Foundation. It was through the Mandel Foundation that this project was originally launched, and, financially and otherwise, it has continued to support this effort enthusiastically. In this regard, special thanks are due to Morton Mandel, whose generosity, wisdom, and good sense gave rise to a foundation that appreciates and supports research on education and Jewish education that insists on the importance of addressing basic questions in a serious spirit. I am also very grateful to the professional leadership of the Mandel Foundation, Annette Hochstein and Seymour Fox. They have encouraged me in this effort consistently and enthusiastically, and both of them have read and commented helpfully on various parts of the manuscript. In the case of Professor Fox, who founded the Mandel Foundation's Visions of Jewish Education Project, the debt has other dimensions as well. Not only is he the person most responsible for bringing me into the field of Jewish education, his work on vision and its relationship to practice has profoundly influenced my own thinking on these matters. The research agenda associated with vision that I have been pursuing in recent years and that has given rise to this project strongly reflects this influence.

I also want to note the summer support I have received through the Esther Leah Ritz Fund, established by the late Esther Leah Ritz to promote work at the University of Wisconsin-Madison at the intersection of education and Jewish Studies. Those of us who were privileged to know Esther Leah appreciate what a wonderful human being she was, and it is gratifying to know that the fund she established has helped to facilitate this project.

I want to acknowledge my gratitude to several individuals associated with the Jewish Theological Seminary publication series on Jewish education. As editor of the series, Barry Holtz played an invaluable role in shepherding the manuscript through the review and editorial process, while offering me encouragement and wise counsel along the way. I was, of course, delighted by the favorable assessment of the manuscript by the anonymous reviewers to whom it was sent for review; but I am also grateful to them for their insights and suggestions. I also want to thank Tamar Frank, the copy editor associated with the project, for her good judgment, her sensitivity, and her patience in the last stages of the project. The final product has been improved in discernible ways through her efforts.

Many friends and colleagues have offered insights, questions, and advice that have contributed to this project. Prominent among them are a number of individuals with whom I have worked on different Mandel Foundation projects. In addition to Barry Holtz, whom I have already mentioned in a different capacity, these individuals include Jonathan Ariel, Gail Dorph, Daniel Gordis, Michael Inbar, Mordecai Nisan, Nessa Rapoport, and Michael Rosenak. Alan Hoffmann and Karen

Barth, who at different points directed the Mandel Foundation's efforts in North America, were always supportive of the project. Daniel Marom, who directs the Foundation's Visions of Jewish Education Project, has also supported the project and the final product has benefited from his questions and advice. As individuals and as a group, the Visions of Jewish Education Professors Group organized through the Mandel Foundation has also given me terrifically helpful feedback. Members of the group include: Isa Aron, Gail Dorph, Sharon Feiman-Nemser, Carol Ingall, Barry Holtz, Bethamie Horowitz, Jon Levisohn, Jeffrey Schein, Susan Shevitz, Alex Sinclair, and Rami Wernik.

In addition to colleagues who have read all or parts of this manuscript along the way, there are also some who have commented on closely related pieces of work. Feedback of this kind from Vivienne Burstein, Jonathan Cohen, Elie Holzer, Alick Isaacs and Herbert Kliebard has been helpful to me in thinking through certain questions in this book.

I have used parts or all of the manuscript in two teaching situations: first, with the Jerusalem Fellows program, and second, with HaSha'ar, an educator preparation program that was developed under the auspices of Drisha in collaboration with Beit Rabban. Student responses to the text brought me new insights and helped me to identify both points of unclarity and issues in need of further discussion. I am grateful to Daniel Gordis, then the director of the Jerusalem Fellows, and Ruth Fagen, then the director of HaSha'ar, for making these opportunities possible.

Among the other individuals who have commented helpfully on the manuscript, there are three whom I would like to single out. The first is Professor Israel Scheffler, my advisor and mentor in graduate school and among the wisest human beings I have encountered. The second is my long-time colleague at the University of Wisconsin-Madison, Francis Schrag, who, on this and other projects I have undertaken, has consistently given me the benefit of sympathetic but honest, judicious, and thought-provoking responses. The third is my good friend of blessed memory, Joy Rochwarger Balsam, whose recent death at a tragically young age has left deep voids in the lives of so many, including her husband, her extended family, and numerous people like myself who counted her as a teacher and/or a friend. It saddens me that she is not here to see this project come to fruition.

I also want to thank my friends, including my sister, Davida Pekarsky, for their support as this project unfolded. Last but certainly not least, I would like to acknowledge my profound debt to my family: to my son Zach who, as he has grown up, has nourished my thinking in all sorts of ways he does not yet recognize; and to my wife Stephanie, who carefully reviewed the manuscript and helped me think through many of the issues that arose as the project unfolded. Most importantly, though, I thank her for being a life-giving blessing since the day we met.

General Introduction

Aspirations, Agenda, Approach

Schools organized around inspiring conceptions of what they are trying to achieve—what I will be referring to as vision-guided institutions—are few and far between. More commonly, school practice embodies multiple agendas, some of which may be at cross-purposes. These agendas grow out of different circumstances and typically reflect long-standing tradition, educational fads, local, regional, and/or national movements and pressures, and the idiosyncratic concerns of particular superintendents, principals, and teachers.[1]

That this is the case is unfortunate because we are not likely to witness significant improvement in the practice and outcomes of education until schools are guided by conceptions of the kinds of human beings and communities they aspire to cultivate, conceptions that inspire and engage the energies of educators and the communities they serve. I will be referring to such conceptions as *existential visions,* and it is my hope that this study will help to establish their pivotal role in the development of quality education. But I want to emphasize at the outset that in addition to an existential vision, a vision-guided institution requires an *educational vision.* An institution's educational vision includes but is broader than its existential vision: informed by a set of integrated beliefs concerning human nature, growth, and learning, as well as concerning present

---

[1]For a discussion of the failure of American schools, especially secondary schools, to declare themselves in any serious way for a well-conceived educational agenda, as well as of the troubling consequences of this failure, see Arthur G. Powell, Eleanor Farrar, and David K. Cohen, *The Shopping Mall High School* (Boston: Houghton Mifflin, 1985).

circumstances (cultural, technological, economic, etc.), the educational vision specifies an approach to education that is designed to achieve the outcomes identified in the existential vision in the world as we know it.[2]

I draw this distinction at the outset because it helps to fill in what I have said about the weakness of contemporary education. In suggesting that there are few adequate examples of educating institutions that are vision-guided, I am advancing a threefold claim. First, few educating institutions have a clear conception of what they are trying to achieve. Second, even those that are associated with such a conception are unlikely to have identified, much less enacted, a coherent stance concerning the way (in light of a particular interpretation of such matters as human nature, human growth and human learning) to make progress in the direction staked out by the existential vision under real-world conditions. And third, although the presence of a vision-guided institution of any kind is already a rare achievement on the contemporary educational scene, even when we can point to such an institution, we may for a variety of reasons not find the educational vision that it embodies a defensible one. We may, for example, find the existential vision that is at the heart of this educational vision problematic; or we may doubt that the recommended approach to achieving the outcomes associated with this existential vision is likely, even if implemented effectively, to achieve these outcomes; or, assuming we do affirm the approach in principle, we may doubt that it's possible, now or perhaps ever, to implement it effectively; or we may find this approach ethically problematic or too costly.

There are many reasons why vision-guided institutions in the sense just described, especially ones we might judge to embody exemplary educational visions, are not more prominent on the landscape of contemporary education; but one of them is surely that educators and the communities they serve do not regularly aspire to create them. That they don't do so can

---

[2]Although I don't know that they explicitly draw this distinction, or would draw it in the way that I have, my thinking about the distinction between existential and educational visions has benefited from conversations with Seymour Fox and Daniel Marom. An important point that has grown clearer through these conversations is that the relationship between these two senses of vision is more complex than is implied by the idea that the educational vision is a conception of education that identifies the way to achieve the outcomes identified in the existential vision. In the life of a vision-guided institution there will typically be a complex interplay between the existential vision, the other elements that make up its educational vision, and practice, an interplay through which any or all of these elements may change.

also be attributed to a number of different circumstances, none of them alone sufficient to account for this phenomenon. But of these circumstances, I want to single out an important one that gives rise to the present study: most people, educators included, have not encountered such institutions in their educational experience or even in literature and therefore lack any serious understanding of what a school guided by a powerful vision would look like. Moreover, even those who do appreciate the potential of vision-guided educating institutions are often skeptical that we can create such institutions under real-world conditions; they may therefore feel that as citizens and educators, our energies will be better spent on what they take to be more practical matters.

These considerations make it important to identify and offer portraits of vision-guided institutions that thrive in the real world. Such portraits can serve a number of useful purposes. First, far more effectively than would a bare, abstract characterization, portraits of vision-guided educating institutions will illustrate what they are and will suggest their educational potential. Second, as will be further developed below, they can serve as demonstration proofs that such institutions can come into being and flourish under real-world conditions. Third, portraits of vision-guided institutions will offer parents and educators mirrors in which to examine practice in their own institutions and an opportunity to struggle with basic questions concerning the aims of education and their reflection in practice. And finally, such portraits may inspire parents, educators, and those who make educational policy to do what needs to be done to encourage vision-guided educational practice.

Hence this study, in which I offer a philosophically-oriented portrait of Beit Rabban, a vision-guided Jewish day school located on the Upper West Side of New York City. If one were to try to capture the spirit of Beit Rabban in a nutshell, one might reasonably say that in its ethos and practices it is a cross between the Dewey School, the University of Chicago and a yeshiva.[3] Beit Rabban is like the Dewey school in its

---

[3]For a wonderful portrait of the yeshiva as an educational institution, see Moshe Halbertal and Tova Hartman Halbertal, "The Yeshiva," in Amelia Rorty, ed., *Philosophers on Education* (London: Routledge, 1998), 458–469. Of the yeshiva, the authors write: "Yeshiva life is a life of an ongoing conversation, a conversation that takes place in the *Beit Midrash*—a large, simple study hall—where students sit and study. In the famous and big Yeshivas the *Beit Midrash* holds a few hundred students whose ages range from 16 to 40 years old or even older." (458)

commitment to progressive pedagogy, a commitment that is exhibited in many ways. It is, for example, discernible in the school's emphasis on problem-based inquiry, intellectual openness, and thoughtfulness; it is also exhibited in its approach to moral education and in its conception of the classroom as a microcosm of what a human community should be.[4] It is like the University of Chicago in its intellectual seriousness; it's a place where everyone learns to take ideas and books seriously, where the activity of thinking is at the heart of the enterprise.[5] It is like a yeshiva in part because of the rich opportunities it offers its students to grow familiar and competent with fundamental Jewish texts like the Torah and the Talmud. But its yeshiva-like character also has to do with the fact that the activity of learning is regularly organized as it is in the yeshiva environment, so that the visitor encounters a room buzzing with the sounds of young children, broken into small study groups ("in *hevruta*"[6]), poring over and together trying to make sense of classical Jewish texts, each group proceeding in its own unique way.

It is hard to capture the vision that informs Beit Rabban in a simple formula, and I make no effort to do so in this introduction. But there is reason to highlight one aspect of the vision that is captured in a comment of its founder, Devora Steinmetz, now a professor at the Jewish Theological Seminary of America. "The radical idea that cuts across all of the edu-

---

[4]The discussions that follow include many references to similarities—and sometimes differences—between Beit Rabban and the Dewey School that John Dewey established in Chicago at the end of the 19th century. For useful descriptions of the Dewey School, see John Dewey, *The School and Society/The Child and the Curriculum* (Chicago: Phoenix Books, 1956). See also Katherine Mayhew and Anna Camp Edwards, *The Dewey School* (New York: Atherton Press, 1966), and Louis Wirth, *John Dewey as Educator* (Huntington, NY: R. E. Krieger, 1979).

[5]I am thinking here not just of the spirit that has historically suffused the University of Chicago but of the writings of some of the major figures—individuals like Mortimer Adler, Robert Maynard Hutchins, and Leo Strauss—associated with its approach to liberal education. See, for example, Leo Strauss, "What is Liberal Education?" in *An Introduction to Political Philosophy: Ten Essays by Leo Strauss,* ed. Hilail Gildin (Detroit: Wayne State University Press, 1989), 311–320.

[6]"In *hevruta*" is the traditional way of referring to the sustained engagement of study-partners, typically twosomes, in the effort to better understand traditional sacred texts. Etymologically, the word *hevruta,* Aramaic *companion,* is connected to the Hebrew word for *friend.* The suggestion that one's partner in learning is also one's friend is also found in Greek thought, for example, in the dialogues of Plato.

cation that goes on at Beit Rabban," Devora observed, "is that there should be reasons for the things we believe and do," an idea that's coupled with the belief that discovering these reasons requires sustained, open, and thoughtful reflection. This theme is important to mention at the outset because Beit Rabban's belief that there should be good reasons for what we believe and do finds expression not just in the school's aspirations for its students but also in the design of the school. That is, as interpreted by Devora, almost every feature of Beit Rabban (and in her aspiration, every feature) is the product of thoughtful reflection; and if it's discovered that in a certain arena practice is not adequately aligned with the school's purposes, there is a genuine interest in engaging in the kind of inquiry that will remedy this problem. In other words, there is a deep symmetry between what the school tries to nurture in the young and its own design; the school itself (as does its founding, visionary leader) embodies the approach to life that it wishes to nurture in its clientele (in the same way as John Dewey's commitment to experimentalism was expressed both in his aspirations for the students in the Dewey school and in the school's design). It is important to emphasize that Beit Rabban is vision-guided in the strong sense discussed above. It is committed to an existential vision that identifies the kinds of human beings and community education should be striving to cultivate, *and* this existential vision is situated within a broader educational vision that represents a developed set of ideas concerning the way to make progress in the direction staked out by the existential vision with the school's particular clientele. That said, it is relevant to add that in discussing Beit Rabban's guiding vision in the pages that follow, there is often no need to specify whether I'm talking about the school's existential vision or its broader educational vision. In most cases, this is because the context will make this clear; in others, it's because the point being made applies to the vision in both senses.

The nature of the portrait. This portrait of Beit Rabban is based on a number of varied encounters with the school and its guiding ideas, most of which took place in a period that began in 1996 and extended through 1998. These encounters included observations of the school at work on some seven day-long visits and the opportunity to review different kinds of written documents. These documents included the school's characterizations of itself in publicity, in letters to parents, in application materials, and in its regular newsletters; formal policy statements relating to such matters as homework and community service; and detailed summaries of several sequences of class sessions. Other materials made available to me include articles about the school written by Devora Steinmetz and one of the teachers. Of critical importance during this period were numerous conversations with Devora, several of them two or more hours long, in which she worked hard to help me develop deeper understandings of the school and the outlook it embodies. It was also my good fortune that Devora continued, beyond that period (indeed, down to the present), to contribute her time and energy to this project: not only did she continue meeting with me in person and through long-distance phone calls in response to new questions that I had, but she also responded carefully to my efforts to articulate my emerging understandings in successive drafts of this manuscript. I also benefited from the fact that many of my conversations with her were preceded or followed by her written responses to questions under discussion.

When Devora ceased being the director of the school at the end of the 1996–97 school year, the school was directed for a year by Pearl Mattenson, who already knew the school very well and whose educational outlook was in many respects continuous with Devora's. She too offered me ready access to the school and generously gave of her time in response to my questions. Following Pearl's tenure, which, due to personal reasons, was brief, the school seemed, under its newest director, on the verge of changing direction, if only temporarily. Though I was no longer actively studying the school in this last period and do not feel prepared to speak in this volume about the changes that may have been introduced at this time (or later on), I do, near the end of the manuscript, consider the potential impact of the departure of an institution's visionary leader, with attention to the challenges, dangers and opportunities that may attend such an important change.

I refer to the portrait I offer as philosophical for three interrelated reasons. First, I am primarily interested in Beit Rabban as an attempt to embody, under real-world conditions, some serious ideas about the aims and the nature of education. I try to identify what these key ideas are, to understand why they are taken to be important, and to examine how they get interpreted and expressed in the school's daily life. Second, I describe the portrait as philosophical because embedded in my discussion of Beit Rabban is a claim concerning the centrality of philosophy to education: education, especially the education of the young, is at its core a philosophical enterprise in the sense that it ought to be guided by our deepest convictions about the way to approach life (both, in general and in the circumstances in which we find ourselves). Finally, I refer to the account as philosophical because it implicitly suggests that those deep convictions that establish the core of an educational agenda should themselves be the product of careful reflection.[7] The genesis of Beit Rabban and its work-ings exhibit a philosophical orientation in all of these senses. That is, Beit Rabban is not just a vision-guided institution in the minimal sense that it is informed by a coherent educational conception that elicits the support of its core stakeholders, but also in the stronger sense that this conception embodies deep convictions concerning the nature and aims of education, convictions that have themselves survived thoughtful examination.

The genre to which this research belongs. As already intimated, this research stands close to, but does not fall squarely within the tradition of philosophically-driven utopian portraits (represented by Plato's *Republic*[8] and, more recently, by Aldous Huxley's *Island*[9] and B.F. Skinner's *Walden II*[10]). Like such portraits, the one I paint is designed to enlarge our understanding of the possible, to get us to reflect critically on the merits and practical implications of a certain constellation of ideas con-cerning life and education, and to guide us towards an appreciation of what it means to inhabit a community in which, in contrast to much of "real life" as we know it, ideas truly guide practice.[11] More specifically, the aspiration that guides the selection and description of the settings, sit-uations, and episodes that make up my portrait of Beit Rabban is to ex-hibit and explore the rationale for the ideas around which the school is organized, as well as to illuminate how a school that is serious about its guiding ideas struggles to interpret and embody them in practice. Put dif-

---

[7]While I am sympathetic to the notion that a community's guiding educational ideas should be the product of systematic reflection, I can imagine circumstances under which I would not encourage a community to enter into this kind of a process.

[8]Plato, *The Republic*, trans. G. M. A. Grube (Indianapolis: Hackett Publishing Com-pany, 1992).

[9]Aldous Huxley, *Island* (New York: Bantam Books, 1962).

[10]B. F. Skinner, *Walden II* (New York: MacMillan, 1948).

[11]One recalls here the opening passage of Plato's *Republic* (327a-328c), in which a group of friends playfully insist that their collective strength will suffice to get an un-willing Socrates to change his plans so as to join them in conversation. Socrates re-sponds with another possibility—that he will succeed in convincing them to let him be on his way. The vignette highlights the difference between a world in which power dictates practice and one that is guided by rationally defensible ideas. The passage not only prefigures the major themes of the *Republic* as a whole, it also points to the tension in social life and education across the ages between practices that reflect ex-isting relations of power (as well as blind allegiance to tradition) and those that re-flect our best thinking.

ferently, I try, as do the authors of educational utopias, to reveal the school's intellectual infrastructure and its reflection in practice.

There is, however, a significant respect in which the school I describe differs from portraits of educational utopias: it is based on a real, living institution. That is, although I am not a trained social scientist, this portrait is anchored in empirical observations of an existing school, and it purports to offer a true-to-life picture of this institution—one that captures the school's spirit and that would be recognizable to those who spend time there or visit it. I emphasize this because the fact that I'm describing a real school is central to this project's agenda. In explanation of this point, note, first, that had my aspiration been limited to illustrating the nature of vision-guided educational practice, I could have accomplished this through the construction of an educational utopia that is a figment of my imagination. But though this might have been a useful endeavor, it is predictable that some thoughtful readers who are interested in educational reform would have been intrigued but also dissatisfied. "Yes," they might have said, "the idea of vision-guided educating institutions is inspiring, but it's no more than a philosopher's pipe dream, incapable of realization under real-world conditions." In adopting this stance, they would be placing themselves in a long tradition of educational pessimism—a tradition which may, unfortunately, contribute to a destructive self-fulfilling prophecy. For the conviction that the institutions of our dreams can be no more than dreams may undermine fruitful efforts to build such institutions. If the pessimism that discourages such efforts is unwarranted, it is important to dislodge it.

Perhaps the most effective way of challenging the pessimist's view that the kinds of schools we would like to see can be no more than pipe dreams is to show that such schools have come into being and continue to exist. The intuition at the heart of this approach to vindicating the possibility of creating exemplary institutions is captured in Robert Merton's observation: "Whatever is, is possible."[12] Our ability to point to institutions which skeptics believe impossible is thus a kind of "existence proof" that such institutions can come into being.[13]

---

[12]Charles Silberman, *Crisis in the Classroom* (New York: Random House, 1970), 95.
[13]I owe the term *existence proof* to Seymour Fox, who, in turn, credits Lee Shulman with coining it. For a discussion of the idea, see Seymour Fox, Israel Scheffler, and Daniel Marom, eds., *Visions of Jewish Education* (Cambridge, England: Cambridge University Press, 2003), 262.

The present project is very much within this "existence proof" tradition. As against those who believe that vision-guided practice is an impossibility under real-world conditions, I point to Beit Rabban as a living counter-example, with the hope that its existence will give pessimists pause and will inspire others to try to build imaginative and well-conceived vision-guided educating institutions. At the same time, I don't want to minimize the difficulty of doing so in the real world. Not only is it hard to establish such schools, it is also difficult to sustain them once they have come into being. As a way of reminding the reader of this point and giving it more substance, my account of Beit Rabban will pay serious attention to some of the problems and challenges the school has had to face. Attention to these matters is very relevant to our thinking about the challenges that are likely to be encountered when one attempts to translate ideas into practice under the complex, ever-changing conditions that life presents. More practically, awareness of some of the difficult challenges that educators are likely to face in their efforts to develop viable vision-guided institutions that run against the grain of contemporary educational practice has the potential to enhance the effectiveness of these efforts. The other side of this coin, however, is that an appreciation of these challenges becomes destructive if it gives rise to a paralyzing pessimism concerning our ability to achieve vision-guided practice. Such pessimism is, I believe, unwarranted, and I will be disappointed if my discussion leads readers to the contrary conclusion.

There is, finally, yet another tradition of research to which the present study belongs, a tradition that explores the principle that a serious guiding vision or conception is integral to education at its best. Though this idea is as old as Plato's *Republic*, it is often honored in the breach and is sometimes challenged on theoretical grounds by those who do not believe that quality education requires the presence of a guiding existential vision.[14] The result has been that much educational theorizing and planning today proceeds on the assumption that guiding visions are not necessary and may well be undesirable. The contrary view, the one

---

[14]Such a view is often associated with, and may have actually been asserted by John Dewey. As I have argued elsewhere, however, Dewey's outlook tacitly embodies a vision which gives powerful direction to his educational agenda and practice. See Daniel Pekarsky, "Guiding Visions and Educational Planning," in Barry Franklin, ed., *Curriculum and Consequence* (New York: Teachers College Press, 2000), 15–29.

that informs this project, has been convincingly articulated in recent years by a number of thinkers who have been focused on the challenges of Jewish education in the contemporary world. More specifically, the Mandel Foundation has encouraged important research—research with implications for general as well as for Jewish education—that has high-lighted the nature of, the case for, and the implications of a vision-guided approach to education.[15] My own work on this project has benefited immensely from the opportunity to learn from those who have been engaged in this work, both through conversation and through their published work; and my hope is that the present project will contribute to the further development of this tradition of inquiry.

To whom is this study addressed? This study is addressed to two different but overlapping audiences. One of them is a general commu-nity of individuals, both lay and professional, who are interested in the challenges of contemporary education. I believe that this study can en-rich their thinking about the potentialities of vision-guided education and strengthen their interest in fostering vision-guided educational prac-tice; and, because of the character of Beit Rabban's vision, it may en-courage educational progressives who have come to view serious religious education as hostile to their liberal agenda to revisit their as-sumptions in a critical spirit. More specifically, though we have some examples of vision-guided educational institutions in general education (the schools described in Lightfoot's *The Good High School*,[16] Deborah Meier's portrait of Central Park East,[17] descriptions of the Dewey School, and Summerhill[18] come to mind), such portraits are still less common than one might hope. And even rarer is a portrait of a vision-guided institution which, though avowedly sectarian and religious in its orientation, is nonetheless suffused with intellectual openness, curiosity, and a commitment to thoughtful inquiry. The tendency among many

---

[15]See, for example, Seymour Fox with Bill Novak, *Vision at the Heart: Lessons from Camp Ramah on the Power of Ideas in Shaping Educational Institutions* (Jerusalem & New York: The Mandel Institute and the Council for Initiatives in Jewish Educa-tion, 1997); Fox, Scheffler, and Marom, eds., *Visions* (Cambridge, England: Cam-bridge University Press, 2003); Mordecai Nisan, *"Educational Identity" as a Factor in the Development of Educational Leadership* (Jerusalem: Mandel Institute, 1997).
[16]Sarah Lawrence Lightfoot, *The Good High School* (New York: Basic Books, 1983).
[17]Deborah Meier, *The Power of Their Ideas* (Boston: Beacon Press, 1995).
[18]A. S. Neill, *Summerhill School* (New York: St. Martin's Press, 1992).

liberals to view religion and intellectual openness as necessarily in oppo-
sition is challenged by the Beit Rabban experiment—challenged not just
at the level of theory but also at that of practice and lived experience.
Here is a school that insists that serious religious commitment and participation in the life of a cultural subgroup can, and indeed should, walk
hand in hand with a life of open-minded, rigorous, and thoughtful inquiry, with an interest in the events and cultural currents transpiring in
American society, and with the desire to ameliorate the suffering found
in this society.

This is not to say that I expect every thoughtful person to be sympathetic to the idea of educating Jewish children in separation from children who come from different cultural and religious groups. Even after
encountering the Beit Rabban experiment, surely some thoughtful readers will continue to believe that the road to a multicultural society in
which the members of different religious and ethnic groups treat each
other with respect and appreciation travels through schools where the
children from these different groups meaningfully interact with one another on a daily basis in classrooms and other settings.[19] This is not the
occasion to systematically enter into the controversy between those who
hold this view and those who champion more parochial forms of education. Suffice it to say that it is far from clear that the children who go to
Beit Rabban will grow up ill equipped to enter into productive, mutually respectful relationships with the members of other groups: the
habits of heart and mind that the school encourages, its interest in the
groups and the problems of the larger society, and the fact that the children in this school inhabit a culturally, racially, and ethnically mixed
community outside of school, may jointly prepare these youngsters to
enter into such relationships with individuals from groups other than
their own. In fact, in view of the troubling educational and social realities in many urban schools whose populations do include children from
a rich mix of backgrounds, it would not be surprising to discover that
the graduates of Beit Rabban are often better prepared than the graduates of these schools to enter into positive relationships with the members of other cultural subgroups. Though this is, at this point, no more
than speculative, it ought at least to be considered before dismissing sectarian schools like Beit Rabban as enemies of the liberal aspiration of

[19]See, for example, Mary Metz, "Desegregation as Necessity and Challenge," *Journal
of Negro Education*, 63:1, 1994, 64–75.

encouraging mutual respect among the different economic, cultural and religious groups that make up American society.[20]

There is also another way in which Beit Rabban challenges misleading stereotypes held by some liberal educational and social theorists. Just as such individuals may wrongly assume that religious educating institutions have agendas that are inherently hostile to liberal social and intellectual ideals, so too, some may believe that the very ideal of vision-guided practice is hostile to such ideals. After all, if the job of a vision-guided educating institution is to cultivate human beings who will embody a particular conception of how life should be lived, is not such an institution indoctrinatory?[21] Though it's surely true that some vision-guided institutions are indoctrinatory, the existence of educating institutions like Beit Rabban, whose guiding existential visions and practice embrace respect for, and an aspiration to cultivate, the learner's potential for intellectual autonomy and rationality, is a powerful counter-example to any facile equation of "vision-guided" with "anti-liberal" or "indoctrinatory." Indeed, a guiding principle of this project is that our capacity to achieve liberal ideals through education may actually require the development of vision-guided educating institutions. Whether or not readers come to agree with this view, it is my hope that the example of Beit Rabban will provoke fruitful dialogue concerning the kinds of educating institutions that will facilitate efforts to realize liberal social ideals.

The second audience to which this study is addressed is made up of educators and others who are interested in the challenges of Jewish education at the dawning of the new millennium. Anxiety concerning survival and internal strife concerning direction are at the center of American Jewish life today, and many have turned to education as a

---

[20]For a rich discussion of the significance and effectiveness of parochial schools in American life, see Anthony Bryk, Valerie Lee, Peter Holland, *Catholic Schools and the Common Good* (Cambridge, MA: Harvard University Press, 1993).

[21]In this context I use the term "indoctrinatory" in a very crude, intuitive way and don't enter into the sometimes fascinating (and sometimes tedious) debates concerning the nature of indoctrination and its place (if any) in child-rearing and education. For those who are interested in these debates, see I. A. Snook, ed., *Concepts of Indoctrination* (London: Routledge and Kegan Paul, 1972), I. A. Snook, *Indoctrination and Education* (London: Routledge and Kegan Paul, 1972), and George Counts, *Dare the School Build a New Social Order?* (New York: Arno Press, 1969).

major vehicle for addressing some of the community's most difficult challenges.[22] The extent to which education, or education alone, can successfully address these challenges is uncertain; but the likelihood that Jewish educating institutions will make a significant difference will be enhanced to the extent that these institutions are guided by powerful conceptions of the whys and wherefores of Jewish education. But the truth is that, except perhaps in the ultra-Orthodox, or *haredi,* world,[23] Jewish educating institutions are no more likely to be organized around well-conceived and inspiring visions of what they are trying to achieve than are public schools; like most public schools, they, too, tend to be amalgams of "this and that," ungrounded in any coherent, larger sense of the nature of the enterprise. Since, moreover, the kinds of portraits that might inspire relevant constituencies to foster the development of vision-guided institutions are even rarer in Jewish education than they are in general education, the need to make available descriptions of institutions like Beit Rabban is especially strong.

It is important to note, however, that in its interest in expanding our sense of the possible in Jewish education under modern conditions, this portrait does not stand alone. Two significant studies have already emerged in response to similar concerns: Seymour Fox's study of the Camp Ramah movement, *Vision at the Heart,*[24] and Daniel Marom's study of the Magnes School (a pseudonym for a Jewish day school in a suburban Jewish community in the Midwest).[25] The development of a third portrait, one that paints a school that attempts to be true to a different vision of Jewish life, is important, among other things, because in combination with the other portraits, it will allow the reader to investigate some challenging comparisons and contrasts.

[22]See, for example, *A Time to Act* (Lanham: University Press of America, 1991), the manifesto produced by a blue-ribbon panel, called the Commission on Jewish Education in North America, made up of very senior and influential Jewish leaders from the worlds of philanthropy, Jewish religious life and education, and academia.

[23]For an illuminating discussion of education in the *haredi* world, see Samuel Heilman, *Defenders of the Faith* (New York: Schocken Books, 1992), especially 168–177 and 213–225.

[24]Seymour Fox with William Novak, *Vision at the Heart* (Jerusalem and New York: The Mandel Institute and the Council for Initiatives in Jewish Education, 1997).

[25]See Marom's "Before the Gates of the School: An Experiment in Developing Educational Vision from Practice," in Fox, Scheffler, and Marom, eds., *Visions* (Cambridge, England: Cambridge University Press, 2003), 296–331.

As will soon be seen, I develop my discussion of Beit Rabban with attention to the difficult challenges currently faced by American Jewry and to current debates concerning how education might help to address these challenges. I do so in order to help the reader think about how, and how adequately, the institution I describe and the others just referred to speak to the situation of contemporary American Jewry.

Before leaving behind the question of audience, I want to add that it would be a mistake to think that through this study I am primarily hoping to reach those who are interested in the reform of schools. Although I am, of course, hopeful that such individuals will find the study of interest, it is, I believe, as relevant to the work of those who want in enhance the effectiveness of other kinds of educating institutions, for example, summer camps. If my references are usually to schools rather than to educating institutions, more generally, it is only because the case I am considering concerns a school; but the reader is encouraged to generalize and apply the major points to other kinds of institutions as well.

Terminology. Several comments concerning terminology are necessary. First, and most importantly, I want to speak to my decision to characterize the kinds of institutions I am pointing to as "vision-guided." Neither of the words that make up this phrase is unproblematic. To some the word "vision" may seem hopelessly vague or may carry connotations that suggest disconnectedness from the real world. Believing, though, that this term healthily straddles the real and the ideal ("vision," after all, refers to what we see both with our eyes and with our ideals) and invites us to create bridges between them, I have chosen to hold on to this term. But I hope to employ it in ways that will be responsive to the concerns that warn against its use. In the case of the term "guided," it is relevant to note that up until recently (and in previous publications) I have shunned this and kindred terms in favor of the word "driven." What I liked about the latter term is that it seemed to signal the powerful conceptual and energizing role that an existential vision should play in the development of an institution. However, over time, the insights of teachers and colleagues, especially Professor Israel Scheffler, have persuaded me that, on at least two scores, the term "driven" is problematic. First, it may steer us away from the important insight that, inevitably, a host of factors other than an existential vision influence the development of any living institution, as well as our assessments of its merits; indeed, this is one of the reasons why I have felt the need to insist above that a credible educational vision depends on much more than the possession of an attractive existential vision that identifies the aims of education. Moreover, even the concept of educational vision doesn't fully capture the various circumstances, often unforeseeable, that are likely to play a role in the evolution of any thriving institution. Second, the term "driven" may carry the suggestion that a vision-driven institution is one in which the driver, the vision, has gained the kind of ascendancy that stands in the way of its being challenged and transformed by the institution's constituencies in response to new realities, data and ideas; even more strongly, it may carry the unwelcome connotation of "unthinking compulsion." In the end, these considerations have led me to abandon the phrase "vision-driven" in favor of "vision-guided," a phrase that better captures what I have in mind.

A second point relating to terminology concerns the use of Hebrew and references to Jewish culture. Beit Rabban is a Jewish day school and the Hebrew language is central to its identity and mission; and it would be very hard to discuss the school's agenda and challenges without regular reference to the Jewish landscape in which it is situated. But because, as already suggested, I intend this study for an audience that goes well beyond the Jewish community, I have tried to make the text more user-friendly by translating most of the Hebrew terms that are used and by offering rudimentary explanations of practices, ideas and institutions that may be unfamiliar to individuals who are unacquainted with Judaism or contemporary Jewish life.

Format. As the reader will soon discover, the book takes shape as a series of letters written by Daniel (the author) to Alice, an educational director of a congregational school who is on a personal and professional odyssey of her own.[26] In these letters, Daniel offers Alice his observations and emerging understandings of Beit Rabban; he also shares with Alice conversations that have transpired between himself and Devora, the

---

[26]For those unfamiliar with Jewish communal and religious life, many synagogues in America include educational institutions for the children of congregants that supplement the general education they receive in public or private schools. Designed to offer these children a Jewish education, these schools typically meet at least on Sunday mornings and, not uncommonly, on one to three late afternoons per week. They go by such names as "Religious School," "Sunday School," or "Hebrew School." Such "supplemental" Jewish schools are to be contrasted with Jewish day schools, which are essentially Jewish parochial schools which offer youngsters both a Jewish and a general education. Beit Rabban is a day school.

school's founding director. These conversations illuminate the nature of the school and the ideas that stand behind it and explore basic questions concerning its conception and design. Although Daniel's letters to Alice include sometimes detailed accounts of, and quotations from her responses to his letters, the reader does not encounter Alice's letters directly.

Lest the reader feel that I am doing Alice an injustice in not offering direct access to her letters, I want to emphasize something that may not otherwise be apparent: Alice's letters and Alice herself are fictions that I invented to advance this project. Although the character of "Alice" with which I begin is loosely based on a couple of educators I have known, I have allowed the character to unfold (in ways that sometimes surprised me) as I tried to imagine how a smart, practice-oriented, but perhaps somewhat jaundiced educator would respond to the ideas I articulated to her concerning vision-guided education, in general, and Beit Rabban, in particular.

The idea of developing my account of the school through a series of letters to a working educator, a person who is thoughtful, smart, honest, but not guided by particularly philosophical concerns, is a device I adopted because it promised to help me keep the discussion (both the themes and the language) tied to the concerns of everyday people working in educational arenas. Although they are by no means my only intended audience, such individuals are certainly prominent among them, and I believe that, if we are concerned with the improvement of educational practice, the concerns and questions that working educators are likely to raise need to be prominently included in discussions of educational ideas that have the alleged power to improve practice. In addition to this, my sense was that a letter format could, without sacrificing rigor, allow for a kind of informality that would be less forbidding and more engaging than academic texts on education often are. It is relevant to add in this connection that in order not to interfere with the narrative flow, I have included citations and references to scholarly treatments of issues I take up in the footnotes rather than in the main body of the text.

Unlike Alice, "Devora," the educational director I describe in the book and my conversation partner in many of the letters, is very much based on a real person. Devora Steinmetz is the moving spirit behind Beit Rabban, whose knowledge and thinking concerning Judaism, children, and education, combined with her passion, practical idealism, ingenuity, and sustained hard work over a long period of time, gave rise to the school. I met Devora in the mid-1990s, first at a conference concerning Jewish education organized by the Wexner Heritage Foundation and then, in Israel, at a conference organized by the Mandel Foundation around the idea of vision-guided educational practice. As I heard about her school and marveled at her ability to articulate its intellectual infrastructure, I thought to myself: "This would be a fascinating institution to study (and, if warranted, write up) as an example of vision-guided education." And so this project was born.

Although Devora and I spoke on numerous occasions, the conversations recounted in the text are decidedly *not* verbatim summaries of actual conversations that she and I had. Rather, based on a variety of inputs that included conversations with her, observations of the school, and a review of many written materials, I set about creating focused conversations that would vividly capture ideas central to the school, the responses these ideas evoked in me, and what (based on my varied opportunities to encounter her ideas) I believed Devora's responses to my questions and concerns would be. Though some of the conversations I report may include snippets of our actual discussions, overall the conversations are inventions designed to communicate the ideas that inform the school in an accessible way, as well as to investigate their merits and implications.

The reader may reasonably wonder what relationship the ideas attributed to Devora in the conversations I invent have to the real Devora. The answer is this: although the real Devora often complains that "I don't talk like that," that the character of "Devora" as I represent her doesn't sound like her, both of us have insisted that the ideas attributed to this character not misrepresent her own understandings of what the school is about. She has read the entire manuscript from beginning to end, and at a number of junctures I have revised the comments of the Devora character so that they cohere with Devora Steinmetz's actual views.

A few words about "Daniel," the writer of the letters that follow. Daniel is very much myself in the sense that the concerns, questions, ideas, and beliefs that he expresses are generally my own. I say "generally" in order to signal the fact that, now and then, the Daniel that appears in the letters voices certain positions in order to ensure that certain views get expressed and examined in his conversations with Devora. Perhaps the best example of this is that I may be somewhat less optimistic than Daniel sounds in the letters about the likelihood of significantly improving existing educational institutions.

I turn now to the vignettes described in the text. These vignettes emerge out of three different contexts: my actual observations of the school at work; conversations with Devora as well as written communications from her in which she describes situations she witnessed or participated in; and published materials, especially the school newsletters, that describe the work of the school. I want to emphasize that none of the situations I describe is invented, but that, with the exception of Devora, I have used pseudonyms for all the other individuals, both adults and children, that the reader will encounter in my descriptions. Moreover, in one case which focuses on the children's attempt to decide how to spend the money they had raised for tzedakah (a word that refers to what is required of us by something that stands somewhere between *charity* and *social justice*), the dialogue between students and between them and the teacher is, in some of its details, an imaginative reconstruction, based on, but not identical with, a published account written by the teacher who led this project.[27] Although my account honors the spirit and direction of the class's deliberations, in reconstructing the event (one which I did not actually witness), I allowed myself to imagine in more detail how the discussion might have unfolded, using this as an opportunity to emphasize the *social* character of deliberation in Beit Rabban's classrooms. The result is the dialogue included in the text. For comparison's sake, interested readers are encouraged to review the teacher's published account of the episode.

Now, some more specific comments concerning the form and content of the letters that make up this book. As with real letters, the seventeen letters found below are looser in their structure than are essays. The tone is more conversational, and certain themes sometimes surface briefly, then disappear, and then, in response to a question, reappear later on. But although the conception of the project gives rise to a measure of zigzag back and forth among themes, and although the letters overlap one another, a general trajectory is at work in their sequence.

More specifically, the first letters continue the work of the introduction: they explain the nature of the project and its rationale, and they establish its intellectual and cultural contexts. The letters that immediately follow the first two letters offer a portrait of the school, identifying its aspirations and practices, with attention to its guiding beliefs concerning Judaism, education, and human development. These are followed by letters that further probe Beit Rabban's assumptions concerning human

---

[27]Ilana Blumberg, "Learning Chesed: Community Service in a Kindergarten Classroom," *Kerem: Creative Explorations in Judaism* (spring 1995), 53–56.

development, quality education, and evaluation; these letters also include a lengthy discussion of the challenge of identifying and cultivating teachers who are competent but not contaminated by too much experience in less-than-adequate educational environments. The letters that follow offer an account of some of Beit Rabban's real and alleged problems and weaknesses. Consideration of these matters offers an opportunity to further clarify Beit Rabban's conception, to discuss some nuts-and-bolts issues concerning money, and to explore both the place of imagination in education and the challenge of educating children with different levels of ability. The very last letters investigate, in some cases for the first time, some larger questions—questions concerning the nature and significance of visionary leadership, the accuracy of my portrait (and whether this matters), and the nature, emergence and maintenance of vision-guided educational practice.

Because, as already observed, the letters are designed to form a developing, organic whole, the reader is encouraged to follow the sequence in which they are presented. But for some purposes, it may be helpful to know what themes are emphasized in particular letters, and, for this reason, each letter is given a title that identifies its major themes. Significantly fuller detail concerning the content of the letters is offered in the brief italicized summary that precedes each letter. As an additional aid to the reader, immediately below I identify the themes that are central to my study, indicating where in the manuscript they are principally discussed.

The rationale for the project and its direction are introduced in the first and second letters. In these letters, recent interest in the improvement of Jewish education is explained in relation to the larger concerns of American Jewry, and the argument is advanced that the various educational reform strategies that are being discussed are unlikely to bring about serious improvement unless and until Jewish educating institutions become organized around compelling visions. Beit Rabban is pointed to as an example of a vision-guided institution outside of the *haredi* world, and this establishes the context for the examination of Beit Rabban. This examination begins in the third letter, where the reader will find a preliminary snapshot of Beit Rabban's outlook and practice.

The ideas that make up Beit Rabban's basic outlook and their embodiment in practice are developed in a number of letters. The core practices and activities around which Beit Rabban is organized, practices and activities that are constitutive of the school's identity and embody its deepest aspirations, are identified in Letter 4.

The nature of intellectual autonomy and its place in Beit Rabban's understanding of Judaism, as well as in its vision and practice, are examined in Letters 3, 4, 6, 7, and, briefly, 13. In these letters, careful attention is paid to the interdependence, but also the possible tensions, between autonomy and tradition.

The place that serious study of Jewish texts plays in Beit Rabban's understanding of Judaism and in the life of the school is explored in Letters 3, 4, 5, and 9. Related to this, the school's approach to text study, including the way it treats so-called "difficult texts," is explored in Letters 5 and 9.

Beit Rabban's openness to diverse interpretations of Judaism and its approach to pluralism are discussed in Letter 5.

Letter 8 explores the aspirations and assumptions that give rise to Beit Rabban's approach to moral education.

The place of imagination, empathy, and creativity in Beit Rabban's approach to education is discussed in Letter 13.

Beit Rabban's focus on very bright children is explained and examined in Letters 13 and 14.

Beit Rabban's understanding of itself as "a learning community," understood to be a microcosm of a perfected world, is explored in Letter 9.

Beit Rabban's understanding of and approach to evaluation, as well as its perspective on praise and prizes, are explored in Letters 3 and 12.

Some guiding beliefs that enter into Beit Rabban's educational vision and practice that are distinct from its conception of the kind of human being and community it aspires to cultivate are explored in Letter 10.

The challenge of identifying and cultivating adequate teachers is explored in Letters 10 and 11.

Some of Beit Rabban's major problems—both those identified by the school itself and those alleged by its critics—are explored in Letter 13.

Letter 16 explores whether this portrait of Beit Rabban is true to life and why this is important.

Although all of the letters are concerned with the nature of vision and its relationship to educational practice, this theme is also systematically addressed in a number of places. The concepts of vision and vision-guided institutions are explored in Letters 1, 2 and 16. The role of leaders in the development of vision-guided institutions and the challenges posed by change in leadership are discussed in Letters 5 and 17. The question of whether it's possible to turn typical existing institutions into vision-guided ones is explored in Letter 15. The Postscript explores whether vision-guided institutions will always be exotic, fragile flowers, the existence of which depends on rare constellations of circumstances that cannot readily be created. It also considers whether, if the latter is true, calling attention to such institutions, as I am attempting to do, has the potential to influence mainstream educational practice in useful ways.

An additional aspiration. The preceding discussion has already identified some of the major hopes that inform this project. Here I want to add—and this will explain some of the directions I go in the text—that I also intend the discussions that follow to stimulate reflection on a number of very basic educational questions, some of which have significant philosophical dimensions. Among the topics that are discussed in this spirit are the following: autonomy—its nature, its relationship to tradition, its significance as an educational ideal, and the implications of this ideal for educational practice; the ethics and effects of giving praise, prizes, and other extrinsic rewards to mark and/or encourage educational progress; the nature of standards and their place in the educational process; competing approaches to the study of fundamental, or canonical, texts; the difficulties, possibility, and conditions of change at institutional and individual levels; and the wisdom (or foolishness) of creating special educational arrangements for the gifted. My hunch is that encountering such issues in the context of a living institution's struggle to define itself and to thrive, combined with the fact that this school's approach to these matters is often very fresh, may render these matters more compelling than they may feel in more traditional educational theory text books. Put differently, this book is also intended as an introduction to some of the questions and debates that are central to educational theory, especially philosophy of education.

O chestnut-tree, great-rooted blossomer,
Are you the leaf, the blossom or the bole?
O body swayed to music, O Brightening glance,
How can we know the dancer from the dance?

— William Bulter Yeats,
"Among School Children"

Setting the Stage

Contemporary Jewish Life, the Potential of Education, and the Case for Vision-Guided Practice

This is the first of many letters written by Daniel, an educational philoso- pher with strong interests in Jewish education, to Alice, a Jewish educator serving as the director of a congregational school. Following up on a con- versation he has had with Alice, in this first letter Daniel situates contempo- rary Jewish education in relation to some of the larger concerns that preoccupy American Jewry, especially its anxiety over it own survival (or, as it is often referred to, continuity). In doing so, he expresses concern over the unthinking way in which "continuity" is trotted out as an aspiration and rejects the idea that bad Jewish education is the cause of American Jewry's ills or that good education is sufficient to cure them. Having set forth these qualifications, he agrees that Jewish education can make valu- able contributions to American Jewish life, if it is suitably improved. While he expresses enthusiasm for recent strategies that are being deployed to strengthen the field of Jewish education, he advances the thesis that there is unlikely to be significant improvement until Jewish educating institutions are organized around clear visions that elicit the enthusiastic support of the communities they serve. The letter concludes with a critique of Jewish edu- cation in America which emphasizes how far the reality is from a world in which such visions guide the work of educators.

Dear Alice:

Greetings! It was great meeting you the other day at the conference of Jewish educational leaders. As I mentioned when we spoke, I was excited to hear about the efforts under way in your community and institution to improve the quality of Jewish education. The amount of money now avail- able is hard to believe, and it is being put to some good uses: upgrading the profession by creating more engaging and challenging positions and in-

creasing salaries; providing resources for stronger inservice education programs—programs that actually contribute to effectiveness; and helping to
cover the costs of Israel experiences and summer camping. All these devel-
opments are wonderfully exciting. And as you well know, what is going on
in your community is happening elsewhere as well.

We agreed that these changes could not come at a better time. But this
agreement also gave rise to our first disagreement. As I recall (and not without some embarrassment), I reacted somewhat critically when you tied these
initiatives to the need to stem rising intermarriage rates and to the challenge
of ensuring Jewish continuity. And as I thought about our conversation later
on, I was concerned that it might have sounded like I am against Jewish continuity and untroubled by the state of American Jewish life. Since this is far
from the truth, I thought I should take this opportunity to clarify my position.

To begin with "Jewish continuity:" to my mind, it's too simple to say
"I'm for it," without asking, "What am I for when I say I'm for Jewish continuity? What kind of continuity is to be encouraged and for the sake of what
should it be encouraged?" After all, not all forms of continuity are desirable;
all sorts of groups have an impulse to preserve themselves, and sometimes
they do so in ways that are an affront to their ancestors and to humanity at
large. It's true that, with an eye towards meeting this kind of concern, recently some have begun to speak not about "continuity" alone but about
"*meaningful* Jewish continuity." But here I find myself wondering: what is to
count as "meaningful Jewish continuity?" It seems to me that one can't really
begin to address this question seriously without some positive conception of
the nature of Judaism and why its preservation is important. And, though I'm
uncomfortable saying this, my impression is that many of the people who
wave the continuity flag are not guided by convictions about these matters
but by a kind of knee-jerk reaction to rising interfaith marriage rates.

As I see it, these rising rates of intermarriage are but a symptom of the
much deeper problem that so many of our contemporaries have ceased to
find their spiritual, intellectual, social and existential needs met within the
framework of Jewish life.[28] My hunch is that if Jews today found participa-

---

[28]This formulation is indebted to the much more eloquent words of Franz Rosenzweig: "What is new is not so much the collapse of the outer barriers; even previously,
while the ghetto had certainly sheltered the Jew, it had not shut him off. He moved beyond its bounds, and what the ghetto gave him was only peace, home, a home for the
spirit. What is new, is not that the Jew's feet could now take him farther than before
. . . The new feature is that the wanderer no longer returns at dusk. The gates of the
ghetto no longer close behind him . . . To abandon the figure of speech—he finds his
spiritual and intellectual home outside the Jewish world." Franz Rosenzweig, *On Jewish Learning*, Nahum Glatzer, ed. (New York: Schocken Books, 1955), 96.

tion in Jewish life fulfilling, there would be a significant drop in interfaith marriage rates.

Of course, the fact that contemporary Jews don't seem to find Judaism responsive to their deepest questions and needs might mean that Judaism is less profound than are competing systems of ideas and spiritual practices. It may be that Judaism has little to offer contemporary Jews who are not prepared to leave modernity behind. While this hypothesis cannot be ruled out of bounds, I know that neither of us finds it compelling. For me, this is in part because I am so impressed by the ability Jewish civilization has exhibited to claim the intellectual, moral, and emotional energies of Jews of all kinds across a multitude of cultural contexts and eras. If it's true that there is widespread indifference to what this civilization has to offer, I doubt that this is best interpreted as evidence for the irrelevance of Judaism in the modern world; rather, I suspect that it's a symptom of the fact that so many American Jews have, at best, a superficial appreciation of what Judaism is and, at worst, some serious misconceptions.

Assuming this to be true, many would be quick be put the blame for this state of affairs on our educational institutions: "If only Jewish congregational schools were better [or "If only day school education had a different form," or "If only. . . ."], we would not be in the mess we're in." But we should be well beyond the stage of scapegoating educational institutions for a larger and complex cultural problem. Surely we need to recognize the fault of the larger Jewish community that has failed to support and fund adequate Jewish educational institutions. We must also recognize that, however good educational institutions might be, they cannot take the place of appropriate experiences in the family and the culture at large.[29] If we assign to schools the job of counter-

---

[29]That formal educational institutions don't have the power to override the powerful influence of the popular culture and the family is a view at least as old as Plato's *Republic* (see, for example, Book III: 491d–492, 165–166). Nonetheless there has been a strong tendency in American educational history to suggest that schools have this kind of power. For one of the earliest and most influential statements of this view, see Horace Mann, *The Republic and the School* (New York: Teachers College Press, 1957). With apparently unbounded optimism, Mann writes (79–80): "Under the Providence of God, our means of education are the grand machinery by which the 'raw material' of human nature can be worked up into inventors and discoverers, into skilled artisans and scientific farmers, into scholars and jurists, into the founders of benevolent institutions, and the great expounders of ethical and theological science . . . Without undervaluing any other human agency, it may be safely affirmed that the Common School, improved and energized, as it can easily be, may become the most effective and benignant of all the forces of civilization."

acting the outlooks acquired in the family and in the general culture, we are setting them up for failure and ourselves for disappointment.

And yet, as we said when we spoke, educating institutions are not blameless, either. They must also shoulder responsibility for our present predicament—and, more to the point, for remedying it. That is, both of us felt that although educating institutions are not sufficient to transform American Jewish life, they are probably critical ingredients in any serious approach to the problem. And we also agreed on the need to strengthen the qualifications of communal educational planners, of the directors of educational programs, and of front line educators. In addition, we agreed on the importance of informal education. But then we came to our major disagreement. While you seemed to feel that such improvements would suffice to make Jewish education as effective as it could be, I was skeptical. All these improvements will not amount to very much, I suggested, until Jewish educating institutions and programs are thoughtfully organized around inspiring yet realizable ideas that both identify the aims of Jewish education and explain their importance. Even as I said these things, I think you began glazing over; and as I have thought about our conversation, I have come to realize that what I said must have sounded hopelessly abstract and perhaps irrelevant. And so, because I feel strongly about this, I want to clarify what I had in mind. I think this might prove useful for me because, if I'm right, it's important for me to be able to convey my point in a way that will ring true, and useful for you because, should you come to agree with me, this may have a bearing on your work.

What I had meant to convey is not unrelated to what I said earlier about continuity advocates whose pronouncements aren't anchored in any understanding of why Jewish continuity is important. Like them, most Jewish educating institutions that I'm familiar with are not guided by anything like a conception of what Judaism is about and of what we should be trying to cultivate in learners. Instead, when we see these institutions up close, we encounter a hodgepodge of aims and practices which are individually underdeveloped and which don't hang together in a credibly coherent way. Imagine building a new house without any clear architectural plan: one person is given the responsibility for the living room, another for landscaping, a third for interior design, a fourth for plumbing, and so forth, without anyone overseeing the entirety of the project and asking, "What should the final product look like? What purposes should it serve? What will it need to look like if it is to be esthetically pleasing and functional for those who will be using it? How will the various pieces hang together?" Too often this is the situation in Jewish education!

Look, for example, at the typical curriculum of a congregational religious school. Here you are likely to meet up with subjects like Hebrew, Bible, holidays, prayers, customs, Jewish history, and Israel. But take any one of these subjects—say, the Hebrew curriculum—and try to enter into a conversation with the teachers, the principal, or members of the Education Committee about its aims, and you don't get very far. It's not just that none of them has a systematic approach to the teaching of Hebrew; there also isn't clarity or agreement among them concerning the importance of teaching this subject. When you ask about aims, one of these folks may look at you in bewilderment, a second might speak about Bar Mitzvah competence or the ability to read the prayer book, a third might make reference to conversational or biblical Hebrew. You are, unfortunately, unlikely to discover in their views any clear and shared aim for Hebrew education; and none of the teachers or the other interested parties is likely to say anything about the kinds of attitudes towards Hebrew that they are hoping to nurture. And if you move beyond this, and ask about the connection between Hebrew, other curricular domains, and the kind of Jewish life the school is hoping to encourage, you are, I regret to say, unlikely to encounter more than blank stares.

Adequate responses to such questions would, I think, depend on the presence of a larger conception of the kind of Jewish human being a community is trying to cultivate, a matter that requires thinking seriously about the nature and significance of Judaism. But such matters have typically not been contemplated in serious ways in the context of efforts to improve Jewish education. Discussions of educational aims rarely move beyond the banalities of "strong Jewish identity" (whatever that means) and "feeling comfortable in a synagogue anywhere around the world" and "eschewing intermarriage."

And so I return to my original contention: more dollars, better trained personnel, opportunities for informal education in summer camps and in Israel—these are no doubt important. But they are no substitute for thinking about the most fundamental questions: Education for what? What kind of a Jewish human being should we be cultivating? What kind of a Jewish community should we be striving to become? Only if we answer questions like these that speak to the point of the whole enterprise of Jewish education, will we be in a position to thoughtfully plan adequate educational environments. Put differently, what we need are vision-guided educating institutions.

I hope this has clarified my views somewhat. I look forward to hearing from you.

Sincerely,
Daniel

LETTER 2
Setting the Stage (II)

In response to Alice's claim that Daniel is unjustifiably critical of those trying to repair Jewish life and education without the guidance of an inspiring conception of what a well-lived Jewish life looks like, Daniel makes the case that their efforts would be more successful if they were guided by a vision of a flourishing Jewish life at the levels of the individual and the community. But after saying this, he backtracks: he acknowledges that he was in error in suggesting that a typical leader has no vision at all; it would be more accurate to say that he or she operates with some kind of a vision of what Jewish life at its best is like, but that it's likely to be a vision that is neither well articulated nor the product of careful reflection that includes attention to its foundations and implications.

At Alice's request, Daniel offers an account of "vision" and "vision-guided institution" (an account that is revised significantly in Letter 16). He also introduces Beit Rabban, which will serve as his example of a vision-guided institution. Beit Rabban's origins are described in relation to the concerns that animated its founder, Devora Steinmetz, and some of its basic tenets are articulated in a preliminary way.

Dear Alice:

Thank you for your response to my letter. Since receiving it, I have been pondering how to respond to the important questions you raised. Let me begin by saying that you were right to take me to task for one of the things I said. You wrote: "I think I detected a judgmental tone in your comments about Jews who, though perhaps not sophisticated about the nature of Judaism, give their money, their time, and their voice to the effort to strengthen Jewish life and education. Many of them do have deep beliefs about Judaism, even if they may be unable to articulate them. Besides, in an age when Jewish life is threatened with erosion, I am troubled by the

7

derisive tone I sense in your comments about those who are working to stem the tide."

To be honest, I had no clue that my comments might be construed as contemptuous, and for this I am genuinely sorry—not just because I have no desire to offend but because, like you, I have deep respect for those in the Jewish community who are devoting their energies and funds to the improvement of Jewish life. That said, honesty compels me to add that there probably was a judgmental tone to my comments, because I think that their efforts are much less effective than they could be, if only they had a clear conception of what aspects of Judaism are the most important and essential to preserve. Is it our tradition of studying texts? our sense of peoplehood? certain moral insights or insights into the human condition? strict halakhic practice grounded in certain beliefs about God? Clarity about this would prove invaluable in deciding what kinds of continuity initiatives to support. To which you might want to say, "Let's support *all* expressions of Jewish vitality!" But this is problematic both pragmatically and as a matter of principle. Pragmatically, it's problematic because we have limited resources to expend, and this necessitates making choices among competing possibilities. And as a matter of principle it's problematic because, to be blunt, not all initiatives that claim the mantle of Jewish continuity are necessarily worthy of support, and some such initiatives will probably not do us proud. To which perhaps you would respond, "From where does *your* authority come to decide which initiatives are and are not authentic expressions of Jewish life and continuity?"

A fair enough question, to which I have, I think, a reasonable answer. And this answer is that all of us draw the line somewhere between what is and is not an authentic expression of Jewish life that is worthy of support. I can't, for example, imagine supporting Jewish continuity as understood, say, by Meyer Kahane or Baruch Goldstein, or Yigal Amir, or Jews for Jesus[30]—or for that matter, and perhaps more controversially, by those

---

[30]Meyer Kahane, Baruch Goldstein, and Yigal Amir are individuals on the extreme Right Wing of Israeli's religious-political universe who have endorsed and/or perpetrated horrible violence towards Arabs, as well as towards Jews (e.g., Yitzhak Rabin) whom they view as hostile to what they take to be the interests of the Jewish people. "Jews for Jesus" refers to a group, sometimes also described as "Messianic Jews," who are born Jewish, accept the Christian view that Jesus is the Messiah, and insist that they can meaningfully maintain that view *as Jews*. For most Jews, on the other hand, one of the markers that separate Jew from Christian is that Jews do not acknowledge that Jesus was the Messiah.

haredi communities that delegitimize the rest of the Jewish world. Now you may not agree with me about this; it could well be that you draw your lines somewhere else. But I'm not asking you to draw lines where I do; what I am asking you to do is to agree that you, too, draw lines, and that those lines reflect a certain conception of authentic and inauthentic (or, more weakly, of acceptable and unacceptable) forms of Jewish continuity.

So now I hear you saying something like this: "First, you complain that supporters of Jewish continuity aren't guided by any sense of meaningful Jewish continuity; and now you tell me that somewhere, deep inside, they are guided by some such understanding. Well, you can't have it both ways." This is a reasonable criticism, and it tells me that I was wrong to say that supporters of Jewish continuity are working with no conception of meaningful Jewish continuity. What I really should say is that the conception of Jewish continuity that typically underlies the continuity agenda is not the product of reflection, study, and conscious decision; and this I find very problematic.[31] Or, to put it differently, precisely because those who

---

[31]Embedded in this view is an assumption that we will be better off if we surface and critically examine our guiding assumptions. Since this assumption is at work in a number of the discussions that follow, a few words concerning it are in order. Two variants of this assumption can be distinguished. One of them, associated with Socrates and his descendants, holds that "the unexamined life is not worth living"—that it is always desirable to subject our guiding assumptions to critical examination. The second variant, one which seems to embrace the old adage "If it ain't broke, don't fix it," recognizes that there are circumstances when life proceeds very well without our analyzing why we do what we do—this, despite some philosophers' qualms that this way of proceeding puts tacit and unwarranted trust in unexamined assumptions concerning what it means "to live well." But there are, according to this second view, some circumstances (for example, rapid economic and social change) under which our basic orientation may become confused and our intuitions distorted and unreliable. Under these circumstances, careful reflection on our guiding beliefs, with the aim of reestablishing a better fit between our outlook and the situation in which we find ourselves, can be of great value. On either of these two views, thoughtful attention to the whys and wherefores of Jewish life is warranted in the present; that is, even if one rejects the Socratic insistence that it is always desirable to reflect on the most basic questions, the problematics of contemporary Jewish life would warrant examining such matters.

are working so hard to ensure Jewish continuity will inevitably be guided by some kind of conception of Jewish continuity, it's very important that they thoughtfully scrutinize this conception—first, so as to assure themselves that it represents a kind of continuity that is worth encouraging, and, second, because the resultant clarity could make for much greater strategic effectiveness. Enough on this.

In your letter you asked me to say a little more about what I meant when I spoke of "a vision-guided institution," and also, if possible, to give an example. The first part of this request is not difficult for me to honor. To my mind, a vision-guided educating institution is one that is, *down to its smallest details,* organized around a vision, or image, or conception, of the kind of person and community it's hoping to cultivate through the educational process. In saying this, I want to emphasize that it's not enough for this vision to live in the minds and hearts of the educators who make up this institution; it also has to suffuse daily life in areas as diverse as curriculum, architecture, the physical organization of classrooms, evaluation and grading practices, admissions forms and policies, and so on.[32] And this means that, informed by a set of beliefs concerning human nature, growth, motivation, learning, clientele, and other such matters, as well as by financial and other real-world conditions, this vision has been translated into a coherent and practicable approach to educational practice.

This brings me to your second request: can I give you an example of a vision-guided institution? A very reasonable request, but I must confess that my initial response to it was a feeling of uncertainty that I could point to a satisfying example. Not that there have not been, and are not now, significant instances of vision-guided institutions. A famous example is the school built by John Dewey at the end of the nineteenth century in Chicago, a school that was selfconsciously organized around his beliefs concerning the nature of life, work, learning, and the relation-

---

[32]To anticipate: this definition gets revised in a systematic way in Letter 16. For a more systematic discussion of different senses of "vision" and of the nature of vision-guided institutions, I refer the reader to three articles in which I have explored these matters: "Vision and Education," in Haim Marantz, ed., *Judaism and Education: Essays in Honor of Walter Ackerman* (Beer Sheva, Israel: Ben-Gurion University of the Negev Press, 1998), 277–292; "The Place of Vision in Jewish Educational Reform," *Journal of Jewish Education* 63, no. 1–2 (1997), 31–40; and "Guiding Visions and Educational Planning," in Barry Franklin, ed., *Curriculum and Consequence* (New York: Teachers College Press, 2000), 15–29.

ship between the individual and the group in a thriving community. Anything you might point to in the Dewey School—be it the architecture, the curriculum (in math, history, shop, or whatnot), evaluation practices, the desks used by the children, and so forth—was designed with explicit attention to the school's aspiration to cultivate human beings with certain attitudes, beliefs, and habits of mind and heart.[33] And, by the way, I could also point to examples of vision-guided schools in the *haredi* world; here, too, you could find communities supporting educating institutions that have a very clear conception of the aims of education, as well as practices and personnel that are at one with these aims.

But while these examples may help to give the flavor of what a vision-guided institution is, they may seem too far removed from the world you and I inhabit—a universe that is Jewish but non-fundamentalist and that wants to nurture a commitment to Judaism along with openness towards and respect for diverse groups, both Jewish and non-Jewish. Are there, I asked myself after reading your letter, examples of vision-guided institutions within this universe? Most of the institutions I know of that are committed to this kind of open community are not vision-guided: eager to avoid any appearance of imposition, and in order not to alienate any of their constituencies, they adopt a rhetoric of aims which is so vague and abstract that it would be hard to dissent from it; but the reason it's hard to dissent from this litany of aims is that it entails no commitments to any particular understanding of Jewish life. So, yes, these schools have a shared conception of what they are about; but it's a conception that is, as Seymour

---

[33]This general point is wonderfully exemplified by the care that was apparently taken in the Dewey's school to select teachers—rank and file educators—who understand and identify with the school's experimentalist educational ethos. Consider, for example, the way the shop teacher in the Dewey School describes his approach to education: "Because we teach a child to saw or plane, it does not follow that we expect the child to be a carpenter. What we do wish is to make the child think—to question—to wonder. One day a child was pushing a plane straight on a piece of wood and remarked to his neighbor how hard the plane worked. The small boy thus addressed said, 'If you put your plane so (showing how to place the plane at an angle and be perfectly level with the edge of the board) it will work easier.' When questioned why it worked more easily, he said it was because all of the plane was not on the board at once. The child, knowing almost nothing of friction, had discovered its principle in a concrete applied case, through his own efforts at experimentation." In Mayhew and Edwards, *The Dewey School* (New York: Atherton Press, 1957), 262.

Fox put it, so pareve[34] that it doesn't succeed in enlisting the passion of the teachers, parents, and children or in giving educators much guidance in determining what and how they should teach.[35]

Now the good news: I recently heard about a Jewish day school outside the *haredi* world that sounds precisely like the kind of vision-guided institution that I have in mind. With the promise that I will follow up with more information shortly, let me begin by telling you what I have so far heard about this school. Called Beit Rabban, this school on the Upper West Side of New York was founded in 1991 by Devora Steinmetz, a young woman with a doctorate in Comparative Literature who was at that time the mother of four children; now, I'm told, there are several more. The school started with four kids, with three more added during the first year. In the course of the 'nineties it grew bigger, and eventually had a population of between fifty and sixty youngsters, ranging in age from about four and a half to ten or so.

As I understand the story of the school's beginnings, when Devora's oldest son, an intellectually very able boy, the kind of youngster who might be described as gifted, reached school age, she found none of the available Jewish day schools acceptable. True, she had fond memories of some very traditional Orthodox schools that she herself attended as a young girl, schools in which everything testified to the supreme and unquestioned value of learning; but, unfortunately, these schools tended to be intellectually straitjacketing, offering the children one particular understanding of Judaism as the single authoritative interpretation. Devora didn't just object to the imposition of this interpretation on moral grounds; as far as she was concerned, this insistence on a single interpretation was also untrue to the

---

[34]The word *pareve*, which will also appear below, needs explanation. As many readers already know, kosher food, as well as the dishes and utensils used to prepare, eat, and store it, fall into three categories: there are *meat* foods, dishes, and utensils; there are *dairy* foods, dishes, and utensils; and there are foods, dishes, and utensils which are *neither meat nor dairy*—for example, fruits and vegetables or breads/pastries that include neither dairy nor meat by-products and that are prepared with utensils that are not used in the preparation of meat or dairy dishes. This last category—neither meat nor dairy—is called *pareve*. On this natural foundation in the world of food, pareve has also acquired the secondary meaning embedded in this discussion— namely, boringly uncontroversial, the Jewish equivalent of vanilla.

[35]See Seymour Fox, "Towards a General Theory of Jewish Education," in David Sidorsky, ed., *The Future of the American Jewish Community* (Philadelphia: Jewish Publication Society, 1973), 260–271.

spirit of Judaism, which at its best, she believes, encourages members of the community to wrestle with multiple interpretations of texts and ideas and of Judaism itself.

As for the "more modern" traditional schools associated with what is usually called the "modern Orthodox" community, the situation was even worse: the emphasis on the preeminent value of learning which she associated with the schools she attended as a child was all but gone. As Devora sized up the situation, the real agenda of these schools, their heart and soul, is to prepare their charges for success in American society as it is; they are prep schools in Jewish dress.

Nor were the so-called progressive Jewish day schools that she encountered significantly more promising. True, they emphasized creativity and supported the idea of autonomous choice with respect to various streams in Jewish life. But, from what I've been told, she felt that they approached these ideals in a superficial way. Most fundamentally, these schools were not intellectually serious and challenging environments. While there was a strong emphasis on making learning fun and against blindly following the dictates of authority, there was no sense in these institutions that serious engagement with texts was an essential life activity, that getting on the inside of these texts was critical, and that these texts, like life itself, pose problems that can only be adequately solved through imaginative and rigorous thinking. Perhaps these environments were friendly, but they were not sufficiently challenging or organized around serious study.

So what kind of school was she looking for? Here's what I've been told: a school that was progressive in orientation (in a sense that I don't yet fully understand), serious about initiating children into the Jewish textual tradition, open to different interpretations of Judaism, and intellectually challenging. She wanted to find a school that would allow her child to learn a lot in an open spirit and in a way that would foster a love of learning.

Feeling that none of the schools that surrounded her met these criteria, Devora took the bold step that most parents who are unhappy with extant educational alternatives only dream of: she set out to start her own institution, to build a school around her own understanding of the kind of Jewish human being Jewish education should endeavor to nurture. And now comes some bad and good news. The bad news is that I don't know much more than I've just told you; but the good news is that I've arranged to visit the school and to meet with Devora next week. I'm pretty excited and will share with you what I've learned shortly.

All the best,
Daniel

LETTER 3

A Day in the Life:

First Encounters with Beit Rabban

Daniel takes Alice through a day at Beit Rabban, offering a description of the physical and social environment as well as some snapshots of what goes on in the school. This letter serves to deepen our understanding of key elements in the school's vision and introduces a number of themes that will be further explored in other letters. A brief discussion of the school's preference for inexperienced teachers (further developed in Letters 10 and 11) leads into a discussion of the place of praise and standards of excellence in education, as understood by the school's founding director, Devora. Her claim that the kind of reliance on praise that is common in child-rearing and education functions to undermine the development of autonomy leads into a discussion of autonomy, which is a key element in the vision that informs Beit Rabban practice. This discussion begins to explicate the nature of autonomy and its place in Judaism, as these matters are understood by Devora. Central to this understanding of autonomy is not just the idea that our beliefs should be grounded in reflection, but also that our conduct, for which we are responsible, should grow out of thoughtful attention to the purposes it is intended to advance. Towards the end of the letter, a question concerning how autonomy and tradition live together in Judaism and in the school gives rise to a preliminary discussion of a school project that illustrates their relationship. This project, which engages the youngsters in thinking about whether turning on lights is consistent with the spirit and laws of Shabbat, is further discussed in the next letter.

Dear Alice:

In the last few days, I have undergone some very exciting experiences! Beit Rabban is every bit as interesting as I expected, and I'm not sure whether my excitement has to do with my identification with the school's animating vision or with the fact that this really is a school whose guiding vision seems to truly inform day-to-day decisions and practices. But let me start at the beginning.

On my first visit, I arrived at the very old, but stately synagogue from which the school rents two floors in an annex building at about 8:20 in the morning. I found myself in the company of several children and their parents who were waiting to be buzzed into the building. True, this is Manhattan, but I must say I was surprised that this is the way a child's day begins in this school. The wait afforded me a chance to speak to the father of two children who were standing nearby. When I mentioned that I was interested in the school, he told me proudly that he's had kids in the school for five years and began raving about it—something like "the only school we can imagine for our children . . . a very special place." Soon we were buzzed in and traveled, all six or so of us in a rickety old elevator, to the second floor, where we exited into the school.

Thinking that first impressions might be particularly significant, I tried to take it all in. Straight ahead of me was a small room that served as a library; to my right was a very small school office and to my left was a wall with a bulletin board, underneath which was an old couch. The physical space was clean and very simple, perhaps even a little primitive. I took note of this as I headed into the office, where I introduced myself to an informally dressed, smiling young woman of about twenty-two. Judith—that was her name—said that Devora was expecting me and would soon find me; in the meantime, I should have a seat outside the office. Rather than sitting, I looked at the bulletin board above the couch and at the other walls surrounding me. What immediately impressed me was that the walls were alive with challenging games (for example, "Family Math Games") and questions of various kinds. As an example, in one envelope on the wall that was labeled "FAMILY *CHUMASH* LEARNING" there were sheets of paper containing an uncommonly interesting assignment. I immediately took a copy with the intention of sending it to you. I didn't stop to ask if it was okay to take it; I had only been there for a few minutes and already felt that taking this liberty was not just okay but something praiseworthy at this place. Anyway, I copied it verbatim because I want to share with you some of my reactions to it. So take a couple of minutes to look at it before reading further.

FAMILY CHUMASH[36] LEARNING

So many fascinating questions have come up over the last few days as we've been learning the story of Qayin and Hevel[37]. Here are two of the interesting things which we've been wondering about. Please choose one or both for this weekend's discussion. Remember to read over the relevant passages with your child (let your child find them!), and please help your child write down the ideas which emerge in the course of your family learning.

**The children noted a number of similarities and differences between what God says to Adam after he ate of the fruit of the Tree of Knowledge and what God says to Qayin after he killed Hevel. One similarity and difference is in the curse: God curses the *adama* (earth) in response to Adam's disobedience, but God curses *min ha'adama* (from the earth?) in response to Qayin's crime. Why this difference?
**God tells Qayin that he will be *na'vanad* (a wanderer), yet Qayin settles down—and in a land called *nod*! How can we understand this? (Children might also be interested in discussing what it means to leave *milifnei hashem* [from before God, from God's presence] and what Qayin means when he says *umipanekha estater* [I will be hidden from God's face or presence].)[38]

So here's what struck me about this exercise. First, I absolutely loved the questions. Grounded in a careful reading of the biblical text, the questions are real—nothing school-bookish about them. And when you consider that these questions come not from a scholar or the teacher but out of

---

[36]The *Chumash* refers to that part of the Bible known as the *Pentateuch* or *The Five Books of Moses*. The Bible is only one of a number of classical Jewish texts that play a prominent role in Beit Rabban. Readers interested in developing some understanding of the major genres of classical Jewish literature and of approaches to their study are referred to Barry Holtz, ed., *Back to the Sources: Reading the Classic Jewish Texts* (New York: Simon and Schuster, 1984). In the pages that follow, I often substitute "Torah" for "Chumash." I do this because although it is true that "Torah" sometimes has a broader meaning, it is often used synonymously with "Chumash" and may be more familiar to many readers.

[37]"Qayin and Hevel" is a transliteration of the Hebrew names for Cain and Abel in the story in Genesis.

[38]For those who are interested, I am including in an appendix to the main text a few other examples of the Family Chumash Homework that was sent home with the children.

discussions that take place with and among the children—well, I was blown away. Even as an adult, it's all too rare for me to encounter thought-provoking questions like these in relation to Jewish texts, and I'm pretty sure I was never invited to think about such matters as a child. Other aspects of the activity also impressed me. Specifically, not only were the parents offered rich information about what their children were doing, but the information came packaged as an invitation to review the pertinent texts *as a family* and to struggle together with the questions that had emerged in the classroom setting. Talk about family education!

As I was looking through this exercise, a woman who looked to be in her thirties approached and introduced herself as Devora. I informed her that I already had lots of questions but she suggested that before talking about the school, I do some observing, and she led me up a set of stairs to the classroom of the third, fourth, and fifth graders. Physically, this room resembled what I had seen downstairs: unimpressive but serviceable. There were fifteen or so children in the room, dressed informally in jeans and T-shirts; all the boys and two of the girls were wearing *kippot;* [39] *tztitzit* [40] were discernible on one or two children, but not most. At this moment, seated around three or four tables, they were quietly reading to themselves or writing in small journals. As best I could tell, they were completely absorbed in what they were doing, and I was amazed by the complete absence of goofing around, by the atmosphere of rapt attentiveness to what they were doing that emanated from this group of eight- to ten-year-old children. Devora introduced me to two young people, probably in their early twenties, who were quietly engaged in setting up the room for the day; she described them as the teachers of this class, and then she left. The two teachers and I conversed for a few minutes. I learned that both of them were recent college graduates and was surprised to hear that neither of

[39]*Kippot* (*kippah* is the singular), called *yarmulkes* in Yiddish, are the skullcaps that have traditionally been worn by Jewish males—in some communities during all their waking hours, in others only when they are present in sacred places or engaged in religious activities like prayer and study. In the contemporary world, some females have also adopted the custom of wearing *kippot.*

[40]*Tzitzit* are the fringes that the Torah commands Jews to wear as a reminder of God's commandments. *Tzitzit* are found on the prayer-shawls that traditional Jews and many who are not traditional don when praying; in the case of most Orthodox Jewish males, *tzitzit* are worn as part of an undergarment during their waking hours. Regarding it sometimes as custom and sometimes as commandment, in the modern world, some women have begun wearing *tzitzit* as well. In the school, it is mostly the boys who wear *tzitzit,* though some girls do so as well.

them had trained to be an educator prior to working at Beit Rabban. I promised myself that I would ask Devora about this later on. For now, I simply listened as they explained that each class day began with a period of quiet, individualized work.

I used the time to look around the room. There was one—only one—old computer in a corner, and on the walls I saw written instructions for the way the children should study Torah in *hevruta*. The instructions emphasize understanding the text and searching for interesting problems to bring to the attention of the group. There were similar instructions for the study of Mishnah;[41] both sets of instructions emphasized working in partnership with others. "*Brachot Acharonot*"[42] were also on one of the walls, along with one bulletin board that identified facts and questions relating to the moon, and another that offered descriptions of books of interest under the heading "Historical Fiction." One of the authors featured was Mildred Taylor, a black writer whose works describe the African-American experience. She is quoted as saying something like "I wasn't a particularly good writer, but I believed I could achieve whatever I set my mind to." The other author represented on the board was William Steig, and from what was written on the board, it looked like the children had read and sought to identify commonalities among several of his books. There was a rich mix of Hebrew and English on these walls. As I scanned the wall, I was struck by the absence of any references to Israel.

After some twenty minutes, *tefillot*[43] began, with the children still sitting where they had been. The *tefillot* were entirely in Hebrew, and the chanting was loud and in unison. Though the children had *siddurim*,[44] many seemed to know the prayers by heart. Following the *tefillot*, one of the two teachers, Yael, introduced the next activity, which was focused on geographical facts, principles, and questions. I was struck not only by the fact that her instructions were given completely in Hebrew but that without exception the children seemed to understand her. When she was done talking, they dispersed to seven stations, each offering different chal-

---

[41]The Mishnah is recognized as the first part of what is called "the Oral Law." The Oral Law includes rabbinic debates and dicta, largely concerned with questions of religious/ethical practice that grow out of efforts to apply the Torah to the challenges of life under changing circumstances. Ingeniously pieced together by Yehuda Ha-Nasi around 200 of the Common Era, this text reflects rabbinic conversations and opinions that span more than two hundred years.

[42]*Brachot Acharonot* refer to the blessings that are said after the eating of a meal.

[43]*Tefillot* means "prayers." The singular is *tefillah*.

[44]*Siddurim* are prayer books.

lenges, that had been set up around the room. The exercises were a mix of imaginative tasks demanding real thought. Some asked the children to be physically active and to do measurements requiring maps, globes, rulers, and strings, and some required interaction and sharing with others; others were quieter activities that emphasized reading. One of them asked the kids to chart travel routes on a map, a second was concerned with climate in different parts of the world, a third focused on time changes, and yet another asked them to find certain places on the globe. Perhaps the most popular of the activities was the one that invited a response to the question: "If you met an alien, what characteristics would you point to, to explain to him where you live?" followed by the instruction that each child should compare his or her answer with someone else's. The room was filled with the sound of children's voices discussing their various explorations in animated tones, moving from one station to the next with inquisitive interest and with no obvious goofing around. They were pretty much on their own for this activity, and the room was bustling with talk and movement—a sharp juxtaposition with the ordered, almost lock-step feel of the *tefillot*. The teachers were present for this activity, but largely as resources or guides, offering help as needed (in English now rather than in Hebrew) and handling one or two minor behavior problems that arose. They were so confident of the children's engagement with the activity that some of the time they were off in another part of the room preparing materials for a later activity.

When the activity was halted, they had been at it for a little less than an hour; it was now 10:10, and, in preparation for their snack, the children cleaned up the room quickly and, though it may be hard to believe, with what at least looked like considerable enthusiasm. The snack itself was preceded by some announcements. Noam, one of the teachers, voiced the concern that some of the children were not turning in their Torah/Mishnah homework. He reminded them that this is part of their responsibility, and then, instead of telling them why doing homework is important, he asked *them* for the reasons. The children were quick to respond. It shows the teacher you understand, said one child; as a result of reviewing, you will be better prepared for what's to come, said a second; if you don't do your homework, you will be less able to participate in class discussion the next day, offered a third. Noam affirmed these points and then commented: "Homework shouldn't be purposeless. If you feel it's too easy, come to a teacher to ask for a more challenging assignment. If you don't do a homework assignment, hand in a note with an explanation. What is unacceptable is 'No note' **and** 'No assignment'."

Snack followed, with the other teacher, Yael, beginning to read out loud to the children from a book entitled *Zeke Pippin*. But in the middle of the story a very tall man wearing a suit and a *kippah* walked in. He was, it turned out, the father of Hadassah, a girl in the class celebrating her birth-day. Because one child had a dairy allergy, there was a question from the teacher concerning whether the cupcakes he brought were pareve; he as-sured her that they were, his confidence grounded in the fact that he had baked them himself. As he distributed the cupcakes, he asked the kids to advise him concerning how to improve them next year. As the kids were happily enjoying the cupcakes, he noticed that I (whom he didn't know) hadn't gotten a cupcake, and he immediately came over to offer me one. After responding as I would have hoped to my question about cholesterol content, he gave me a cupcake and inquired in a friendly way about my name and the purpose of my visit.

The snack concluded with traditional prayers that follow eating, and Noam set the stage for their Mishnah class, which, he told them, would proceed in *hevruta*. I was eager to see what this would be like, but because I wanted to get a feel for the whole school before meeting with Devora, I decided to go downstairs to another classroom. On the way out of the 3/4/5 classroom, I stopped at the class's bathroom, and was reminded again how stark and primitive the physical environment of the school was. Small, almost closet-like, and very old, it featured an old toilet and sink, and nothing at all on the walls. The only utensil or object in the room other than soap, toilet paper, paper towels and garbage can, was a cup, presum-ably there for *Netilat Yadayim*.[45]

On my way out of the room, I mused about the juxtapositions I had encountered over the last couple of hours—the quiet engagement that marked the day's first activity as compared with the cheerful spirit animat-ing the activities that came later on; the univocal, singsong, almost rote rendition of the *tefillot,* juxtaposed with both the intellectual excitement with which the children greeted the other activities of the morning and the informality of the environment; the primitiveness of the school's physical facilities juxtaposed with the richness of the ideas and content on the walls and the warmth of the social environment.

A few minutes later, I found myself in what turned out to be the end of a class for some second graders. It was a group made up of five or six chil-dren about 6 and 7 years of age and a teacher in her twenties, all sitting around a small table. The conversation among them was entirely in He-brew, and I was awed by the children's fluency. Apparently, they had been studying vitamins, and they were now in the middle of working on a play in which the vitamins would figure prominently as characters. The feeling

[45]*Netilat Yadayim* refers to a ceremonial hand-washing, accompanied by a prayer, that precedes meals in traditional Judaism.

around the table was almost familial, with the teacher making sure that all of the kids stayed involved and had a chance to participate. A couple of times in the course of the conversation, the teacher turned to the kids, and then to me, in search of a Hebrew word she didn't know, and at least once one of the children was able to help her out.

Later, she explained to me that though her Hebrew level was not as high as she would have liked, the school was committed to the idea that American Jews can become speakers of Hebrew, and that speaking it is not an all-or-nothing affair. One can and should continue learning, and for her to model this possibility and desire at her modest level of proficiency was, from the school's vantage point, a plus. In response to my questions, it emerged that she had a Master's degree in Jewish education from the Jewish Theological Seminary, which is only a few miles away, and that this was her first year of full-time teaching. About the work I had seen her do with the children, she explained: she had some background in drama and, having discovered that the children loved it, she decided to make it central to her Hebrew curriculum. Her idea was to make the language-learning an integral part of an activity (writing and performing a play) that the children would find exciting.

Still later in the day, I wandered back up to the third/fourth/fifth grade classroom where I found the children grouped in pairs, engaged in Torah study, and I heard the sounds of Torah-trope[46] all over the room. I joined one such pair, and found that one of the two boys was chanting a passage, while the other was following along, periodically translating the passage into English. They smiled at me when I sat down but continued with their activity. After a while I asked them what the assignment was, and they told me that there was no specific assignment. They were to move along in the study of the text, they said. When I asked them how they arrived at the process I was witnessing (one of them chanting, the other translating), they told me that they had decided themselves to proceed in this way. Both boys read very well, and one of them (who turned out to have spent two years in Israel) was a superb reader; they moved along steadily until the whole class was called together by the teacher to consider the passage together. The passage (Gen.1:27) declares that "in the beginning God created the Adam[47] in His image, in the image of God He created him; male and

---

[46]*Trope* is the musical notation that accompanies many printed versions of the Hebrew Bible. Like more familiar forms of musical notation, the *trope*, made up of individual notes called *te'amim*, gives the reader/cantor guidance in the way to chant the written words and frequently illuminates the text's meaning.

[47]Literally, *adam* means "man" and derives from the word *adamah* or *earth*.

female He created them." Immediately a question from the teacher: " Why are we told three different times that God creates the human being?" followed by a succession of hypotheses from the children. And then it was the children who were asking the questions: What does it mean to say that the human being was created "in His image?" Does God have a physical image—and if not, what can "b'tzelem" ("in the image of") refer to? Does it mean that we are "like God," and if so, in what sense? Are we, one child wondered, like God by virtue of having eaten from the Tree of the Knowledge of Good and Evil?

For me, once again, the experience of being "blown away." Here were young children not just investigating but themselves raising thought-provoking questions about the text in a serious spirit. What I was witnessing was light-years removed from the kind of Torah study that I encountered as a child or that I have typically seen in Jewish religious schools—you know, the kind of learning that begins with decoding the Hebrew words and ends with uncovering the surface meaning.

The class was still in full swing when I suddenly noticed Devora, standing at the door, apparently waiting for me to become aware of her presence. She waved me out of the room, and I followed her to a barren little room that looked like a cross between a storage room and an office. She had a free hour and thought that this might be a good time for me to ask my questions about the school.

Actually I had many questions, but I was so excited by the Torah study session I had just witnessed that I began by telling her how impressed I was. When she asked me, "By what?" I responded, "By the children's proficiency in Hebrew, by their ability to work so well independently at such a young age, and by the high quality of the discussion I had witnessed. I was especially taken with the way the teacher was able to structure the discussion so as to elicit an interesting array of hypotheses from the children."

Devora seemed pleased with my appreciation of what I had seen. "What you just saw in action is our *Beit Midrash*,[48] and it's a very special part of Beit Rabban. The *Beit Midrash* is a multi-age setting in which children third grade and beyond study classical Jewish texts: on any given day, they will participate in one *Beit Midrash* session focused on rabbinic texts, and in another one that is organized around the biblical narratives. The *Beit Midrash* you visited was the one organized around learning the Bible. Typically the children work in *hevrutah,* making their way in pairs through the biblical narrative. Though the teacher will often give them

[48]*Beit Midrash* is a traditional term for a "House of Study" in which classical Jewish texts are learned.

some general goals to structure their efforts, we encourage them to develop a plan of learning that will allow them to explore the text in a way that makes sense to them. The result is that often their interest is piqued by all sorts of questions that might not have occurred to the teachers or to me. This is very different from the kind of classroom I grew up in, where we approached the text with an assignment made up of questions framed exclusively by the teacher. And the result is that although today, in the class you witnessed, it was the teacher who posed the initial problem that triggered a larger group discussion, often it's the children who take the lead."

"Can you give me an example of this that you particularly like?"

"Sure," she responded, pausing until the right situation came to mind. "On the occasion I'm recalling, a few of the children were busily investigating the episode in Genesis where Yaakov[49] tore his garments because he thought Yosef[50] had been ripped up by an animal.[51] Well, one of these kids, a girl, got the idea that maybe tearing garments in the *Tanakh*[52] was done not as a general act of mourning but only when there was significant uncertainty concerning the circumstances of the death. Yaakov, after all, didn't really *know* what had happened to his son Yosef. The girl's hypothesis excited the kids in the class, both those in her group and others who had been studying other biblical passages. So what happened? She and the others found their way to concordances in the room and looked up other places in the *Tanakh* where people tear their garments in order to see whether this hypothesis would survive."

I liked the example very much. For me, it powerfully captured the sense of whole-hearted engagement in learning that I had begun to sense in this school: it's not just that an intriguing question and hypothesis emerged spontaneously from a small group in the class, but that pretty soon others in the room enthusiastically joined in the inquiry to which this question gave rise. And for the nth time that day a measure of envy welled up within me as I compared these children's experience with what my own had been.

After expressing my sense of excitement and our further discussing this incident, I felt ready to turn my attention to the larger concerns that had brought me to visit Beit Rabban. So, when there was a lull in our conversation, I went on to say that what drew me to her school was the hope of dis-

---

[49]The biblical Jacob.

[50]Jacob's son, Joseph.

[51]The reference here is to Genesis 37.

[52]*Tanakh* refers to the totality of the Hebrew Bible.

covering and getting to know a vision-guided educational institution. "Vision-guided institution?" she asked, and I explained, "An institution informed, down to its very details, by a conception of the kind of person you're hoping to cultivate and of the kind of community we should be striving to achieve." She nodded, as if to say, "I know what you mean" and without any suggestion that I had been misled in my decision to visit the school. And the more we talked, the more I understood why: while the practices of most schools reflect the interplay of a diverse number of often idiosyncratic, fortuitous circumstances, Devora really did seem to have a guiding idea that informed her every decision! Not that she doesn't regularly have to deal with unexpected circumstances the way other institutions do, for I'm sure she does; but it was already clear to me that the presence of a serious guiding idea to which the school is committed proves invaluable in determining how to interpret and respond to these circumstances. Now what I wanted was to better understand this idea, and this led to my next questions.

Hoping to jump-start the conversation concerning the school's vision, I thought back to the comment of a friend who had tried to summarize the school for me "while standing on one foot,"[53] and I decided to try out this person's formulation. Was my informant right, I asked, in suggesting that Beit Rabban is a progressive school whose guiding idea was to be found in its commitment to nurture three elements: comfort in the textual tradition; the skills, dispositions, and attitudes associated with problem solving; and openness?

Devora smiled weakly and suggested that while she found these three ideas congenial, listing them the way I just had didn't capture their interrelatedness; for example, you can't really speak about nurturing the cluster of attitudes and skills associated with problem solving without also encouraging intellectual openness. "After all, the willingness to see things in a new way, to recognize that there are alternatives to the way we're used to thinking about a situation—and this is the heart of intellectual openness—is inseparable from being a good problem solver. And by the way, this kind of openness is also intertwined with the school's understanding of Judaism."

When I asked her what she meant, she explained that for her (and presumably for the school) Judaism is to be identified not with one particular

---

[53]The phrase "while standing on one foot" comes from a famous story, found in rabbinic literature, about the different responses that a heathen gets when he approaches the two most famous rabbis of his day, Hillel and Shammai, with the request that they explain the whole of Judaism to him while he is standing on one foot.

perspective or set of beliefs but with a multitude of outlooks, all of them grounded in Jewish texts or ideas but representing different answers to fundamental questions. Becoming aware that there are other ways of understanding things, she explained, is integral not just to the way we approach science, history, and math but also to the way we approach Jewish studies. In fact, if we were to present Judaism as representing just one view, *that* would be inauthentic to the tradition.

I was eager to further explore what Devora had just said; but, for now, in the spirit of getting some rudimentary but broad clarity concerning the school's outlook, I tried to move the conversation in a different direction. Commenting that it wasn't obvious to me what it meant to describe Beit Rabban as "progressive" in orientation, I asked if she could explain this to me.

"You're probably right not to be satisfied with that term, since it means such different things to different people. What I mean when I describe Beit Rabban as progressive is that it takes the children seriously as learners. That is, the school offers many opportunities to be fully engaged as thinkers and interpreters who take responsibility for their own learning, challenging themselves, day in, day out, to move beyond where they are at the moment. This is not to imply that they have sole responsibility for charting the direction of their learning; but within the framework of broad learning goals identified by their teachers, the kids are encouraged to identify and figure out problems for themselves, pursuing paths of interest defined by goals and plans that they themselves develop."

Devora's words helped me to interpret, not just the anecdote she had just shared concerning the youngsters exploring the meaning of "tearing your clothes" in the Bible, but also much else that I had been observing. I was about to comment about this when Devora continued in a different vein. "Something that's missing for me in the way you tried to capture the school's character is that it doesn't get at the spirit of the school, at its uncompromising, but often playfully expressed, insistence that there be good reasons for the things we believe and do; it's a commitment with powerful implications for the life of the school." I asked her to say more about this. "Well," she responded, "whatever arena of the school's life you look at, whether it be a classroom activity or a teachers' meeting you happen into, you will find an emphasis on doing things for good reasons, that is, with thoughtful attention to the goals we want to accomplish. When, for example . . ."

Surprising me, Devora suddenly broke off midstream and said, "Look before getting further into this, why don't we start with some of your impressions. I'm hoping to learn something from your perceptions of the school."

"Okay," I responded and found myself articulating something that had been making me a little uneasy. With more time to consider, I might have raised a more innocuous matter; but as it turned out, the question I raised led to a rich conversation. Here's what happened.

I commented on the fact that the teachers seemed bright but also young and inexperienced; as best I could tell, some of them had had virtually no formal training or prior experience as educators. Devora nodded, adding that this was not an accident: given who's available, she actually prefers such teachers. When I asked her to explain, she responded with a story about an experienced teacher who used to work at the school and on whose bulletin board she (Devora) was disturbed to find, above a series of student assignments, the phrase *AVODAH METZUYENET* [EXCELLENT WORK].

Perplexed, I interrupted Devora. "What was disturbing about this?"

"I'm generally suspicious of these exhibits of 'excellent student work.' Often it turns out that, by design, these displays include examples of everyone's work. The effect of this is to destroy the currency of the word 'excellent;' and the kids, who are not dumb, realize soon enough that the inclusion of their work doesn't necessarily mean anything except that their teachers desire to include everyone's work."

"But surely this is not the only way teachers organize such displays. Isn't it often the case that they only include those pieces of work that they judge to be truly excellent?"

"That's true," Devora responded, "but I have a problem with that kind of practice as well."

I waited, and an explanation soon followed. "I'm not sure it's a good idea to heap praise on children whose work satisfies our standards of excellence. For one thing, whether a child is capable of satisfying these standards substantially depends on whether he or she has been fortunate enough to acquire certain abilities through heredity or a favorable familial environment. It's just not right that one child should be rewarded for achievements that are due to gifts for which he or she can take no credit, while other children who are not so blessed should go unrewarded and unacknowledged; and it's wrong that one child who can do an assignment beautifully (by the teacher's standards) in five minutes should be praised, while another child, who is perhaps less able, works for hours on the same assignment and receives only a lukewarm response because he or she has produced something that, by the teacher's standards, is less accomplished."[54]

---

[54]Embedded in Devora's view is a perspective that is at the core of a significant strand of recent liberal social philosophy, especially as expressed in the writings of the late John Rawls. Rawls's conception of a just social life is predicated on the idea that it is, from a moral point of view, arbitrary that some of us, as the result the operation of what he calls "a natural lottery," i.e., whom we happen to be born to, have abilities that others are not blessed with. See John Rawls, *A Theory of Justice* (Cambridge, MA: Belknap Press of Harvard University Press, 1971).

"So what do *you* think children should be praised for?"

"I'll try to answer that, but I want first to say that I think we lavish too much praise on children. Not that praise is a bad thing, but the way Americans tend to use it has the effect of either emptying it of all meaning or of nurturing a tendency to engage in an activity for the sake of the praise rather than for better reasons.[55] And if there aren't better reasons—and I mean reasons that the child can appreciate—then one ought to rethink the activity."

"And yet you say that praise isn't a bad thing. So how and when *would* you praise children?"

Devora went on to explain that children should be praised for doing the best they can and for growing beyond their previous levels of achievement. Not only would this avoid invidious comparisons between students, it would communicate to all the children, whether particularly able or not, that there is always a possibility for growth, as well as for stagnation. In a well-designed school, the particularly able student shouldn't feel smug or able to rest on his or her laurels; nor should less able students be feeling inadequate. Both types should be encountering and seriously responding to challenges that take them beyond their current levels of understanding and achievement; and their sense of themselves as learners should be grounded in this, rather than in where they stand relative to one another or to some absolute standard of excellence announced by the teacher.

I commented that what she was saying seemed to suggest a radical rejection of "standards of excellence," and that I wanted to verify whether this is what she intended. Devora paused for a moment, and then said, "Well, not exactly. Let me approach this by explaining some other reasons I was bothered by the teacher who claimed to identify examples of excellent work on the bulletin board. More often than not, the children have no real understanding of those standards of excellence to which their work is being compared."

"So would you be happier if teachers gave children a clearer idea of what the standards are in relation to which they are being evaluated?"

"That would probably be better, but not much. Because the kids would still be getting the idea—and I think this is problematic—that standards of excellence are just 'out there,' and that it's our job in school and in life to internalize and conform to them."

---

[55]In the paragraphs that follow, as well as in Letter 12, the place of praise and prizes in education is explored in the context of articulating the outlook that guides Beit Rabban. For a popular discussion in the general education literature of the dangers of relying on external rewards as a tool of education and child-rearing, see Alfie Kohn, *Punished by Rewards* (New York: Houghton-Mifflin, 1993).

"And what do you see as the alternative?" I asked.

"Well, let me give you an example. A few years back the children in the kindergarten/first grade were reading a series of books that had received Caldecott Awards, and at some point the question arose—I don't remember whether it came from the teacher or the children—how was it decided which books get this award? It was agreed that a letter should be written to the Caldecott people, requesting their selection criteria. But what we got back was a vague answer which gave us no real information. So the teacher suggested an idea which caught fire with the children: let's invent our own book award, to be given to books that we ourselves judge to be outstanding! The kids loved the idea and found themselves embarked on a successful effort to develop their own standards for book excellence. Instead of spending their early years just internalizing others' standards or inhabiting a world in which, in the spirit of 'I'm OK; you're OK,' adults tried to shield them from all standards, the children had a chance to develop some understanding of how and why standards come into being and to begin developing their own."

"So your objection isn't to standards, but to thoughtlessly absorbing other people's standards, rather than acquiring the capacity to develop and assess the standards that govern one's judgments and conduct."

"Yes, I think that's right. In fact, I probably wouldn't have objected to a wall display entitled EXCELLENT WORK, if it was guided by standards of excellence that had been developed by the children. This is actually what the kids did with the book standards that they created. These standards became the basis for something very much like a display case that they filled with examples of excellent work."

"It sounds to me," I said, "like a great example of the school's commitment to progressive pedagogy and to an ideal of autonomy, and I definitely want to ask you more about this. But I don't want to lose track of the question that first led us down this path. What does all this have to do with the fact that your teachers tend to be young and inexperienced?"

"The answer is pretty straightforward," said Devora. "The teacher who created the *avodah metzuyenet* bulletin board was a very experienced teacher; but, unfortunately, those many years of experience in more conventional schools and probably also her training had led her to think about teaching and children in a particularly narrow and rigid sort of way. In my experience, it's difficult to bring such a person to see things in a new way. So what does this mean? If I had to choose between bringing in someone who, though inexperienced, is excited about the school's approach and an experienced educator whose educational intuitions, though perhaps highly developed, are out of sync with the school's outlook, there's no question whom I would choose."

I told Devora that I was intrigued by the position she was sketching out, that I found it simultaneously insightful and troubling, and that we should definitely explore it further. But as I first wanted more time to better understand my own inchoate responses to what she was saying, I suggested that we bracket this issue and go back to the other theme we had just begun to explore: the nature of autonomy and its place in the school. When she nodded agreement, I asked her to explain what she means by autonomy.

"Actually, it's something pretty simple," Devora began. "It's not just about having one's own views about the world, about life, and about one's conduct. The key idea is having good reasons for the things that we do and believe. This is why, and I think I mentioned this before, everywhere you look in Beit Rabban, you'll see an emphasis on there being reasons for the way even seemingly minor things are organized. For example, instead of inviting the young children to gather in a circle, the teachers will say something like, 'Let's sit in a circle so that we can all face one another.' The *so that we can all face one another* is a critical part of the message. It transforms a mere custom into a practice that is grounded in a reason that connects what the participants are being asked to do to a purpose that makes sense to them. And it's integral to our effort to encourage in the children a reflective ethos, a problem-solving orientation, that will be reflected in the ability and disposition to shape their own behavior in relation to goals.[56] Though very simple, this is what is really radical, even subversive, about the school: the idea that things have to make sense, that we should expect there to be sensible reasons for doing things this way rather than that."

"Well, that idea certainly seemed to be present in the teaching that I observed this morning," I commented, and I mentioned the conversation concerning homework that I had witnessed. Devora nodded and added that this orientation is to be found across the various domains of school life in Beit Rabban: the children are regularly encouraged to think of "the way we do things" (and of the way *they* do things) as attempts to effectively achieve our purposes.

Pondering what she had just said and recalling the questions and conversations I had heard in the classes I had visited, I commented that it seemed to me that the school's interest in there being reasons for things is

[56]In the course of our various conversations concerning the problem-solving orientation that Beit Rabban embodies, Devora Steinmetz expressed her debt to Dr. Lisa Wright and Ms. Connie Coulianos of the Hollingsworth Preschool (a program of the Hollingsworth Center for the Study of Education of the Gifted at Teachers College, Columbia University), whose work, she believes, demonstrates the power of a problem-solving model in the education of even very young children.

also discernible in arenas that don't have to do with shaping our conduct in relation to goals. For example, it's also seen, but in a somewhat different way, in the way texts are investigated. Devora nodded affirmatively. Yes, she agreed, Beit Rabban children are regularly encouraged to identify and think about challenging questions or problems in the text; and in trying to make sense of the problem, we always ask them to anchor their views in reasons: what's the evidence in the text for the view that you are offering, and is this view consistent with the grammar of the text or other ideas we are encountering? In other words, not all answers are on a par; a worthy one is grounded in reasons, which themselves can be judged as appropriate or inappropriate. In this respect, Beit Rabban differs from both traditional schools that mainly care about whether the learners have gotten "the right answer" and so-called progressive schools that reward "creative" or "imaginative" answers, whether or not they are grounded in relevant evidence.

Though what Devora had just said resonated with what I had so far been witnessing, it also seemed to sit uneasily with some of the other things that she had said. My mind was buzzing with bewilderment, and a lot of it came out at once. "In complaining about the teacher who put *avodah metzuyenet* on the board, weren't you objecting to the idea of conveying to children that they are accountable to other people's standards? But isn't this exactly what you are doing when you demand that they offer reasons of a certain kind to support their views?" Devora started to answer, but I continued: "And another thing: how does this commitment to autonomy fit in with the Jewish outlook of the school? After all, this certainly seems to be a modern Orthodox kind of school which takes halakhah[57] seriously. And . . ."

Now it was Devora's turn to interrupt me. Though she wasn't exactly bristling, she seemed agitated or perhaps irritated. "Though people outside the Orthodox orbit often identify us as 'modern Orthodox,' Beit Rabban is *not* a modern Orthodox school, any more than it's a Conservative or a Reform or a Reconstructionist School.[58] It never ceases to amaze me how much people feel the need to categorize us, and how unhappy they are when they can't! I think one of the main reasons the Orthodox community is suspicious of us and mistakenly assumes that we're not *frum*[59] is that we don't wear the *Orthodox* label."

---

[57]Literally "the way," halakhah refers to Jewish Law, as found in the Torah and elaborated by the rabbis, which guides the conduct of traditional Jews.

[58]That is, the largest religious denominations that are found in American Jewish life.

[59]*Frum*, in this context, means "religiously committed and observant in a very traditional way."

Here Devora paused for a moment, before adding, "But there are probably other reasons as well, reasons which you pointed to when you asked about Beit Rabban's commitment to autonomy. Some members of the Orthodox community feel that when you convey to children that they are right to expect reasons for beliefs, you undercut the idea that we are commanded to act in certain ways whether or not we understand the reasons. They are so fearful of nurturing an autonomous outlook that even in small matters that are not governed by halakhah they would be wary of encouraging the children to think for themselves, lest the seeds of a dangerous disposition be planted."

"But," I responded, "why are you not worried about planting this disposition?"

"Well, for one thing, because the cultivation of autonomy is one of my aspirations as a Jewish educator!"

"Your aspirations as a *Jewish* educator?" I repeated in surprise. "Since when is autonomy a Jewish virtue?"

"Since almost the very beginning," Devora answered, and reaching into the top drawer of a nearby desk, she pulled out an article she had written that compared human agency, sin, and the consequences of sin in our earliest ancestors, Adam, Cain, and Noah.[60] She suggested that I read the article and that, after we had both had more time to think about some of the issues we had been discussing, we return to our conversation the next day. And off I went, eager to read what she had to say, and pleased that I had been invited for a second visit.

Here, in brief, is what I made of her article. Devora observes that the history of the world, as described at the beginning of Genesis, can be broken down into three eras. The first era, that of Eden, ends with the sin of Adam and Eve and their expulsion from Eden; the second era, from the expulsion until the flood, includes the sin of Cain as a central event; and the third era, which is the postdiluvian era in which we now find ourselves, begins with the sins of Noah and his son. Devora argues that if we look carefully at these three stories of sin, we discover, as we move from Adam to Noah, that human beings assume an increasingly autonomous role in relation to their responsibility for their conduct. Whereas, for example, in Adam's case, the rule that he violated was explicitly given to him and the urge to sin is viewed as emanating from outside him (via the serpent), in the case of Noah, there is no explicit prohibition (he himself is responsible

[60]See Devora Steinmetz, "Vineyard, Farm, and Garden: The Drunkenness of Noah in the Context of Primeval History," *Journal of Biblical Literature* 113/2 (1994), 193–207.

for determining what is right and wrong) and the locus of agency is completely in himself. As Devora sees it, early on in the Bible, long before Kant and modernity, the image of human beings as moral agents, responsible for determining their own conduct and living with its consequences, is already present. And, as best I can tell, it is this image of human beings that informs Devora's aspiration to nurture autonomous human beings.

As I thought about this, I wondered to myself whether this image of human beings as autonomous is an aberration, with the weight of Jewish tradition emphasizing not autonomy but obedient fulfillment of the Divine commandments. It did occur to me, though, that in the Talmud we find some powerful images of intellectual autonomy in the rabbinic figures who argue the merits of different halakhic positions with reference to higher order standards that involve faithfulness to the text and to the spirit of the tradition. Perhaps, then, Devora is on solid ground in suggesting that there is a tradition, or at least a current, of intellectual autonomy in Judaism, a tendency which, at least in this respect, is close to the spirit of modernity.

By the way, the article also helped me realize that Devora's understanding of autonomy includes far more than the notion that our ideas should be grounded in our own critical thinking and reasons. For her, as for the philosopher Kant, autonomy is also a *moral* notion, one that enters into her understanding of what it means to be a human being.[61] As she understands it, to be autonomous is to be responsible and accountable for one's conduct and its predictable consequences. As I pondered this, I found myself thinking in a somewhat new light about the homework incident I described to you: rather than reading the kids the riot act concerning homework or trotting out the reasons for doing the homework, the teacher, Noam, had asked the children themselves to articulate the reasons for homework. As if to say: your conduct should flow from considerations that you yourself recognize as reasonable.

To be honest, though, even as I was appreciating the school's emphasis on there being reasons for the things we are asked to do, I found myself wondering how Jean-Jacques Rousseau, the eighteenth century French philosopher, might have responded to this approach. As you may remember from one of those philosophy of education classes you probably had to take on the road to becoming an educator, Rousseau is sharply critical of Locke's notion that one should "reason with children," for he is convinced that children beneath what he calls the age of Reason cannot really appreciate our reasons. While they may pretend to be convinced by our reasons,

---

[61]See Kant, *Groundwork of the Metaphysic of Morals*, trans. H. J. Paton (New York: Harper & Row, 1964).

really they are convinced by the bribes or threats which they know lie be-hind our words.[62] Then again, perhaps the homework incident I have been thinking about would not be subject to his criticism. After all, this is a case in which the youngsters weren't asked to embrace the teacher's reasons but to identify their own. (I can already hear Rousseau asking: But are these really the children's reasons or just the reasons they know adults expect them to mouth? A good question.)

When we met the next day, I let Devora know how helpful I had found her article; and I commented that it enriched my understanding of various things I had been seeing—for example, the emphasis placed on giving the children plenty of room to design and pursue plans of work that reflect issues of interest to them. But there was also another matter on my mind, and at what felt like an appropriate moment to shift the direction of our conversa-tion, I asked if she could help me better understand how this commitment to autonomy coheres with the school's apparent seriousness about halakhah. Once again Devora suggested that a concrete example would be helpful, and she went on to describe a fascinating project concerning whether it was halakhically okay to use lights on Shabbat. The example is pretty long, and it's already late at night, but let me at least begin describing it.

Here's the background. After three years of intensive Hebrew in kindergarten through second grade (and I'll vouch for the fact that the third graders speak, understand, and read Hebrew with ease), from third grade on the children participate in the twice daily *Beit Midrash* that I have al-ready described. As you may recall, the youngsters study Torah in one of them and rabbinic literature in the other; and there is also a strong empha-sis on the interrelationship between the two literatures and on the perti-nence of what's studied to their own lives. In this particular year, the children were studying *Seder Moed* (a section of the Mishnah concerned with Shabbat and the holidays). In the course of a unit on Shabbat, the children looked intensively at everything that is said about Shabbat in the Torah: they tried to understand the relationship, pointed to in the Torah, be-tween Creation, Shabbat, and the *mishkan*,[63] and they also tried their hand at identifying the kinds of prohibited labors that might emerge from atten-tion to the Torah alone. Then they went on to consider the thirty-nine

.

[62]See Jean-Jacques Rousseau, *Emile*, trans. Barbara Foxley (New York: Everyman's Library, 1911), 53–56. See also Daniel Pekarsky, "Education and Manipulation," *Philosophy of Education* (1977) (Champaign, IL: Philosophy of Education Society, 1978), 354–362.

[63]The *mishkan* is the tabernacle built by the Israelites in the desert on the way to the Promised Land.

labors proscribed on Shabbat in the Talmud: they examined different explanations for why there are thirty-nine prohibited labors; they worked to understand the major categories of prohibited labor; and they tried to understand the underlying principles at work in what is prohibited. Beyond this, they wrestled with the implications of the Ramban's (Nachmanides') commentary on Leviticus 23:24 in which he suggests, though in different words, that it is possible to keep the letter of the law regarding Shabbat but violate its spirit. The children were asked: "What place do you think a conception of the spirit of the law ought to have in shaping our attitudes and our actions?"

Now, what's important for you to know is that at the same time the children were studying what is and is not permissible on Shabbat, they were also engaged in an interdisciplinary study of American history. And in this context, they had been learning about the effects of the Industrial Revolution on our lives and on the nature of the work we do. All of this led to a detailed study of the incandescent bulb, an inquiry which included reading primary and secondary sources about its invention, exploring basic electrical concepts, building circuits, and creating simple electrical gadgets.

As I said, this is all just background to the project that excited me, a project in which these two streams of activity—an inquiry into Shabbat and a study of the Industrial Revolution and incandescent bulbs—flowed into one another. Briefly, the children were asked to imagine how the invention of the incandescent light bulb might have been greeted by Jews who had heretofore relied on candles and kerosene lamps for light. Here's the exercise:

Imagine hearing that Edison has invented an electric bulb and imagine seeing a light bulb for the first time. You find yourself over Shabbat in a home which has electric lights, and you wonder whether you may turn one on. What considerations are pertinent? And what do you decide?

Well, Alice, I wonder how you would address this question. In fact, why not give it a try, and let me know what you think? In response, I'll let you know how I'd approach the problem, before going on to describe the curricular journey that was planned for Beit Rabban students. I suggest this not to be coy, but because this letter is getting way, way too long, and I'm very tired. I look forward to hearing from you.

Daniel

P.S. I neglected to mention that Devora seems to be enjoying our conversations about the school and has conveyed that she would welcome my continuing to visit when I can. As you might have guessed, I was delighted by this invitation and intend to take her up on it.

LETTER 4
First Encounters (II)
and
Autonomy, Tradition, and Text-Study in Beit Rabban's Outlook

In response to a question from Alice, Daniel fills in a gap in his description of the school by sketching out the schedule of a typical day and week; in the course of this sketch, some of the school's curricular elements and priorities also emerge. After this, the light bulb activity introduced in the preceding letter is more fully described and, as promised in the preceding letter, is used to illustrate Beit Rabban's understanding of the relationship between autonomy and Jewish tradition. Along the way there are some more general theoretical explorations of the nature of autonomy and the ways in which it may not only cohere with but may actually presuppose a surrounding social framework or tradition. This letter concludes with a review of the ways in which the light bulb activity exhibits both the school's progressive character and its commitment to serious Jewish learning.

This letter also emphasizes a second core dimension of Beit Rabban's vision: the place of serious text study in the life of a Jewish human being. Although Devora does not dismiss the idea that study helps Jews address issues of practice that arise in their lives as Jews, she emphasizes that, as understood by Beit Rabban, study has a much more fundamental significance: it is a defining characteristic of Jewish culture, a key way in which Jews express their participation in this culture. This discussion of the pivotal role that text study plays in the life of Beit Rabban gives rise to the identification of other activities (for example, those intended to relieve human suffering) which are at the core of the school, that is, which are embodied in school life in ways that communicate that they are constitutive of the school's identity and its understanding of Jewish life.

This letter concludes by highlighting the gap between conception and reality in the light bulb activity, and this provides an occasion to re-

37

flect on the significance of such gaps. This theme is revisited later on (especially in Letters 13 and 16).

Dear Alice:

Thanks for your latest letter. I am more than a little pleased that you are sharing my excitement about Beit Rabban—and I am grateful that you pressed me for more concrete detail concerning the school. You are entirely right: though I offered you a picture of the school's physical space and gave you some sense of its spirit, I said very little about what a typical day at Beit Rabban is like. And the reason is that in my initial encounter with the school I was so focused on its guiding ideas that I paid very little attention to this matter. This may be an occupational hazard—not one to be proud of!—for people like me whose work focuses on the philosophy of education. In any case, thanks to your question, I decided to remedy this in my next conversation with Devora. And she was quick to respond when I asked her to give me a sense of the structure of a typical day and week.

In a nutshell, here is what I learned from that conversation; and, following the lines of her description, my own begins with the schedule for the youngest kids, and then explains how things differ for the older ones. As you'll see, along the way, I've included a few words of commentary, some hers, some mine. Anyway, starting with the kindergarten/first grade (a group of up to fifteen kids, most of them five or six years old but some as young as four and a half), here's what it looks like:

8:30–8:45 Hello

During this period the children are greeted by their teachers and can choose between two activities. One of them is quiet reading, and the other is a "morning challenge" prepared by the teachers. The morning challenge consists of an engaging problem or puzzle to struggle with, a problem that might come out of very different domains, for example, math, logic, or Hebrew.

8:45–9:15 Morning Meeting and the Morning *Tefillah*

At the center of this period are the communal prayers that traditional Jews recite every morning. But because the school believes that the children should not utter prayers they don't understand, and there is still much they don't understand, the prayer service (especially for the youngest children) tends to be quite short; and some of the time devoted to *tefillah* actually focuses on coming to an understanding of the prayers.

As an aside: Devora mentioned the point about not saying prayers you don't understand almost in passing; it's an approach I've never encountered in Jewish day schools I have visited. In its own way, it's very radical, I think. And it's certainly consistent with the school's message that the things people ask us to do should make sense—what she described at one point as the simple but radical idea behind the school. That said, it might be interesting to hear a response from a thoughtful educator who believes, as I suspect many do, that it sometimes makes better educational sense to encourage, and even regularize, certain practices (including *tefillot*) in advance of exploring their meaning.[64]

Anyway, back to the morning meeting/*tefillah* period. The rest of it is rich with other activities that usually include some of the following. Over and above discussing matters that may need attention as the group makes the transition from the preceding day to today's agenda, part of the time is given over to various routines: they will together review and revise their job chart, which specifies the responsibilities of different youngsters; and they'll update their upcoming calendar of events, as well as the weather chart that sits in the room. Depending on the day, this period may also include reviewing a text together and/or a substantive discussion. The discussion might be about current events, about the Torah portion for the week, or about a theme or question that will be the focus of their activities later in the day or week, such as an upcoming holiday or a unit of study. Not uncommonly, this period also includes singing one or more songs in Hebrew and/or English.

9:15–10:15 *Explorations*

Initially, it wasn't obvious to me what this referred to, although I had already experienced an instance of it (which I earlier described). During *Explorations,* the kids are typically offered the chance to choose from a variety of activities, some of which relate to the larger course of study they're engaged in. So, for example, if they're learning about geography, there is likely to be a broad range of activities, each of which offers a chance to acquire geographical knowledge or to struggle with a question that has significant geographical dimensions. This is also the time when youngsters who have grown interested in certain questions or topics have the chance to explore them in a more individualized way. Typically, some of the available options involve opportunities to read and to write. Devora emphasized that during this period the youngsters are responsible for planning their own time in order to accomplish individualized purposes. When I asked her how much choice the children have during *Explorations,* she explained that this varies with the particular teacher, with the time of the year, with the age of the youngsters, and so on.

---

[64]This idea was once nicely captured by philosopher of education Richard Peters who was trying to articulate Aristotle's position. According to Peters, we enter the palace of reason through the courtyard of tradition—assuming, that is (and as Peters does), that our apprenticeship in this courtyard can be accomplished in a way that won't incapacitate us for a reflective life. See Richard Peters, "Reason and Habit: the Paradox of Moral Education" in Israel Scheffler, ed., *Philosophy of Education* (Boston: Allyn and Bacon, 1966), 245–262.

10:15–11:15 Hebrew (including snack)

Devora emphasized that though Hebrew is heavily used throughout the day, in the Hebrew immersion period, there is no English. The children learn Hebrew through what she described as a "natural language" approach to language learning, an approach that emphasizes the acquisition of language through participation in ordinary, but language-rich, activities. Thus, because of the way the children are encouraged to participate in activities like acting and cooking and to communicate about what they are doing, they do more than acquire some general vocabulary and the more specific vocabulary that is tied to these activities; to the extent that the program succeeds, they are also picking up the larger structure of the language, including syntax and grammar.

11:15–12:00 Math

Not much (at least yet) to report about this activity, except to mention that in contrast to several periods of the day during which the youngsters are grouped together based on age categories, they learn math in cross-grade groups, based on their level of mathematical thinking.

12:00–1:30 Lunch and Park

Typically, the kids eat lunch at the school. Since the school is across the street from Central Park, weather permitting, on Monday through Thursday the youngsters usually go out to the park to play for about an hour.

1:30–2:30 Hebrew

This is the second Hebrew immersion period of the day, and its presence seems to me to be a good index of the school's seriousness about this subject. Think about it: when you add it up (and take into account that in addition to the Monday-Thursday slots, there is a Hebrew class for the younger kids on Friday morning), it sounds like there are about nine hours a week (two hours a day, four days a week, as well as one hour on Fridays) devoted to learning the Hebrew language. And since the teachers use and encourage Hebrew in other parts of the day, adding up the language immersion hours actually underestimates the amount of language learning that's going on.

2:30–3:30 Reading/Writing Workshop

As Devora explained it, this workshop resembles what one is likely to encounter in typical progressive schools. For some part of this period the teacher will read to the kids, and in another the kids will disperse into reading/writing activities. There may also be conversations concerning the nature of language. There might, for example, be a conversation organized around the challenge of interpreting a poem or a story the children have read, around the various writings of an author the children have been studying, or about literary devices. The workshop is typically a mix of individualized, small group, and large group activities.

On Fridays, the schedule for all the children is somewhat different. For one thing, the kids go home early and do not usually eat lunch in school. For another, the time devoted to math is replaced by community service activity. When I commented that this didn't seem like a long time to engage in community service, she readily agreed, but explained that some or all of the time following the 11:15–12 slot (up to 1 or even 1:30, depending on the time of the year) was also available for community service activities. If the children were involved in actually implementing a project, all of this time might go to community service; on those days, though, when their agenda was limited to discussing or planning such activities, other activities (not necessarily connected to community service) would be introduced near the end of the day. The message seemed to be twofold: first, that that we try not to skimp on time devoted to social service activity, and, second, that there's some flexibility built into the design.

Though I had some questions concerning what she had described, I first wanted to understand how the schedule differed for the older kids. Devora explained that for the first/second grade group, an hour devoted to Torah replaced one of the two daily Hebrew sessions. Actually, she added, some years this substitution was only made for the second graders. By the way, Devora emphasized (in what was for me an extremely telling comment) that once Torah is introduced into the schedule, it, like Hebrew in the kindergarten/first grade class, is never displaced by other activities.

Bigger changes take place when the kids reach third grade. For one thing, henceforth the day goes until 4:30 in the afternoon. For another, the afternoon is now divided into two one-and-a-half hour slots, one of them for "Torah she be'al peh," the study of the Oral Torah,[65] and the other for the integrated humanities. (When I asked Devora what she meant by "integrated" in this context, she explained that it signals the fact that subjects like literature, history, and social studies are joined together in addressing whatever subjects the kids take up during this period.) By the way, if it's not already clear, the morning slot devoted to the study of Torah and the afternoon slot devoted to the study of the Oral Torah correspond to the two kinds of *Beit Midrash* I told you about in my last letter, the *Chumash Beit Midrash* and the *Torah she be'al peh Beit Midrash*. Both of these are multi-age educational settings, with the children ranging in age from seven to ten or so.

Devora's concise sketch gave me the general picture that I wanted; and, figuring I would be learning more about the different elements that made up this schedule as I continued observing the school, I didn't feel the need at this time to press her for much more specificity and explanation. I did, though, raise a couple of questions. For one thing, from the looks of

[65]The "Oral Torah" includes a variety of Rabbinic texts, including the Mishnah and the Talmud.

the schedule, there didn't seem to be much room for traditional subjects like social studies and history. Was there a real place for them in the school's curriculum?

Devora laughed, adding that she gets that question a lot when she describes the school's schedule. She went on to explain that such subjects aren't treated as separate time slots but are woven into the rest of the curriculum. Across the year, the faculty identifies some broad themes or questions that they want the children to engage with in an interdisciplinary way. With the younger kids (through the second grade), the teachers identify three broad units around which the year will be organized. If, for example, the teachers decide to do a unit on buildings and homes, they will seek out questions, stories and books that get the children to think about the different kinds of habitations people have dwelt in at different times in different places, such as caves, tents, houseboats, igloos, and so forth. In *Explorations,* the children might have the chance to engage in activities that allow them to think about the way environmental constraints and resources limit and guide the kinds of homes people dwell in; and in the time devoted to social service, they might deal with the problem of homelessness. Depending on the time of the year, there might also be an attempt at appropriate times in the day to think about dwellings the children encounter within Jewish life and history (for example, the *sukkah* or the *mishkan*).[66]

Things change some from the time the kids enter third grade. Rather than doing three interdisciplinary units per year, they engage in the integrated humanities program I mentioned above. Typically, each of the next three years is organized around a major theme. In one such sequence, the children studied the cultures of Africa and Asia in the first year; ancient civilizations relevant to the development of western and Jewish civilizations in the next; and American history at the last stage.

Now you might think that this integrated humanities program doesn't leave much room for science, but this wouldn't be accurate. Not only is time for science protected in the *Explorations* part of the day, the integrated humanities program by no means excludes it. This is beautifully illustrated in the light bulb project I began describing in my last letter, and I want to come back to that in a minute. But, first, I want to mention a couple of other things that emerged in my conversations with Devora about the school's schedule. One of them concerned the place of art in school life, a topic that we began to explore when I commented that I was struck by the absence of any reference to the arts in her characterization of the school. "How, if at all," I asked, "do they figure into the life of the school?"

---

[66]*Sukkah* is the word for a temporary booth, associated with Sukkot, the biblical Festival of Tabernacles.

"The general answer to this is very similar to the answer to your question about other subjects," Devora responded. "That is, at Beit Rabban we don't typically segregate art from other activities. But there are some things that are worth highlighting. For one thing, various art materials are available for the kids to work with during *Explorations,* and some of the activities which they can choose call on them to work with these materials; and sometimes, during this period, our teachers offer them more focused opportunities to develop certain skills—say, using water colors, or trying to match a color palette with tempera paints.

"Art also enters into other parts of the day. As an example, although it's true that the visual arts don't figure prominently in the Reading/Writing workshop, in this arena as well as in Hebrew classes, there is a chance to engage in more literary arts (as when the kids write and perform plays in Hebrew). And when, under the guidance of the faculty, the children take on an interdisciplinary theme that cuts across the day, there is often an artistic dimension. For example, the hypothetical unit on human habitations we were just discussing might very naturally lead to encountering works of art in which human habitations play a central role, or to attempts to imaginatively represent, with paint or with clay, some of the habitations the youngsters encounter in the course of their reading, or even images of homelessness."

"And what about physical education? Is this limited to running around in the park during lunch time?"

"I'll get to that in a second," Devora responded, "but I did want to say one more thing about how the arts figure in the school. There are times when they are not just elements in a multidisciplinary thematic inquiry, but are themselves the subject of the inquiry. If you're interested, one of these days I'll share with you a unit we did on the life and work of Leonardo Da Vinci—a unit that had a strong art appreciation dimension."[67]

Trying to hold on to the various things she had just said so quickly, I didn't say anything in the pause that followed, and Devora went right on to the question about physical education. After reminding me—only half jokingly, I think—not to underestimate the amount of good exercise the children get during their time in the park, she went on in a more serious vein to indicate other ways that physical education goes on in the school. As an example, she cited a movement class which would sometimes take place

[67]The place of the arts at Beit Rabban is further discussed below in Letter 13, which considers the place of imagination and creativity in the school's conception and practice.

during park time. I came away from this last exchange with the sense that, yes, there is *some* room for exercise and physical education at this school, but that it's far from central. This is a school in which it is clear that Hebrew and Torah are never displaced by other subjects; but I'm doubtful that physical education falls into this category.

This thought reminded me that education, or at least vision-guided education, has everything to do with identifying priorities you really believe in, and not pretending to do everything under the sun. Not surprisingly, these priorities show up not just in what and how you teach and in your expenditures, but also in the kinds of activities that do—and don't—make up the school day.

In any case, with the hope that this description is responsive to your interest in getting a more concrete feeling for the way life at Beit Rabban is organized, I want now to go back to the subject I raised at the end of my last letter and to which you responded in yours, the light bulb activity. As you'll recall, when I asked you how you would respond to the challenge that was posed to Beit Rabban children concerning whether to turn on electric lights on Shabbat, you responded by saying that as a non-halakhic Jew, the question of whether to turn on electric lights on Shabbat is, for you, simply moot. In my own case, I confess that I would not have a clue about how to use halakhic considerations to answer this question, but given that Shabbat plays an important role in my life, the question of turning on lights or electric appliances on Shabbat is of interest to me. Were I to address it seriously, I would probably find myself asking the question: what practice (regarding the use of electricity) is most likely to enrich my experience of Shabbat by protecting or strengthening the spirit of the day? To do justice to this question, I'd have to give some real thought to what I mean by the spirit of Shabbat.

Now let me tell you how the Beit Rabban children were asked to approach this problem. Although, like me, the children were interested in, and were invited to explore, what would help preserve, and what might violate, the spirit of Shabbat, the Beit Rabban faculty had in mind a much more multi-faceted inquiry and educational agenda. As you know, the Torah declares that on Shabbat, a day of rest, one is to refrain from all work. But, the rabbis ask, what does and doesn't count as work? As I mentioned in my last letter, the kids had already learned that in the Talmud the rabbis answer this question by specifying thirty-nine forms of labor that are to be included within the biblical prohibition of work on Shabbat. Needless to say, since there was no electricity at the time the rabbis were deliberating over these matters, the Talmud does not explicitly discuss whether turning on electric lights is forbidden. So one is left with the challenge of determining whether turning on a light falls under one of the categories of labor which the rabbis do explicitly forbid or whether it violates the spirit of the day. But this in turn requires developing a deeper understanding both of the nature of the forbidden labors and of what goes on in the lighting of a bulb. This is precisely what the kids are asked to do. Since, for example, one of the labors forbidden on Shabbat is "kindling a fire," the children need to determine whether the defining characteristics of kindling a fire are to be found in the activity of turning on a light bulb. This inquiry leads to the identification of characteristics like heat, light and combustion as defining characteristics of kindling a fire, as well as to an inquiry into whether these elements are sufficiently present in lighting a light bulb to warrant putting this activity under the category of "kindling a fire." As you might well imagine, this turns out to be as much a lesson about science as about Torah, a stellar example of integrating the Jewish and the general curriculum. By the way, some of the children will go through parallel inquiries as they consider the possibility entertained by some *poskim*[68] that putting on a light falls under other categories of forbidden labor.

And now comes what was for me a critical point. (Remember that Devora described this case to me because I was confused about how the school's interest in autonomy and halakhah are related to each other.) Based on all of the foregoing activities and learning, each child is expected to come up with his or her own perspective on the problem. As Devora wrote in a Newsletter describing the activity:

> They will argue their hypotheses based on halakhic thinking, scientific evidence, reflection on the nature of work, and a deep appreciation of the prohibition of labor on Shabbat. They will challenge each other's ideas and they will be challenged by the ideas of scholars, past and present, introduced by their teachers. Each child will emerge with his or her best understanding of this question.[69]

As this suggests, this light bulb project highlights the interplay between autonomy and tradition in the life of Beit Rabban. The children are asked to engage in a number of different inquiries, culminating in the effort to come up with their own judgment concerning whether it's okay to turn on lights on Shabbat. By the time they complete the project, their views will be grounded in reasons that testify to rich familiarity with electricity and with biblical and rabbinic sources concerning Shabbat—as well as to a lot of careful thinking about how these Jewish sources apply to our own cir-

[68]*Poskim* are interpreters charged with authoritatively deciding questions of Jewish law.
[69]*Beit Rabban Newsletter,* Winter 1998—Choref, 5758, 4.

cumstances. So here we can see autonomy within the framework of the tradition: the resources of the tradition provide the concerns, the tools, and the ideas that enter into the effort to develop an autonomous position towards the problem at hand.

Now I suspect that for you this might not be an entirely satisfying solution to the problem of integrating autonomy and tradition. After all, I can hear you (or if not you, many others) saying: wouldn't real autonomy also include not just the ability to make decisions within the framework of the tradition, but also the ability to decide whether to accept the framework of the tradition? I find this an interesting question, one that I'd like to ponder further. But, for now, let me just say this: if, as I believe, the school's view (implicit if not explicit) is that autonomy has its meaning within the framework of the tradition, this would not be an eccentric or unconventional understanding of autonomy. That is, the kinds of autonomy we actually see in the world and admire typically operate within frameworks defined by particular bodies of ideas and norms. When, for example, we think of moral autonomy, we usually have in mind people making moral decisions within the constraints of the moral point of view, and when we think of the autonomy of a scientist, we're not imagining a person who stands outside of the tradition of science but a person who stands on the inside—someone who is steeped in its canons and standards of evidence. When, around the age of eight, my son began developing into an autonomous chess player, he did so not by stepping outside the framework of the game, but by mastering its rules and applying them in a thoughtful way. If we take these examples as a guide, we might say that autonomy is actually defined by the particular "games" or traditions in which we participate.

Anyway, chances are we'll come back to this subject of autonomy.[70] But I want to be sure that my attention to it doesn't shut out an appreciation of the many other benefits of this light bulb activity, benefits that include, but also go well beyond, the acquisition of different kinds of

---

[70]For those readers who are interested, there is a rich philosophical literature that deals with the subject of autonomy in a more systematic way than I undertake to do. The interest in autonomy in modern philosophical literature has its origins in the work of Rousseau, who writes that he alone is free who obeys a law that he gives to himself, and in Kant's ethical writings. See Jean-Jacques Rousseau, *The Social Contract*, trans. Maurice Cranston (Middlesex, England: Penguin Books, 1968) and Immanuel Kant, *Groundwork of the Metaphysic of Morals*, trans. H. J. Paton (New York: Harper and Row, 1964). For a more contemporary treatment of the subject, see Gerald Dworkin, *The Theory and Practice of Autonomy* (Cambridge, England: Cambridge University Press, 1988).

knowledge. To my mind, it has, in the best sense, a very Deweyan character: it offers a chance to engage in a serious inquiry grounded in an engaging problem and necessitating critical thinking and investigation of ideas
drawn from diverse realms of human thought (in this case, science, social
studies, and Torah). Equally important, I think, it's a chance to better understand the entire process of the Oral Law and its relationship to Scripture, as
well as the way in which a Jew can work to fulfill the obligation to apply
Torah to daily life in the midst of rapidly changing circumstances.

For me, this last point—the activity as a model for how Jews in the
modern world can thoughtfully fulfill their obligation to apply Torah to
daily life—is critical. When I mentioned this to Devora, though, she commented that it suggested a "too instrumental" perspective on the activity.
For her, the most important part of the activity is the activity itself. The
body of Jewish learning continues to grow richer and deeper through the
kind of process of interpretation that rabbis and other Jews have engaged in
across the centuries, and you can't understand this process without, as the
children are invited to do, engaging in it. Not only that: engaging in this
process is itself one of the defining characteristics of Jewish culture; and
the children's engagement in this process through the light bulb project
and other activities is a way of their participating in this culture, becoming
rooted in it, and beginning to contribute to the development of the interpretive tradition that they are entering into.

Devora's insistence that engaging in the activity of interpreting Torah is
a defining feature of Jewish life and ought not to be understood as primarily an instrumentally motivated activity was quite striking to me. Part of
what made it interesting was the sharp contrast in which her characterization of this activity stood to the way she spoke about other kinds of activities and practices, in which emphasis was placed on understanding them
as vehicles of the purposes or goals they are intended to serve. Based on
what she said in some of these other contexts, one might have come away
thinking that one of the hallmarks of Beit Rabban is that it conveys to
youngsters the importance of thinking of all activities and practices as vehicles of achieving particular purposes and as therefore assessable by their
success in contributing to these hoped-for results. Think back, for example,
to the way Beit Rabban presents the idea that the youngsters should sit in a
circle. But here I heard Devora saying that in the case of the kind of interpretive activity associated with the light bulb project, the activity is in a
sense self-justifying.

When I asked her about this, she seemed grateful for the opportunity
to more fully explain her view. While it's true that Beit Rabban emphasizes
the desirability of thinking of activities as serving purposes (with these purposes serving as criteria for understanding and evaluating the activities),
there are certain activities—activities like the engagement in learning

Torah, broadly understood—the value of which Beit Rabban takes as a given that does not require justification.

When I asked her for other activities that fall into this category, Devora mentioned "community service" and "treating everybody with respect." When she said this, I found myself wondering whether the three activities she mentioned are an exhaustive list, or just examples, of activities that Beit Rabban regards as needing no justification. I was about to ask about this when Devora elaborated on the place of these activities in the life of the school.

"These activities," she explained, "are our core. We don't try to justify them, or to transmit them by repeating them as a mantra; rather, their importance gets expressed by the ways they are woven into the fabric of the school. They are built into daily life in a way that conveys, mainly tacitly, 'This is who we are; this is what we do.' And, as core values, these activities and aspirations function, through the agency of our teachers, as the goals or reasons that are used to shape, justify, and critique other activities and norms that are found in the school. So the school's message is this: given that we want to learn Torah in a meaningful way (or that we want to treat other people with respect, or that we want to serve the community in a way that genuinely reduces human suffering), what should we be doing, what's the best way for us to act?"

Devora's comments reminded me of John Dewey's ideas about the continuum of means and ends, especially his idea that one brings youngsters to identify deeply with certain activities and values not by treating such identification as a goal to be achieved through some sequence of instrumental activities, but, rather, by building these activities and values into the daily life in which the children presently engage.[71] I think that this is precisely the insight that informs Devora's approach to the school's core values. More basically, I felt that my understanding of the school took a leap forward when I came to realize that within the world of Beit Rabban, a distinction can be drawn between, on the one hand, activities that need to be thoughtfully justified in relation to certain purposes and, on the other hand, activities whose value is taken as a given and that provide the purposes that justify the first set of activities.

---

[71]The way in which the values and ways of thinking and being that are at the core of the principal activities we engage in get absorbed and come to spill over into other domains of activity is discussed by Dewey in *Democracy and Education*, for example, in the chapter entitled "Education as a Social Function." Also relevant is his early article "Interpretation of the Savage Mind," in *Philosophy, Psychology, and Social Practice*, ed. Joseph Ratner (New York: Capricorn Books, 1965), 281–294.

This insight helped me to recast the significance of the light bulb activity. Yes, it was about developing an autonomous approach to life and to Judaism within the framework of the tradition; but perhaps more fundamentally, it was an opportunity to come to share in and identify with one of those core activities that are constitutive—so Beit Rabban views it—of Jewish life and identity. But this line of thought also raised a new question for me: what is the relationship, and is there a tension between coming to identify with these core activities through pre-reflective participation in the routine life of the Beit Rabban community, rather than via a process that involves rational deliberation, and the school's commitment to autonomy?

To put this concern more provocatively, I think that some advocates of autonomy may find it ethically problematic that these core activities and the values they embody are not themselves autonomously chosen. But, having thought about this matter, I'm not sure they would be right about this. Quite apart from my reluctance to embrace the tacit assumption that the ideal of autonomy ought to trump all other value commitments, three other thoughts come to mind. In the first place, all cultural and educational environments inevitably embody core activities and values that are absorbed pre-reflectively by those who participate in them. In the second place, though Beit Rabban matter-of-factly stands for certain core activities, it does not, as an indoctrinatory institution may, strive to educate in such a way that its core commitments can never be seriously questioned. In the third place, the values and activities that are at the core of Beit Rabban are not a threat to a generally autonomous approach to life; that is, they don't serve to shut down or narrow an intellectually open, inquiring spirit.

Over and above these considerations, in thinking about this concern, I found myself recalling, and again identifying with, some earlier thoughts about autonomy that I shared with you, particularly the idea, explained with the help of the chess example, that autonomy may be best thought of as operating within a structured sphere of activity. That is, activities like Torah learning, treating one another with respect, and responding to human need in the community are the arenas or the frameworks within which autonomous conduct is fostered in this environment. Each arena is associated with certain kinds of aspirations and standards of success, and, in each of them, Beit Rabban learners are encouraged to use their minds as effectively as they can to achieve these aspirations in a way that makes the most sense.

In any case, as you can see, I found the light bulb activity enormously exciting: exciting both as an educational activity and as a stimulus to my own thinking about education and other matters. In fact, I was so taken by the project that at first I missed a critical qualification that accompanied Devora's description of it: due, in her opinion, to certain inabilities of the teachers, the project did not fully unfold as she had anticipated, and it fell short of her hopes for it. I hasten to add that in commenting on the teachers' inability to fully execute this project, she did not at all seem to be singling them out for blame. Rather, she seemed to be saying that, at least at present, it would be hard to find many teachers anywhere with the bodies of knowledge (in Judaism, science, social studies) and the ability to integrate them meaningfully in a concrete situation in the way that this project required. She may well be right about this, though I found myself wondering whether, if the school had unlimited financial resources, it might have been able to attract the kinds of teachers who could have pulled off this project more successfully. I didn't raise this question with Devora at the time we spoke about the failings of the project, but I have made a note to myself to find an occasion to learn more about the school's financial circumstances.[72]

Whatever the reasons, for me, the admission—if that's what it's to be called—that the program fell short of its aspirations was, initially anyway, disappointing information to absorb; but, on reflection, it's an important point on which to reflect. For one thing, it's a healthy reminder that building an educationally imaginative school environment is not an easy thing to do, and that, in the end, much depends on having appropriate educators in place; and this in turn may have implications for the way we identify promising individuals, recruit them to the profession, and educate them. These are, no doubt, difficult challenges, and I'd like to come back to these matters later on. The only other thing I would add at this point is that, though the school's failure to achieve the lofty educational agenda embodied in this project may be disappointing, the fact that the school's educational ideology spawned this kind of a project is itself impressive. Equally noteworthy, I think, and an index of the school's seriousness about making real progress, is its willingness to acknowledge gaps between aspiration and actuality.

All the best.
Daniel

---

[72]Questions concerning the school's financial circumstances and their impact are addressed in Letter 13.

LETTER 5
Pluralism

This letter focuses on the place of themes connected to "pluralism" (a term that, as we shall see, is not central to Devora's understanding of the school) in the vision that guides Beit Rabban. The letter begins with a brief discussion of the ways in which Jewish educating institutions sometimes force students to conceal their actual religious outlooks and practices, and this leads into a discussion of Beit Rabban's commitment to intellectual openness regarding the diversity of belief and practice found within Judaism. Respect for this diversity is not just grounded in the sociological fact that contemporary Jews live in very different ways; Devora also believes, and the school tries to communicate, that such diversity is a feature of authentic Judaism. More specifically, three assumptions are key elements in Beit Rabban's outlook. It is important to try, via careful study and reflection, to arrive at an approach to one's life as a Jew that makes the best sense; thoughtful people who make this effort are likely to end up embracing different webs of beliefs and practices; and respect is owed to those whose thinking leads them in directions that differ from one's own. We also hear about Devora's view that the school's commitment to both serious text study and genuinely open, rigorous inquiry makes both liberal and Orthodox Jews uncomfortable.

Finally, this letter includes a brief discussion of the school's view that educators shouldn't shield children, even very young ones, from so-called "difficult texts" in the Torah. Its interesting, and perhaps controversial, approach to text study is further developed later on, especially in Letter 9.

Dear Alice:

No, I don't at all mind digressing from the questions concerning autonomy that we began exploring in our last letters. It's true, I hadn't expected Beit Rabban's "Can we use light bulbs on Shabbat?" exercise to lead you in this direction, but I'm happy to follow your lead, especially since your story about your daughter and the questions you raised in your last letter are pretty compelling. I was saddened, but not surprised, to hear about your eleven-year-old's experience in a local Jewish day school; what did surprise me was how thoughtful and articulate she could be in describing how something in the school environment made her feel ashamed of, and eager to conceal, the fact that she and her family are not very observant when it comes to Shabbat.

She is, of course, not alone in this respect. As you probably know from your work in Jewish education, though it's different when you hear it from your own child, there are many children who feel thrust into this inauthentic position in Jewish educational settings. Certainly there are many children who come from families that are relatively non-observant on Shabbat, families whose Shabbat includes, along with a special Friday night dinner, shopping at the mall and going to the golf course. And many Jewish schools, like your child's, respond to this fact by tacitly encouraging the children to keep this information to themselves. The rarely articulated but powerful rule seems to be: "If you are not identified with the beliefs and practices the school officially stands for, keep it to yourself! Each of us should talk and act as though we are identified with these beliefs and practices, even if we know that we ourselves and some of the others are not." My own feeling is that this rule has disastrous educational consequences, turning the school environment into an artificial, make-believe place where children learn to hide, and to be ashamed of, who they are.[73]

---

[73]This point extends well beyond the issue of religious outlook and practice and is not limited to religious schools. In other educational environments as well, in different ways in different eras, learners—young and old—have felt pressured to keep out of the public arena of school life certain features of their lives that are central to their self-understanding. In the 'fifties, when I was growing up, it was the fact that your parents were divorced; more recently, attention has focused on the pressures on youngsters not to reveal that they are gay. Though I am not prepared to make the claim that the school should be a place where students should feel free to reveal *any and every thing* about their situation, I am suggesting that the cloak of enforced secrecy that surrounds some such topics can have various negative consequences for the learners who are asked to hide significant dimensions of their identity; in at least some of these cases, moreover, the other learners lose out on valuable lessons as well.

And as you well know, it's not just the youngsters who have this problem. There being a dearth of qualified educators to work in Jewish educating institutions, it is not uncommon for an institution struggling to find teachers for their classrooms at the beginning of September to end up hiring individuals who in their personal lives don't embody the religious ethos that the school is trying to nurture. I know one exceptionally gifted young educator (and I'm pretty sure he's not alone) who found the strain of pretending, in the desire to be an approved of role model, that he was more observant than he actually was so uncomfortable and demoralizing that he ended up quitting. And you may have heard of the anthropologist who studied an afternoon Hebrew school in a Conservative congregation some years back. In the class he sat in on for an extended period, he discovered that the very same teacher who engaged the children in thinking about why "we" don't work on Shabbat was known by his students (many of whom were themselves not Shabbat observant) to manage a pizza parlor on Friday nights.[74]

The case of the teacher whose personal pattern of beliefs and practices differs from that of his/her institution is an interesting one for people like me who believe that vision-guided institutions are important and that, at their best, they are staffed by educators who identify strongly with the institution's vision. I can certainly understand the logic that informs the institution's explicit or implicit demand that they act "as if" they embraced the institution's views. On the other hand, the costs and the risks are enormous: the inauthentic, morally awkward postures which compliant teachers adopt are likely to be destructive in various ways; and if, as in the case I just described, the learners become aware of the subterfuge, it is hard to imagine that the Jewish school environment will not come to seem bizarrely unreal. In the case of Beit Rabban, it's clear to me that Devora believes that this is a school in which integrity—the integrity of the school and that of its young and old members—is a (perhaps *the*) core value. In schools that insist on this, there can be no room for this kind of pretending, quite apart from whether the teacher is "discovered." Needless to say, for those interested in vision-guided practice whose thinking moves along these lines, the difficulty of finding educators who do honestly identify with their institution's guiding vision will pose a serious problem and make for some interesting, and very difficult, choices and compromises.

Anyway, I found the story about your daughter troubling, and, like you, I think it would be interesting to see how Beit Rabban would respond to

---

[74]See David Schoem, "Jewish Schooling and Jewish Survival in the Suburban American Community," in Michael Rosenak, ed., *Studies in Jewish Education*, Vol. 2, (Jerusalem: Magnes Press, 1984), 52–64.

someone like her. As you framed the question in the wake of my description of the "Do we turn on lights on Shabbat?" activity, "Am I right to conclude from the fact that using lights and not using lights on Shabbat are both acceptable positions in the world of Beit Rabban that Beit Rabban is committed to Jewish pluralism? Or, to put it more personally: Would my daughter, who comes from a not-very-observant family, feel comfortable there?"

As you intimate, there are actually two questions here, not one: whether Beit Rabban is a pluralistic community and whether your daughter would be comfortable there; and I'm not yet sure whether a positive answer to one of them would necessitate a positive answer to the other. But first things first. Let's start with the question of pluralism; and let's, at least for now, stay with the definition of a pluralistic community that you intimated when you asked, "Is this a school that affirms the legitimacy of very different ways of living as a Jewish human being, so long as everyone respects the legitimacy of everyone else's way of living as a Jew?"

As it turns out, I just came across a recent Beit Rabban Newsletter in which Devora discusses a pertinent passage from the Talmud. First, the passage:

> Rabbi Yochanan said: "What is meant by the verse 'The Lord gives a word: those who announce it are a great host' (Psalms 68:12)? Each and every word which went forth from the mouth of mighty God was split into seventy languages." The school of Rabbi Yishmael taught: '[Is not my word like a fire . . .] and like a hammer which shatters a rock' (Jeremiah 23:29)? Just as a hammer produces many sparks, so each and every word which went forth from the mouth of the Holy One, blessed be He, splits into seventy languages."

Devora comments:

> [It] describes the infinite meaningfulness of Torah, the power of the divine word to create multiple meanings despite its embodiment in human language. The notion of seventy languages, though, focuses not only on the divine power to communicate, but also on the human ability to make meaning. Seventy is the traditional number of the nations of the world . . . If Torah speaks in seventy languages, then it speaks to each and every member of the community which accepted it and, potentially, to each and every human being. This is true despite differences in language, in how we speak and hear, in our world views, personalities, and cultures. This passage, then, suggests that Torah's power lies not only in God's power to communicate but also in the human ability to make meaning. There are multiple ways to hear Torah, and

this multiplicity, rather than undercutting the authenticity of Torah, attests to the power and uniqueness of Torah.[75]

I think this last sentence directly addresses the pluralistic character of the school. Devora seemed to be saying: there are many ways to interpret Torah, and there are therefore many authentic ways to live as a Jew within a Torah framework.

But things got more complicated when I directly asked Devora your question about pluralism. For one thing, though she didn't seem uncomfortable with my references to pluralism in relation to Beit Rabban, she quickly pointed out that she herself does not tend to use this term to describe the school, tending instead to refer to it as nondenominational. That said, here's how she responded when I told her how I had interpreted what she had written in the Newsletter:

"Rabbi Yochanan's idea that the words of the Torah can be interpreted in a multitude of ways is important and it does lead towards pluralism, but it doesn't fully capture the idea of pluralism that guides Beit Rabban. Neither does Alice's idea that to be pluralistic means 'to affirm the legitimacy of very different ways of living as a Jewish human being, so long as everyone respects the legitimacy of everyone else's way of living as a Jew.' This is a popular understanding of pluralism, but I don't buy it."

When I asked her to explain, she pulled out the same school newsletter that included the Rabbi Yochanan quotation and pointed me to a second rabbinic text that is found there. This one records a story about another ancient rabbinic sage, Rava, a story that appears on the same *daf* (page) of Talmud as Rabbi Yochanan's words. It reads:

A certain gentile saw Rava sitting engrossed in study, and the fingers of his hand were under his feet, and he was crushing them so that they bled. The Gentile said to him: "You rash people who put your mouth before yours ears;[76] you still persist in your rashness. First, you should have listened; if you are able, accept it, and, if not, do not accept it!" Rava said to him: "We who walk in wholeness, of us it is said: 'The wholeness of the upright shall guide them (Proverbs, 11:3)"[77]

---

[75]*Beit Rabban Newsletter,* Vol. 5, No. 2, Spring 1996-Aviv, 5756, 1–2.

[76]The reference here is to the biblical story in which the Jewish people respond to God with the words "We will do and we will hear," conventionally interpreted to mean that they agree to abide by God's commandments before they know what these commandments are.

[77]*Beit Rabban Newsletter,* Vol. 5, No. 2, Spring 1996-Aviv, 5756, 1.

When I inquired about the relevance of this passage to the problem of pluralism, she began by suggesting that Rava is pointing to the difficulty, even the pain, involved in serious study. She reads him as cautioning us against quick-and-dirty interpretations of Torah and against simply dismissing texts that seem nonsensical or that don't immediately speak to us. We are obliged to struggle with such texts, to see if we can make sensible what seems senseless, to try to understand why one interpretation of a text is more plausible than another.[78] "There is no assurance or hope at Beit Rabban that our struggles to make sense of Torah will lead us to the same place, and in this sense we're very pluralistic; but the culture of Beit Rabban is suffused with the idea that our decisions about Judaism (and everything else, for that matter) should grow out of thoughtful and patient reflection."

"So it sounds like Beit Rabban's respect for diversity of outlook and practice goes hand in hand with an ethos that encourages its members, both children and adults, to think seriously about the basis for their beliefs and practices."

"I think that's fair," Devora responded, "but don't forget the other point that's central to the Beit Rabban approach. To think well about a problem requires that we take into account the web of ideas and information that's 'out there' and relevant to the discovery of a satisfactory solution. Just as it would be silly to ask the children to come up with an approach to racial prejudice or anti-Semitism that didn't take into account available knowledge about the sources of such phenomena and about what has been tried in order to combat them, so in the case of decisions concerning Jewish practice. We believe it critical that the thinking of the children grow out of serious struggle with what our tradition has to say about these matters."

"What you're saying about the value of study leads me to wonder whether you are suggesting that text study is valuable because of the ways it helps to ground our thinking about the practical problems we encounter in our lives as Jews."

"Not really. Certainly, the activity of study has this effect, and it would be problematic if it didn't influence how we thought about the nature of Judaism and our lives as Jews. But I'm uncomfortable with this way of formulating its value."

---

[78]Implicit in this approach is some version of a hermeneutical approach that has been described by Moshe Halbertal as a *charitable* approach to the text. For Halbertal's rich discussion of what he calls the principle of charity, see *People of the Book: Canon, Meaning, and Authority* (Cambridge, MA: Harvard University Press, 1997), 27 ff.

"How so?" I asked.

"For one thing, as I mentioned in an earlier conversation, it seems to turn the study of Jewish texts into little more than a tool that will help us make better life choices. In actuality, our relationship to text study is much, much more basic: we engage in this study not in order to accomplish purposes that are external to the activity, but because this kind of study is part of our identity as Jews; it's one of the life activities, perhaps the defining life activity, that mark us as Jews. Children at Beit Rabban are, it's true, encouraged to turn to texts to illuminate questions of Jewish practice; but this is a far cry from making this the justification for studying these texts. From day one, the study of texts is woven into the daily rhythms of Beit Rabban in ways that reflect its central place in our lives as Jews."

"You said 'For one thing . . .' Is there another? I mean, is there also another reason why you're uncomfortable with my formulation?"

"I suppose there is, or maybe it's just an extension of the other. Either way, here it is: when you speak of Torah study helping us live more meaningfully as Jews, it sounds as though I'm to value Torah study because of what the engagement in study does *for me*. I myself would emphasize the ways in which our tradition of Jewish learning grows through the study of Torah by its interpreters."

I felt the need to ponder these comments. I was troubled—maybe because there was some truth in it—by the implied suggestion that the way I had characterized the role of text study in Jewish life bespeaks a kind of therapeutic Judaism, a Judaism to be valued because of what it does for me. But at the time we were talking, we didn't pursue this topic any further, in part because I wanted to stay with the subject of pluralism. I was becoming increasingly aware that Devora's idea of an optimal educational and social environment separates her not just from those who are intolerant of departures from some single, authorized way of doing things. It's also light-years away from institutions whose "we are pluralistic" self-description is equivalent to a proud declaration that however you choose to live as a Jew is fine and legitimate—at least so long as you affirm certain fundamental values like *Ahavat Yisrael*.[79]

Devora's understanding of an ideal Jewish community, though it allows for great diversity in outlook and practice, is very different. Members

[79]Literally, *Ahavat Yisrael* means "love of Israel." It refers to the sense of connection and concern that Jews are supposed to feel for other Jews and for the Jewish people, in general, even those they don't know or who adhere to beliefs and customs that they do not identify with. Some may view it as a kind of tribal loyalty.

of her ideal Jewish community will all be seriously engaged in the study of classical Jewish texts, such as the Bible and Talmud. And because authentic Judaism does not offer any single answer to most questions but embodies and encourages multiple understandings, and because its interpreters bring different sensibilities, concerns and insights to their study, their discussions will be marked by interesting differences in interpretation, differences from which they can all learn and grow. In the end, the likelihood is that their inquiries will lead them, as it has Jews throughout the ages, to different views and practices; but these views and practices will not represent uninformed, idiosyncratic tastes but the products of informed and thoughtful thinking. And because members of this community recognize that Judaism does not represent any single authoritative approach to things, and that they are all co-participants in the continuing effort to understand the meaning, or meanings, of Torah in all its complexity and depth, they won't feel any less a sense of community with one another because their thinking doesn't lead them all to the same place, either intellectually or practically. So, in the end, the fact that some of them are very observant and some are not doesn't affect their ability to share in a single community.[80]

One index of Beit Rabban's identification with this outlook is that the school is not identified with any particular standard of Jewish observance, and Devora's impression is that there is a great range in the levels of observance of Beit Rabban families. But, she reiterated as we continued to discuss this matter, diversity per se is not the important thing. "At Beit Rabban we don't just smugly affirm the diversity represented by our children. At the heart of our community is the idea that the religious life involves choices that are grounded in honest inquiry informed by study, or, in other words, that how we understand ourselves and act as Jews should be of a piece with, rather than set apart from, our lives as reflective people. People who engage in study and reflection may well come to different conclusions and make very different choices. And that's fine."

"So, do you ask children to examine the reasons for the Jewish practices that inform, say, their approach to Shabbat?"

"It's not at all as frontal as your question may suggest; and we certainly don't grill children about what they observe and don't observe, and why. But in units like the one about the use of lights on Shabbat, Beit Rabban children have the chance to do some serious text study and thinking con-

---

[80]Much has been written in a more theoretical vein about the place of pluralism in Jewish life. For an especially useful discussion, see Elliot Dorff, "Pluralism," in Steven T. Katz, ed., *Frontiers of Jewish Thought* (Washington, D. C.: B'nai Brith Books, 1992), 213–233. This article has the virtue of including a bibliography that will refer interested readers to a number of other valuable treatments of this subject.

cerning the nature of Shabbat and the *mitzvot*[81] associated with it. How, in the end, this study and thinking influence their religious life is not something I worry about; but I would be unhappy if we didn't succeed in conveying to them that the commitments that shape a Jewish life grow out of choices that are grounded in serious study and honest inquiry. Beit Rabban's outlook is inseparable from its commitment to this kind of exploration; and if we're successful, the children who graduate from our school will have the tools and the desire to continue participating in such exploration."

Devora's comments about honestly and thoughtfully exploring Jewish texts that may have a bearing on our understandings and choices touched a resonant chord in me. At the same time, I found myself wondering about the limits of such exploration, especially whether certain texts might not be age-appropriate.[82] So I asked Devora about this, and was delighted to get a response which illuminated not just the narrow question I thought I was asking, but also her views on other matters.

She began by observing—and it's something that you and I know well—that many Jewish educators (including some who represent a very traditional Jewish educational agenda) would be very reluctant to offer young children the kind of open access to Jewish texts that would bring them face-to-face with what might prove very disturbing issues, for example (and this was her example), a biblical text which declares that those who don't observe the rules of Shabbat should be put to death. But in this matter Beit Rabban's approach is very different. Reminding me that this was a school based on integrity, she emphasized that for her this meant that the school would not patronize the children by leading them on a journey through Jewish texts that bypasses what may prove difficult issues. This does not mean, she emphasized, that the school forces the youngsters to think about and respond to such issues; what it does mean is that if they feel ready to address such issues, they can.

Correctly reading the look on my face as a request to say more about this, Devora went on to challenge the conventional wisdom that leads educators to shy away from texts which embody what we view as difficult issues like the one identified above. "First of all, the impulse to circumvent or quickly explain away such texts is of a piece with an approach to Jewish education which seeks to inoculate youngsters against challenges to their religious outlook by avoiding, or sometimes simplistically domesticating, potential threats to their beliefs. In the end, this will prove a disastrous

[81] As traditionally understood, "*mitzvot*" are religiously binding, divinely ordained commandments.
[82] Though not necessary for present purposes, the term "age-appropriate" is sufficiently vague as to warrant careful examination.

strategy. Second, you shouldn't think that because an issue is an issue for adults, it will also be an issue for, say, an eight-year-old. The eight-year-olds may be completely uninterested in the passage that speaks about being put to death for non-observance, and they may be much more interested in a text which, to many adults, seems utterly uninteresting."

"My view," she added, "is that, unless pushed by adults to deal with certain issues that the adult has designated as important to address, the children will not take on our so-called 'difficult issues' until they are ready to deal with them, and then they will deal with them in a way that is appropriate to their overall development. The challenge for the teacher is to avoid trying to mediate the children's encounter with the text; it's to let the issues that are of interest to them surface and then to offer them help in exploring them in a way that honors their concerns."

I asked Devora how the parent community felt about this approach. She didn't answer in any systematic way, but told me with a smile that one of the reasons she had used the biblical statement that one should be put to death for not observing Shabbat as an example of the kind of difficult text the school doesn't seek to avoid is that it had been one of the less observant parents in the school who had urged that such statements not be excluded from Beit Rabban's curriculum.

As you know, the question of whether, when and why to include or exclude difficult issues—issues pertaining to such matters as blemished heroes, disturbing events in biblical history, and the Shoah—is a difficult one for educators, and Devora and I continued discussing it for some time. Eventually, though, I brought us back to the question that launched our conversation on this occasion: Would Alice's daughter be happy at Beit Rabban?

Devora paused briefly and then said, "If things Jewish are important to her and her family, so that she doesn't feel that a school organized around Jewish learning and culture is alien or alienating, and if she and her family are comfortable with her engaging in text-informed inquiry into the basis of their beliefs and practices, she might well find Beit Rabban a very congenial place. On the other hand, a child from a very observant home who found it impossible to engage in this kind of inquiry would find Beit Rabban an impossible environment. Not a certain level of observance but a willingness to approach one's Jewish life—like everything else, be it in math or science or current events or grammar—in an inquiring, reflective spirit is what a young person needs to share in the life of Beit Rabban; and certainly this quality is one of the marks of a successful Beit Rabban graduate."

I responded that this commitment to approach the conduct of our lives in a reflective spirit is actually very radical, reminding me of Socrates' dictum that the unexamined life is not worth living—a dictum which, when he practiced it and especially when he encouraged others to do so, got him executed! Devora smiled, and said that though she had faced problems in building and directing Beit Rabban, fear for her life had not been one of them. But, she added in a more serious vein, it is true that in its strong emphasis on examining the reasons for what we do and think, Beit Rabban is a rarity in the world of Jewish schools and occasions a measure of mistrust. And we then revisited a theme we (she and I, and also you and I) had discussed before. Right-wing Jewish schools carefully avoid encouraging reason-asking, reason-giving approaches to life for fear that eventually children will be led to call into question the very fundamentals of Jewish faith. They prefer to educate children in such a way that they are, as it were, inoculated against challenges to their faith. Devora thinks this is nuts—thoroughly counter-productive. As soon as they encounter bright, thoughtful people out in the world, say, at the university, who think differently from them and can muster strong arguments on behalf of their views, these kids who have been systematically sheltered from serious challenges to their belief-systems are going to be terrifically confused and maybe disillusioned. On the other, so-called progressive, side of the educational universe, we find schools that welcome diversity of belief and practice but without any serious interest in the reasons that lie behind different approaches to Jewish life. Sure, teachers in these schools might ask, "Why do you do this or that?" but there is an expectation that the responses that are offered will be smilingly affirmed without attention to whether they make sense or are grounded in real thinking and study. In contrast, the Beit Rabban idea is that careful thinking, enriched by Jewish texts and ideas, about why we do or don't believe certain things and act in certain ways, is not just sensible, it's also the Jewish thing to do."

Well, well. Maybe the digression away from questions pertaining to autonomy occasioned by the story about your daughter was not such a digression after all: though we started by thinking about authenticity and pluralism, we've found our way back to questions about intellectual autonomy and thoughtful self-examination. And that being so, I want to more fully explore, although not today, a Beit Rabban assumption that emerged when we looked at the "lights on Shabbat" problem: namely, that there is no incompatibility between the spirit of open-minded, independent inquiry that she encourages and living within the tradition. Since you and I, and probably many others (both to the right and left of Devora) may not be fully convinced, it may be worth returning to this assumption when I next speak to Devora.

All the best,
Daniel

LETTERS 6 AND 7
Autonomy and Tradition (II)
and
The Possible Significance of Informal Preschool Experience

These letters further examine the relationship between intellectual auton-
omy and tradition. With attention to the figure of Ozzie in Philip Roth's
"The Conversion of the Jews,"[83] *Letters 6 and 7 examine Devora's rejec-*
tion of the widely held view that genuine intellectual autonomy threatens
a person's identity as a "son or daughter of the tradition."

Daniel proposes, but Devora rejects, the possibility that autonomy and
tradition are likely to sit comfortably together only in those who have been
blessed with the right kind of early informal socialization in the family. De-
vora advances her own view that it is the failure of Jewish schools to offer
children serious intellectual challenges and to address their concerns in a
compelling way that leads the Ozzies of the world to grow alienated.

Letter 6

Dear Alice:

I was moved by your reactions to what I wrote about teachers and
children being forced by the norms of Jewish educating institutions into inauthentic roles—into pretending to be other than they are. At the time I
wrote about this, I was thinking about children and classroom teachers, not
about principals like yourself. But as soon as I read your response I realized
that many of them, like you, are also thrust into uncomfortable positions,

---

[83]Philip Roth, "The Conversion of the Jews," in *Goodbye Columbus and Five Short
Stories* (New York: Bantam Books, 1959), 180–205.

with enormous pressure on them to act as though they buy the employing community's religious stance 100%. It can, I am sure, be very trying. So it is not entirely surprising to me, but it makes me sad, that you have made the decision to leave the principalship of your congregational school. Knowing what I do about your talents, I am far from confident that the school will be better off; but I can understand your decision, and I hope that you will find an institution that has an outlook closer to your own. If I can be helpful, let me know. But since your letter suggested that, for now, you would rather not dwell on this matter, I'll honor your wishes and bring us back to our shared interest in Beit Rabban.

I imagine you recall the problem that I brought to Devora's attention. Isn't she—or shouldn't she—be worried that children who have been encouraged to reach conclusions based on good reasons for what they believe and do will eventually call into question the Jewish framework within which they are operating? I'm entirely willing to concede that Devora is right that there is no logical incompatibility between being autonomous and dwelling within the tradition, and I'm also prepared to agree that that it is psychologically possible for many people to function autonomously within the framework of Jewish tradition. Still, it seems to me that some children who are encouraged to expect reasons for what they are supposed to do and believe may well be led to apply this expectation to what the Orthodox and some other communities take to be foundational Jewish beliefs, beliefs that are at the core of Jewish tradition as they understand it.[84] Isn't there something to the Orthodox community's judgment that this is dangerous?

---

[84]A fictional example of something like this phenomenon—or in any case the kind of situation that fuels the anxieties of those who are wary of encouraging youngsters to develop a critical, inquiring spirit—is found in Myla Goldberg's recent novel *The Bee Season* (New York: Anchor Books, 2000). In this story, an adolescent boy, Aaron, the son of a cantor, suddenly realized that he has never applied to Judaism his father's dictum that, before consuming, he should always read the ingredients on the side of the box in a serious way. Guided by this principle, Aaron embarks on a journey of religious exploration that leads him away from Judaism and into the Hare Krishna movement. As Goldberg describes Aaron's situation (79–82): "Ever since Saul [Aaron's father] dissected a Snoopy Snow Cone Machine commercial for Aaron at age seven, Aaron has been aware of the manipulative powers of advertising. 'Never buy a product just because you've seen it on TV,' Saul instructed at an age at which recognizing characters on cereal boxes made leaving aisle three empty-handed tantamount to abandoning a friend. As a result, Aaron has grown to mid-adolescence with an eye for label reading. It is at the [Friday night religious] service's completion, while munching on an *oneg* cookie, that Aaron realizes he's bought Judaism without consulting the side of the box. . . . Aaron decides to apply his father's lessons about advertising to religion. He decides to visit a church!"

"I grant," Devora responded, "that what they fear is a possibility, but it's a pretty remote one. Yes, we try at Beit Rabban to cultivate in the children the disposition to approach their lives as Jews in an inquiring and honest spirit, rather than thoughtlessly; but not only don't I believe that this is likely to push them to call into question Jewish tradition as such, I also think that Judaism will be all the richer—Torah will grow—if its interpreters are the kinds of open-minded, honest, inquiring spirits that Beit Rabban tries to encourage its youngsters to become."

Correctly reading the quizzical look on my face as a request to clarify the intriguing phrase "Torah will grow" that she had just used, Devora then added, "I don't mean anything mysterious by this phrase. It's close to something we've spoken about before. If you think of Torah not just as a set of canonized texts but also as the interpretive tradition that has developed around these texts, what I'm suggesting is this: because each of us brings a unique history of experiences to the study of these texts, we may have the potential to illuminate them and enrich this interpretive tradition in unique ways, adding to its stock of questions, insights, and ways of learning. It is in this sense that Torah can continue to grow through the encounters of different people in different circumstances with the texts and textual tradition they inherit. But this result is only likely if those struggling to interpret these texts approach them thoughtfully, openly and with intellectual integrity."

There was much that I liked in this response to the questions I had been raising. But I didn't feel that what she had said was responsive to the concerns of Orthodox Jews who worried that a Beit Rabban education might threaten the religious outlook of their children; and I continued to feel that their concerns were legitimate. It's not that I think (and I doubt that all these critics think) that all children who get into the habit of demanding reasons will eventually bring this habit to bear on the outer limits of the tradition, but it is conceivable that this will happen to some of them, and that at least some of them will not come back. So in a more recent conversation, I tried to approach the question again, but this time from a different starting point.

"Let me put my concern in the following form," I began. "Is it possible that Beit Rabban's success—and let's assume that it's successful—in nurturing an autonomous approach to life that doesn't threaten the youngsters' embrace of Jewish tradition depends on the circumstance that the school attracts children who, from the beginnings of life, have been immersed in familial environments that are suffused with the rhythms, customs, ideas, and values that typify traditional Judaism? Might it be that it is because this immersion has led to their internalizing very early on dispositions, sentiments, and rhythms that are consonant with the tradition that their participation in Jewish life is not jeopardized by Beit Rabban's unqualified emphasis on intellectual autonomy? And might this emphasis push children not blessed with this background early in life and at home outside the world of Judaism? Might they be more like Roth's Ozzie in 'The Conversion of the Jews:' Ozzie, a boy who does not enter formal Jewish education saturated with traditional beliefs, sentiments, and rhythms and whose pointed, intellectually challenging questions, exhibiting his own autonomous spirit, bring him to disavow—or at least close to disavowing—the tradition into which he was born?

"I am, by the way, thinking about Plato when I say this, about his belief that the attempt to encourage rational judgment in a person who has not, through daily experience in an exemplary culture, acquired appropriate sentiments, rhythms, and pre-theoretical understandings and convictions, is unlikely to produce happy results. Not a worthy human being, says Plato, but a moral monster is likely to result when Reason is cultivated in an individual whose soul has not been rendered good through immersion in a healthy cultural medium."[85]

Devora listened but did not immediately respond. And then I noticed that I was late for an appointment, so we agreed to resume our conversation soon. In the meantime I'm looking forward to hearing from you.

Daniel

Letter 7

Dear Alice:

Sorry—I thought you would get the allusion to Ozzie, the young adolescent hero of Philip Roth's short story "The Conversion of the Jews." Ozzie is a child of modernity, a boy growing up in the 'forties in New Jersey, not far from New York. His father has died and he is being raised by his mother. He is, or could well be, a child of mainstream American Judaism. He lives "an American life" (you know, he goes to public school, loves sports, believes in the Declaration of Independence and so forth), but his mother still honors vestiges of Jewish tradition like the lighting of Shabbat candles every Friday night, and sending her boy to Hebrew school. In Hebrew school Ozzie encounters his nemesis, the teacher Rabbi Binder. Rabbi Binder intones Jewish platitudes the way most people breathe; it comes naturally, with no effort at all. And Ozzie, a successful public

---

[85]See *The Republic* (Book VI, 491d–492), 165–166, for this discussion.

school student in modern America, finds Rabbi Binder's smug, unthinking parochialism insufferable. And so, during "Free Discussion," he asks Rabbi Binder exasperating questions. For example: why do you insist that Jesus must be "historical" (because the virgin birth is a biological impossibility)? If God could create the world in six days, wouldn't creating a baby without intercourse be kid's stuff? Ozzie is enormously clever: his reason, unsupported by sensibilities and understandings that have been cultivated through immersion in Jewish life, lead him, or so it appears, quickly to reject the whole of Judaism. That Devora's students don't, as far as I know, move in this direction makes me wonder whether what saves them is precisely the fact that, unlikely Ozzie, they come from traditional homes that have, as Plato might have said, implanted Jewish sentiments, rhythms, and beliefs deep within the recesses of their souls.[86]

By the way, you're not alone in raising questions about my references to Ozzie. When we next spoke, Devora expressed considerable skepticism concerning my understanding of Ozzie. "I don't think Ozzie angrily steps outside the world of Judaism because he hasn't acquired, along with critical capacities, Jewish sensibilities and ways of being. He rebels because his questions are greeted with disrespectful, authoritarian attacks, because the Rabbi Binders of the world fail to provide him and those like him with intellectually challenging responses to the questions that they raise. Had Rabbi Binder responded to Ozzie's questions differently, these questions, skeptical though they might have sounded, might well have led Ozzie deeper into Judaism, rather than away from it."

So how, I asked, would she have responded to Ozzie?

"Well, Ozzie has posed a problem; and at a school like Beit Rabban that views inquiry as problem solving, Ozzie's questions, grounded in personal concern, could become the foundation for some significant learning: for ideas about Judaism and Christianity; for the acquisition of tools that make for thoughtful problem solving; and for the discovery that even skeptical questions can be asked in Jewish settings and that Jewish tradition has rich ways of responding to them."

[86]Plato has Socrates say in *The Republic* (Book III, 401d–402b, 78): ". . . because anyone who has been properly educated in music and poetry will sense it acutely when something has been omitted from a thing and when it hasn't been finely crafted or finely made by nature. And since he has the right tastes, he'll praise fine things, be pleased by them, receive them into his soul, and, being nurtured by them, become fine and good. He'll rightly object to what is shameful, hating it while he's still young and unable to grasp the reason, but, having been educated in this way, he will welcome the reason when it comes and recognize it easily because of its kinship with himself."

"Do you think it's possible to squeeze this much learning out of this one question?"

"Actually, I think it is; but the truth is that which if any of these learning tracks I would pursue would depend on a deeper understanding of what Ozzie is really asking: what's the question behind the question, and why is he asking it? So perhaps the first thing I would do would be to ask some questions designed to clarify this."

I told Devora that I liked her answer very much but that I continued to feel that she underestimates, or perhaps chooses to ignore, the extent to which the school's simultaneous emphasis on both critical, autonomous thinking and tradition is sustainable because the children have already received, and continue to receive, a rich informal Jewish education through the organization of their home life. And then I reiterated the concern I had already voiced: that youngsters who haven't unselfconsciously absorbed into their very being the social, intellectual, and emotional lexicon of Jewish life through participation in such an environment are much more likely to employ their reasons-demanding, autonomous spirit to call into question the outer limits of Jewish tradition and perhaps to land on the other side, in some cases for good.

Devora shook her head in disagreement. "I've been thinking about this point since you brought up Plato the last time we talked; and while I find it an interesting hypothesis, my experience at Beit Rabban does not confirm it. The fact is that our children do not all come from homes saturated with Jewish rhythms and a Jewish outlook; and those who don't, do not seem to me more likely than the others to challenge the Jewish framework that the school takes for granted."

I was about to respond skeptically, and to reassert my belief that there is probably something special going on in the families of Beit Rabban children which reduces the likelihood that the children will step outside the school's Jewish framework. But before I could do so, Devora continued in a different vein.

"Look, maybe you're right," Devora acknowledged, "that the school's open-minded, inquiry-oriented ethos might conceivably lead some children to question traditional Jewish beliefs and practices. But you shouldn't rule out the possibility that our approach will also have very different consequences; that, by bringing them to deeper understandings, it will bring some less observant children who might otherwise remain pretty indifferent to traditional Jewish beliefs and practices to a real appreciation for them, whether or not they become more observant."

Devora paused for a moment. "I think there are also two other and perhaps deeper considerations that are important here. My criterion for success at Beit Rabban is not whether or not the student passes some litmus test of belief and practice. What does concern me is whether our children grow into adults who are engaged with Jewish life in ways that emerge out of reflection that is enriched by Jewish ideas and texts. If Beit Rabban contributes to this outcome, I will be very happy; and I think the school's design is well fitted to the cultivation of such people."

"One could argue," I interjected, "that adults of this kind will be more successful at integrating their identities as citizens of the modern world with a rich Jewish life than will those in our community whose life as reflective people stops when they enter Jewish arenas."

"That's probably true," Devora responded, "but, again, that formulation—taken alone, anyway—is too concerned with 'what a good Jewish education will do for me.' As I mentioned some time ago, what I would emphasize is that the kinds of thoughtful, knowledgeable, inquiring individuals that Beit Rabban tries to cultivate will prove more powerful bearers of Jewish culture and will be more likely to contribute to its development. True, thinking individuals of this kind may find themselves in tension with various ideas that they encounter in the tradition; but this shouldn't be understood as a problem to be avoided but as a blessing; for it is through such tensions that Torah grows . . ."

Devora again paused briefly, as though groping for another thought, before continuing. "It also comes back to the issue of integrity. In the end, this is a school based on honesty. We don't want to communicate to the children, 'You may inquire this far, but no further.' If a child is led to raise questions that challenge or express skepticism concerning what seem to be foundational Jewish ideas, we need to be respectful and honest in return." Thus ended our conversation for the day.

I would love to hear your responses to any or all of this. All the best.

Daniel

LETTER 8

Moral Education

Along with autonomy, intellectual openness and rigor, and serious study, Beit Rabban's vision of the individual and the community that we should be striving to actualize also emphasizes our obligation to help ameliorate the plight of those who suffer. This letter offers an account of Beit Rabban's approach to moral education. More specifically, it focuses on the way gemilut hesed[87] fits into the vision of the school and how it is integrated with the school's commitment to informed problem-based learning.

Friday afternoon

Dear Alice:

Today, one of the Beit Rabban teachers, Nurit, treated me to a moving account of an activity she was in the middle of with her class. What she described would have excited me, no matter what the circumstances; but as it happened, our conversation took place against the background of some troubling matters that were on my mind when I chanced to meet up with her. Here's the context. When I come to Manhattan, I often stay in a hotel in the middle of the city; and one of the things I most enjoy is step-

---

[87]The term *gemilut hesed* could be rendered "doing deeds of lovingkindness." At least in ordinary parlance, the term overlaps with tzedakah, i.e., deeds that have an element in them of both charity and justice. Both terms concern doing what we can to make the world a better place. Traditional, and many non-traditional, Jews view themselves as under a sacred obligation to make this effort.

ping out in the evening for a brisk walk. It is, after all, so different to be walking the streets of Manhattan, where you routinely hear the buzz of different languages and see people from so many worlds, than to be strolling through the tree-lined, serene, but nearly deserted streets of my neighborhood in Madison.

But, as you well know, not everything that one comes across on such walks falls into the "energizing" or "interesting" category. In fact, some of it is very troubling. In particular, amidst the opulence that I encounter as I walk down a fancy street that is home to some of Manhattan's glitziest hotels (no, these are not the hotels I stay at), there are also signs of serious poverty. Along the same street where chauffeur-driven stretch limousines sit waiting for their clients to emerge from ritzy nightclubs and restaurants, one also finds panhandlers and a surprising number of homeless people camped out in doorways and other empty spaces. Often, all you see is a body covered by old blankets, with feet sticking out at one end and a head on a pillow, usually facing away from the sidewalk so you don't see the face. Taking in such stark contrasts, I am often reminded of the opening lines of *A Tale of Two Cities:* "It was the best times; it was the worst of times." It also reminds me of George Counts, a professor at Columbia's Teachers College, who took in the same contrasts, though probably more extreme, in Depression-era New York:

> Here is a society that manifests the most extraordinary contradictions: a mastery of the forces of nature, surpassing the wildest dreams of antiquity, is accompanied by extreme material insecurity; dire poverty walks hand in hand with the most extravagant living the world has ever seen; and abundance of goods of all kinds is accompanied by privation, misery, and even starvation; an excess of production is seriously offered as the underlying cause of severe physical suffering; breakfastless children march to school past bankrupt shops laden with rich foods gathered from the ends of the earth. . . . One can only imagine what Jeremiah would say if he could step out of the pages of the Old Testament and cast his eyes over this vast spectacle so full of tragedy and menace.[88]

Deeply troubled by what he saw and believing that capitalism was the root of the problem, he wrote a strongly polemical tract entitled *Dare the School Build a New Social Order?* in which he challenges educators to lead the next generation of youngsters to an appreciation of the evils

---

[88]George Counts, *Dare the School Build a New Social Order?* (New York: Arno Press and *The New York Times*, 1969), 32–35.

of capitalism and to a passionate commitment to bring about social change.[89]

Sorry—I fear I've gotten off track and want to come back to the street-people I had started to describe, one of them in particular. Just as some of Jerusalem's beggars have their favorite spots, there is a woman who has a regular perch a few doors down from the entrance to my hotel. She is middle-aged and gaunt, with long grayish hair, and she wears an old pair of pants and a ragged shirt. She sits on the ledge of a street-level window on Lexington Avenue, with a somewhat vacant look and a cup in her hands. She doesn't actively ask for money, she doesn't even look up as you walk by; but the cup contains some coins, and now and then passersby will add to what is there. Though I've passed her many times, I've never seen her do anything but sit quietly, and I've never heard her utter a word. My suspicion is that she is a victim of some kind of mental illness, but I'm not sure; and I've often wondered what her story is.

I don't know about you, but I'm often conflicted about how to respond to street-people who ask for money; I typically don't, reassuring myself—not entirely successfully—that there are good reasons not to, and that it's better to make my contribution to such people through organizations like the Jewish United Fund or a non-sectarian equivalent. But it's hard not to feel cold and heartless when you pass needy people on the street without responding; and there are times when I think that the traditional Jewish idea about leaving the gleanings of your field for the poor might be applied to the change you have in your pocket at the time you encounter a person in need.

But though my general tendency is not to give, when I pass by the perch of the woman I've described to you, I often do put a dollar in her cup, an act which she receives almost without any acknowledgment. But this doesn't seem to matter to me; and when I come to Manhattan, I find myself really looking forward to seeing her. Which is why I have been disappointed

---

[89]To sustain the continuity of this discussion, I will not be stopping to critically examine Counts's view that it would be appropriate for educators to actively lead the young towards a particular assessment of their economic and political circumstances and to arouse in them a passionate commitment to work on behalf of social change. Whether it would have been appropriate, or ethical, for educators to undertake the agenda recommended by Counts in the context of Depression-era America, or whether it is ever appropriate for educators working in public and other settings to become, in their role as educators, advocates for a certain social agenda, are matters worthy of serious attention. Though exploring them is beyond the scope of this project, interested readers would do well to start with a full review of Counts's impassioned discussion.

on my most recent trips. I didn't see her here two months ago when I visited, and she has not been here on my current trip. I have found myself feeling sad about this and wondering what might have become of her. Was she sick? Had she died? Was my speculation correct that she was mentally unsound, and could she be in an institution of some kind? Or, was she just pushed away from her stoop by the police or by some hotel manager who thought that her presence was not good for business? I have no idea.

The relevant point is that these matters were on my mind when, late this morning, I bumped into Nurit, a woman of about twenty-four and a graduate of an elite college, who teaches Beit Rabban's kindergarten/first grade group. We chatted for a couple of minutes, until I asked her matter-of-factly what she had done that day. Immediately her expression grew animated, and she asked whether I had a few minutes to spare. When I said that I did, she proceeded to describe an extraordinary conversation that had gone on in her class that morning. Because we didn't have that much time, the account of this conversation that she offered was somewhat sketchy, leaving me some room to imagine some of its details; and it is this somewhat imaginative reconstruction that I am passing on to you.[90]

Nurit began by explaining to me that today was to have been the culmination of a year-long tzedakah project. At the beginning of the year the children had made a tzedakah container, and every Friday morning they added coins to the collection. Today, the children were to decide where this money would go.

Nurit also told me about the background preparations that had preceded this day. Most importantly, in the course of the year, the children had become familiar with a number of social service projects and agencies

---

[90]The account that follows is based substantially on an article by the teacher who executed this project. See Ilana Blumberg, "Teaching Chesed: Community Service in a Kindergarten Classroom," in *Kerem: Creative Explorations in Judaism* (Spring 1995), 53–56. Although my account is faithful to the direction and spirit of the activity as described by Blumberg, it differs from hers in a critical respect: in order to illustrate the school's emphasis on deliberation that is strengthened through the thoughtful contributions of more than one person, I take the liberty of imaginatively reconstructing some of the dialogue in order to emphasize this point. To mark this departure from Blumberg's account, and because later on in the text I include this teacher in an imagined conversation concerning the school's educational outlook that also includes myself and Devora, I use the pseudonym *Nurit* rather than *Ilana* in the text. As already mentioned in the introduction, Blumberg is aware of and comfortable with my having filled in her account of the tzedakah project in the ways that I have.

through regular community service activities. More recently, earlier this week, Nurit and her co-teacher had posted a sign on the wall which asks: WHERE WILL WE GIVE OUR TZEDAKAH?, and in the course of the week the children had generated a list of possibilities that reflect their encounters with various programs and other ideas they have about how to help those in need. And today, the final decision was at hand!

At around 10 o'clock, the kids clustered around Nurit, who was standing near the list of possible charities. Here were the candidates on the list (in the children's own words):

- Todah [an organization that tries to meet the needs of the Jewish elderly]
- Project Sukkah [care for Jewish homeless people]
- "Learn how to help sick people in hospitals" [medical research]; the Jewish Hospital
- "Poor people/people on the street"

Nurit introduced the activity. "This year we have been meeting our responsibility to help people in need in two ways. Every week we have tried to help needy people directly, and we have also collected tzedakah money, which can help needy people in other ways. But, you know, collecting money is only half the challenge; it's also important that we think carefully and wisely about how to use this money so that it will do some real good."

We will, she went on to say, take a vote, but before voting it's important that we all have a chance to think about the various possibilities. And she then invited each person who had contributed a possibility to defend it by explaining how the proposed allocation would meaningfully fulfill the purposes of tzedakah. The kids, Nurit reported, were incredibly eloquent in pleading the case for their favorite candidates; and when it seemed appropriate, Nurit or her co-teacher would ask a question that elicited more information that seemed pertinent.

And then H-Hour arrived and the children voted: Todah got five votes; medical research, two votes; poor people/people on the street, a whopping seven votes, the clear winner! Already strong democrats, losers and winners alike were getting excited about giving their accumulated forty dollars to Joe, the man who regularly stands on the corner. Apparently, Joe always has a kind word for the kids, and many of them look forward to their encounters with him on the way in and out of school. One of the children now proposed bringing him the can of tzedakah money on the spot, and this idea called forth enthusiasm from the others. The only ones who found themselves a little unhappy were Nurit and her co-teacher, who were not entirely comfortable with this unexpected turn of events.

Thinking fast, Nurit finally said, "Seems like an interesting idea. But before we act on it, let's think about whether it will really help Joe."

"What do you mean?" asked one of the girls.

"Well, do you remember when, some time ago, we had a guest, the director of a shelter, who spoke with us about homelessness? One of the things she mentioned is that some homeless people have serious alcohol or drug problems."

"I remember," one boy said with a smile. "Because after she said that people who are alcoholics sometimes can't help themselves, I said that that's the way I feel when I see chocolate."

Nurit smiled back. "That's right. And when people have very bad habits like that—I don't mean with chocolate, but with alcohol or drugs—it may be very hard for them not to use money that comes their way to support these habits rather than to get things they really need." That's one of the reasons why, Nurit went on to explain, it's sometimes wise to give tzedakah money to social service organizations rather than to individuals directly.

"But we've never seen Joe looking drunk or anything!" another child complained.

"That may be true," Nurit countered, "but you can't always be sure. And if he does have a drug or alcohol problem, not only will our money not do him any good, it may actually hurt him. So my suggestion is this: if you're interested in helping homeless people, why not give the money to Project Sukkah?"

"But we don't just want to help homeless people, we want to help Joe," explained the boy who had proposed this option in the first place. "He's poor, and he's always friendly to us. And if we give our money to Project Sukkah, it's probably not going to help him."

Everyone, teachers and children alike, now sat in silence contemplating the situation. The children had taken in the teacher's point but didn't seem ready to abandon the idea of giving the tzedakah money they had collected to Joe. It was Nurit who finally broke the silence. "I've got an idea. Maybe we shouldn't give Joe money; maybe we should give him something else—you know, the things that money is supposed to buy for Joe; that way we don't have to worry about his using the money for bad things or wasting it."

The comment seemed to reenergize the room. Remembering a recent food drive, someone suggested bringing cans of food for Joe, but someone else wondered whether Joe even had the utensils to handle cans of different kinds or to heat up food. Someone else suggested getting Joe a new coat, but others were concerned that they didn't know Joe's size or the kind of coat he might like. Finally, someone said that "maybe we could make Joe a good sandwich to eat."

"That seems like a good idea," said another, "but we have enough money to buy enough food for a lot of sandwiches."

"That's no problem," said a third child. "After all, though we know Joe better, there are lots of homeless people in the neighborhood, and they're probably hungry, too. Let's make enough sandwiches for all of them."

The idea gathered support around the room, and soon it was agreed on. Nurit felt both relieved and pleased; and she announced that on Monday she would bring to school the supplies they would need to make the sandwiches. That, Nurit informed me, was the end of the day's activity, but she promised to pass on the sequel (and I promise to pass it on to you).

When, before leaving the school, I saw Devora, I told her about my conversation with Nurit, and let her know how impressed I was with what Nurit had reported about the quality of the children's deliberations and about the seriousness with which they approached the question of what to do with their tzedakah funds. I was also, I added, impressed with Nurit, who, as best I could tell, avoided imposing her idea of what should be done with the money or manipulating the children into accepting it, while at the same time not simply acquiescing in their wishes. My impression was that she had succeeded in formulating the situation as a problem that needed thoughtful attention; and the kids, having appreciated the character of the problem, embarked on a thoughtful process of inquiry that culminated, thanks to their creative ideas and to Nurit's skillfully introduced input, in an imaginative and sensible solution.

Devora picked up on this. "We try hard to convey to the children that the same kinds of problem-solving skills that are useful in making sense of a math problem or an apparent contradiction between two passages in the Torah are also to be used in approaching real-life problems: not just problems in our own lives but the social problems that abound in our world."

"You know, you're reminding me that we really haven't talked much about Beit Rabban's approach to moral education. How central is this to Beit Rabban's agenda?"

"Very," Devora responded. "The school would be radically incomplete without this element of community service. We take giving tzedakah and *gemilut hesed* enormously seriously in our school, and we try to emphasize that the giving of tzedakah is a moral obligation rather than being a kind of elective activity: we are all—this is the message we try to convey—responsible for alleviating the suffering found in the community that surrounds us, both Jewish and non-Jewish."

Devora paused briefly and then continued. "Actually, this is a hard message to convey to children living in the middle of Manhattan in the late twentieth century. New Yorkers (and they are not unique in this respect) are surrounded by so much suffering and need, day in and day out, that many people often respond in disturbingly unproductive ways. Some are so overwhelmed by the enormity of the problems we face that they develop a paralyzing sense of hopelessness. Others respond by simply tuning these problems out, the way you see some New Yorkers not even taking notice of the homeless people sleeping along the streets they walk along daily."

Reflecting on what Devora was saying in the wake of my own recent musings about poverty and about the homeless woman who had disappeared from her perch near my hotel, I commented that I am, in my own person, familiar with both the tendencies she has described, with both paralyzing hopelessness and becoming oblivious.

"Well, that sets our challenge! To raise children who will avoid these tendencies. Remember the rabbinic dictum that while it is not our responsibility to finish the work (of remedying the world's problems), neither are we free to abstain from it.[91] If Beit Rabban is successful, our children will become people who, though not naïve about how difficult our social problems are, will believe that they can make a real difference if they are determined to do so and approach these problems in the right way."

"The right way?"

"I don't mean anything complicated. In large part, it's just a matter of thinking critically. One of the messages that I hope—and think—the children are beginning to absorb in Nurit's class is that a willingness to think carefully and imaginatively about problems like poverty can make the difference between a real contribution and a well-intentioned disaster.[92] But there's also another important message we try to convey to the children. Do you remember describing to me how Nurit infused the discussion with information the children had learned about the drug and alcohol problems of some street people? This was a critical part of the process that culminated in a wise decision. I mean, without reasonable information about the phenomenon we're trying to remedy, our efforts to help are pretty blind. So it's really important that the children come to recognize that when they respond to a social problem, they need to get hold of whatever information may illuminate it. For this reason, whenever the kids are addressing a problem, we try to infuse the process with information and ideas that go beyond what they would have known or come up with on their own. And often this means bringing in more knowledgeable people, like the woman from the homelessness shelter, to introduce insights and facts that will feed their thinking."

---

[91]This passage, attributed to Rabbi Tarfon, is found in a tractate of the Mishnah called *Pirkei Avot (Ethics of the Fathers)*, Chapter 2:21.

[92]Devora's comment calls to mind Dewey's view, expressed in *Moral Principles in Education* (Carbondale, IL: Southern Illinois University Press, 1975), that *social concern* (the impulse to help alleviate the world's problems) is a dangerous thing if not accompanied by *social intelligence*.

"I'm struck," I commented, "that in talking about the school's efforts in the area of moral education, you haven't said anything about the role of Jewish texts. Can you speak to this?"

"Well, I guess I don't think that studying Jewish texts that voice the importance of tzedakah or *gemilut hesed* is enough. Think for a moment about a very different area like Shabbat observance. Studying about Shabbat is no substitute for rich opportunities to experience it first-hand; and most often it is only people who are already familiar with Shabbat in this immediate way who will find meaningful the texts that discuss the laws associated with Shabbat and its significance. The same, I think, is true in this other area. As I see it, the disposition to give tzedakah and to participate in more direct efforts to address suffering and injustice does not mainly develop through the acquisition of certain religious or theological beliefs. It comes about through immersion, through a kind of apprenticeship, in a community that takes these things seriously. For the children to be part of a community in which it is a given that we have the obligation to improve the world and that our efforts to do so require rigorous, imaginative thinking about how to proceed, is the closest we can come to ensuring that they will grow into adults who will work to improve the world in this way. And this is why the kinds of community service projects that you witnessed today play such an important role in the life of the school."

Well, that's all for now. I think I'll hold off sending this letter to you until I have the chance to learn about Monday's follow-up experience. I'll let you know what Nurit passes on.

D.

Monday evening

Here's my postscript to the last letter. My curiosity getting the best of me, this afternoon I sought out Nurit in order to find out how the project had unfolded earlier in the day. Here's what I learned. True to her promise, she had shown up in class with all the supplies needed to make peanut butter and jelly sandwiches. Divided into pairs, the children devoted themselves to their work, and she overheard one little boy say to his partner, "I'm not going to take one bite, because a lot of people need this stuff!" The other nodded in agreement. By the way, Nurit informed me that she added a whole new dimension to the morning's events by announcing that they were to complete the whole of this activity in Hebrew! The kids were apparently not surprised, and though there were lapses, they responded enthusiastically to this challenge.

When they finished making the sandwiches and packing them into bags, Nurit and her co-teacher led a short conversation about what it might be like to talk with people whom they didn't know, people who might not always be very clean and who might talk very differently than they do. But the kids didn't seem at all alarmed.

They headed out of the building and one of the boys, David, spotted Joe. He grabbed one of the bags and approached him. Joe greeted him in a friendly way: "How ya' doin', David?" David answered, "Great," followed by, "We've brought you some sandwiches!" Joe accepted the bag and smiled. "Thanks, David. I never say no to food!" That's all he said, but it was enough. The children moved along, a look of pride on their faces, a feeling that they had made a real difference in someone's life.

They continued down the street and Nurit spotted a man looking through the window of a restaurant, trying to catch the eye of one of the waiters; but, not surprisingly, the waiters looked the other way. With encouragement from Nurit, Yonatan, a little bit nervous, approached the man. Here's the interaction.

"Sir?"

"Hi there."

"Sir, we have some sandwiches we made. Do you want them?"

The man bent down and stuck out his hand, saying, "Gimme five, my man!" and Yonatan immediately "gave him five" with enthusiasm.

"My buddy," said the man. "That's sure nice of you. You be safe, you and all your friends. Be safe." And then, after Yonatan handed him the sandwich bag, "I sure am hungry. Thanks a lot."

The children and Nurit continued on their way. At the end of their journey, they were left with a number of sandwiches, and the children asked to take the sandwiches home with them so that they could distribute them to needy people in their own neighborhoods.

As on Friday, Nurit was clearly moved by the experience she had watched the children undergo. She spoke of them as having had the chance to take classroom learning and tzedekah out into the world, where they could serve as "*metaknei olam,*" literally, "repairers of the world."

Her description also left me deeply moved. There seemed to be something so much more satisfying about having real human contact with the people they were helping than simply sending a check to some organization, and when I later saw Devora I commented about the sense of satisfaction the children must have felt as a result of their participation in this experience.

Devora beamed with pleasure, clearly very happy about how well this activity seemed to have gone. "You know," she then added, "the children don't always experience these social service projects so positively. Some time ago a group of older kids went to a home for Jewish senior citizens and came back pretty unhappy. It had been a long ride back and forth, and the seniors they encountered did not prove all that rewarding to spend time with. They came back grouchy, and it was pretty clear that they would not be eager to return."

"How did you respond?"

"At first, I was unhappy that they didn't have a good time. But in the course of reflecting on the situation, I found myself recalling something that had happened to me some time back. At the request of a friend, I went to visit a woman who was dying at Jewish Hospital. As I was about to walk in, a Satmar woman was just leaving, having spent much of the day taking care of this ill person.[93] As we talked, it turned out that she came every day. At one point, she said to me, 'People think I do things like this because I enjoy it; but the truth is, I don't find this work enjoyable at all. But it's a mitzvah!' This recollection helped me see the situation with the children in a new light. I realized that the expectation—theirs and mine—that they would find the experience of helping the elderly rewarding was beside the point. It's great if helping people is personally rewarding, but that shouldn't be our reason or motivation. Rather, we should be helping people in need because it's our job. And then I realized what I needed to (and actually did) convey to the kids."

"Which is?"

"That helping people in need is not about meeting our needs but theirs. Sure, there will be times in life when fulfilling our obligations will not be satisfying, but that doesn't mean we shouldn't fulfill them."

"So, would you send the kids back to the same home for the elderly? Aren't you worried about creating a negative attitude towards fulfilling mitzvot?"

"I think this is a matter for good judgment. And I certainly want to be careful to avoid creating negative attitudes towards *gemilut hesed*. But what's clear to me is that, in the end, I would like to see them become the kinds of people whose sense of obligation leads them to meet the needs of others even when the necessary activities may feel onerous or unpleasant."

Reflecting on what Devora was saying, I found my interest in the problem of autonomy resurfacing. "As you have been talking, I've been wondering whether your desire to nurture human beings who will feel a strong sense of obligation to help remedy the suffering and injustice in the world can be harmonized with your interest in the children becoming autonomous beings who decide for themselves their direction and priorities. But, remembering an earlier conversation in which you identified certain activities, including those associated with alleviating suffering, as foundational, I think I have a sense of at least one of the ways you might address this apparent tension from out of your perspective."

---

[93]*Satmar* is the name of a Hasidic sect that is well-known for the place it gives to *bikkur holim* (visiting the sick).

Devora waited.

"Autonomy," I went on, "is a Jewish value, but it's not the only value. And it sits in the company of other values, one of them being our obligation to address the suffering in our world and to help make the world a better place."

"What leaves me uncomfortable with the way you put that," Devora commented, "is that it misses the ways in which autonomy and the obligations associated with *gemilut hesed* don't just sit side by side but inform one another. As Jews, our freedom is inseparable from our responsibilities. It's not the freedom to decide whether we have an obligation to respond to human suffering; it's the freedom to figure out how best to do so. The kind of autonomous thinking I try to foster (problem-solving activity that is independent-spirited, rigorous and imaginative) is an essential part of fulfilling our obligation to meet the needs of others. Without this kind of thinking, and this is part of what I hope they learned, the kids in Nurit's class would have been much less successful in fulfilling their obligation to help people like Joe."

It was now late, and Devora and I parted. It's a long distance from the school back to my hotel, but it was a pleasant day and I needed the walk. As I moved along, I found myself more aware than usual of the needy people who dotted my path. As I approached my hotel, I wondered whether perhaps, today, the woman who had occupied the nearby perch might have returned. She hadn't.

That's it for now. All the best.
Daniel

A Jewish Learning Community

Beit Rabban's vision of an educated Jewish person is organically bound up with its conception of what it means to be a responsible member of a learning community. This letter explores this theme. It emphasizes the ways in which, whether it's a matter of interpreting a biblical text or helping a homeless person, the classroom is designed to encourage the kind of respectful and thoughtful dialogue among members of the class that will eventuate in a rich web of meaning, that is, in the emergence of a web of ideas, themes, insights, and questions which illuminate one another and which advance the understandings of the participants, both as individuals and as a group. Equally important, these emerging understandings help them to arrive at more adequate solutions to the problems they are trying to address.

This letter also looks at the school's belief that it is desirable for the children to come to feel that the Torah is their book, and discusses the pedagogical implications of this belief. In this context, an earlier discussion concerning approaches to fundamental texts like the Torah is extended, this time with attention to the contrast between Beit Rabban's approach and an approach articulated by Professor Moshe Greenberg that emphasizes the need for selectivity in deciding what passages to put before neophyte learners. Near its end, the letter articulates the idea that, at Beit Rabban, the classroom at its best is a microcosm of an "olam metukan" (of the world, or the Jewish community, as it should be). This leads Daniel to compare the Beit Rabban outlook with that of John Dewey, giving rise to an attempt to identify some similarities and contrasts between the conception that guides Beit Rabban and John Dewey's ideas on education.

Dear Alice:

A few days after my conversations with Nurit, I chanced to bump into her and Devora at the end of a staff development meeting. At least once a week, either individually or in small groups, teachers gather with Devora for inservice work of one kind or another. Typically, the work grows out of challenges that the teachers are facing in their classrooms. Given their inexperience, it is, as I think I've mentioned, vital to the success of the school that there be ample time for this kind of consultation, and it appears that Devora and the teachers work hard to make room for these regular meetings.

When they saw me walk by the room where they were sitting, they waved me in, and we continued talking about Nurit's class. Apparently, the children had been so excited about the work they had done that they expressed a strong desire to find other ways of serving the homeless population of Manhattan. Nurit had suggested to them that they would be in a much better position to help if they learned more about homelessness; and as I came by the room, Nurit had just finished telling Devora that she had succeeded in recruiting both a representative of a local homeless people's coalition and a parent who was a social worker to talk with the children.

I commented again about how impressed I was with this project. Building opportunities to address the problems of the community into the routine of the school probably has a powerful impact on the children, I speculated; embedded in the structure of the week is the idea that to be actively and thoughtfully concerned with these problems is part of what it means to be a member of the Beit Rabban community and, by extension, of the Jewish community.

Devora asked whether I had more questions or thoughts about the tzedakah project, and I said that at the moment I didn't, but I did want to ask about something that I was finding fascinating in my classroom observations. Though the kids typically seemed very involved in the questions under discussion, only very rarely did they interrupt each other; nor did they usually raise a hand to be called on while someone else was talking. Could they say something about this?

Devora looked at Nurit, who seemed to grasp that the ball was in her court. Smiling, she responded, "Well, it's by no means an accident; in fact, it's something that we work on with the kids from the very beginning. We try to bring them to the idea that when anyone is speaking, not just the teacher, they should be paying attention. The message we want to convey is not just that it shows a lack of respect not to be attentive, though this is important; we also want to communicate that the person who is speaking may be making a comment that merits serious consideration. But how can you be listening when you're just waiting to be called on so that you can speak?"

I wished, I commented, that the students at my university had learned this lesson. All too often they tune out all but what the professor has to say, and "discussion" turns into a succession of observations with no discernible relationship to one another. It often takes a teacher's intervention to get the students to relate to one another's comments and to come away with the idea that it is important for them to be listening to each other.

Nurit nodded, adding that what I was describing mirrored her experience from elementary school through college. "Comments made in class," she observed, "scored you points with the teacher, but there was often no sense that you were engaged with others in making sense of a problem. Things are very different at Beit Rabban," she said with a measure of pride. "When we talked about how to spend the tzedakah money, did you notice the way the conversation developed, the way in which the different comments built on one another until, in the end, we arrived at a decision that was far more thoughtful and better than what anyone would have come up with alone? We want each child to be an independent-spirited problem-solver, but we also want them to realize that together, through a process of disciplined give-and-take, they can build a richer web of meaning and probably come up with better ideas than they would on their own."

As Nurit spoke, I caught Devora's eye very briefly, long enough to convey, "This is one articulate young woman!" Devora acknowledged my message with a slight smile. And she picked up where Nurit left off. "What Nurit is saying reminds me of one of my favorite moments at Beit Rabban. I was working with a group of younger children around God's announcement near the beginning of Genesis that there would be a flood in seven days time. A discussion ensued about whether this indicated that the flood would begin on Shabbat, but, after a while, a consensus seemed to emerge that it did not. I commented that, even if not, mention of seven days recalls the Creation story, and one of the children said: 'It's like God worked on Creation for six days and it was complete on the seventh; now, God planned the destruction of Creation for six days and did it on the seventh.' Building on these comments, another child commented: 'And at the same time Noah is using these six days to start the world all over again.'"

I was quietly appreciating what Devora had just described—once again, with a touch of envy as I thought back on my own educational experiences—when she continued. "Actually, that wasn't the end of the conversation. After these first interchanges, I led a discussion about the flood as the destruction of Creation and the beginning of a new Creation, and I said that we would look for evidence of this as we read more of the story. I pointed out that the opening of the *arubot hashamayim* (the heavenly flood-gates) and the breaking open of the *ma'ayanot tehom* (the fountains of the great deep) led to the merging of the waters coming from above and the waters coming from below, and that this reverses the separation of waters at the beginning of the Creation story in chapter 1. And I also said that we had seen another passage which talks about water coming from above and below. Mentally scanning our earlier work, the children were silent, and then one of them remembered the fifth and sixth verses in chapter 2, about the earth not yet being watered by rain from above but by an *ed,* a mist which comes up from the earth. 'Yes,' I said, 'but did you notice that there the water brings life to the earth, but here [in the flood story] it destroys the earth?'

"At this point the children began clamoring to share their ideas and took turns doing so. They were so excited that I found it virtually impossible to get them to go down to their movement class, which they were already late for, and which they loved. And finally, one of the children said, 'I had an idea, and then I listened to other kids' ideas, and I put them together, and now I have a better idea,' which he proceeded to share. And as though this was not enough, another child then commented: 'This [the separation of waters at the time of Creation and the destruction-inducing re-merging of the waters in the flood story] reminds me of *queri'at yam suf* [the parting of the Red Sea].'[94] It happened to be just before Pesach. 'I was thinking the same thing,' said another child. At the end of the week, I sent this idea home as the basis for a family discussion of Pesach. For me, this episode really captured much of what defines Beit Rabban."

When I asked her to say more about this, she continued, "Actually, I think that Nurit and the boy who spoke about emerging with a new idea after carefully listening to what others had to say pretty much captured what I had in mind. Beit Rabban lives out the idea that responsible thinking is thinking that engages the ideas of other people. In this as in other situations, the children discover that fresh and exciting ideas, some of which turn out to be quite powerful, will emerge through the process of reflective give-and-take."

"But," I added, "this wasn't just a process of reflective give-and-take; it was give-and-take that was anchored in studying the Torah, which is very different from the kind of conversation that, say, Socrates has with his interlocutors, conversation that isn't mediated by the written word."

"Yes, this is an important point," Devora nodded. "The text is at the heart of the activity in at least two ways. First, and perhaps most important, it's in the course of the activity of studying the text that new questions and problems regularly arise; and, second, whatever interesting ideas the children come up with in response to their questions, in the end they have to

---

[94]What the child seems to be saying is this: "Here, too, the separation of waters makes possible creation and life (the survival of the Israelites), followed by a re-merging of the waters that brings about destruction (of the Pharaoh and his soldiers)."

return to the text to judge whether there is evidence for these ideas. In the case I just described, the youngsters' learning of the text gave rise to a question: what might be the significance of the Torah's comment that God announced the flood *seven days* before its onset? And the rest was a process of trying to understand and address this problem, a process that's constrained and guided by the text itself. At these times it's very exciting to me the way the children try to ground their ideas in the text—which, of course, is only possible because they learn it very carefully, *pasuk* by *pasuk* [verse by verse]."

"But," I asked, "would they be doing that if you weren't there guiding the discussion?"

"At this stage in their lives, probably not, and that's one of the reasons having a teacher is important."

Picking up on what she had just said, I asked, "And what are the other reasons?"

"Well, though important, the teacher's job goes well beyond encouraging the kids to look to the text to find evidence for their ideas and interpretations. It's also to model what it's like to engage with the text in a way that's infused with seriousness and curiosity and with an interest in uncovering challenging questions. And it's also appropriate for the teacher to infuse the children's discussions with ideas that wouldn't have spontaneously occurred to them but that have the potential to enrich their thinking.[95] On their own, the kids might not have come up with the images of water and the role of water in the chapters of Genesis that come before the Noah story; but once the idea is out there, they're able to move with it."

"Would it be right to say," Nurit was now speaking, "that your role in this conversation was similar to the role played by the homelessness expert in my class?"

"What do you mean?" Devora asked, and Nurit continued. "Well, in both cases, an adult with more information about the subject at hand deepened the conversation by introducing this information into the flow of the discussion."

"For me that's a helpful comparison," I commented. "And in both cases the success of the expert's contribution probably depends a lot on a good sense of timing and on the right formulation."

"That's right on target, I think," Devora responded. "But there is one significant difference between the teacher and the homelessness expert.

---

[95]Devora Steinmetz has commented that this understanding of the teacher's role has been fruitfully articulated by Magdalene Lampert in "The Teacher's Role in Reinventing Mathematical Knowing in the Classroom," Institute for Research on Teaching, College of Education, Michigan State University, 1988.

The homelessness expert is a source of information and ideas; but the teacher is much more than this. This teacher may be more knowledgeable than the children about many matters, but, ideally, as I suggested a moment ago, the teacher's distinctive expertise is as a learner. In a community devoted to learning, the teacher is charged with modeling what it means to engage a text or a subject matter in a serious, authentic way. But what Daniel just said about the teacher needing to be wise about when and how to participate in the discussion is very important. The last thing in the world you want to do is to pull away from the children the sense of ownership they feel in relation to their developing discussion."

I commented on Devora's reference to "ownership," a term that I hadn't heard her use before. "Actually," she responded, "I think it's an important part of education: the feeling that we jointly own the discussion and the text on which it is based. The school's message needs to be that this is *your* book."

"And how do you go about creating this sense of ownership?"

"In part, it's a matter of growing familiar enough with the text to be able to travel with ease within it and to apply it to varied questions and circumstances. But other things are also necessary. One of them, which we have already referred to, is to avoid conveying to the children that the teachers are necessary to mediate the relationship with the text."

"You have alluded to this point more than once in our conversations, for example, when, some time back, you indicated your discomfort with the idea that the teacher should shield children from, or quickly explain away, texts that embody ideas that might be troubling to them, given their sensibilities. Can you say more about this?"

"Sure. The teacher's job, particularly in the early period when the children are developing a relationship with the text, is to put them in direct contact with it, not to summarize the story for them or to tell them what they should be looking for or getting out of the encounter. What this means concretely is that, especially with the young children, we don't seek out so-called interesting texts or try to avoid passages that adults have judged to be problematic or boring. No, we go straight through the Torah, with the teacher waiting for questions or problems that emerge for the children from the encounter. What they come up with, what they're interested in, will vary depending on age and on who is in the class, but in the end it's their issues and interests that dictate what we think about together. So when we study any given passage, one year they may be interested in God, another year in ethical issues, and at another time in how long people lived."

"So you wouldn't bring your own questions to the text and invite them to explore these questions?"

"Well, I wouldn't say I never do. One reason why I might sometimes introduce my questions is that if, as I said before, part of my job is to model an authentic engagement with the text, it's important for them to see how questions and ideas emerge for me through my encounter with it. But, again, I have to be careful not to set up the expectation that their encounter with the text is best mediated by my questions and concerns. It can't be that they come away thinking that we're studying *my* text. This criterion is decisive in the early stages of education, when children are forming their relationship with Torah. With older children and with adults who do feel the sense of ownership I've been talking about, I am often less reluctant to serve as a more active guide through the text."

"But aren't there a lot of passages in the Torah that the children are likely to find boring?"

"I know that a lot of teachers think so, and that with the hope of ensuring that the children's encounters with the Torah will be meaningful or interesting, they carefully pre-select what the children will study. But I don't believe that the text needs to be made interesting or fun. Approached in the right spirit, the material is inherently interesting. You would be surprised how often—though of course, not always—fascinating questions and ideas emerge for the kids in the course of reading passages that educators will typically bypass because they think the children will find them uninteresting."

An example, I commented, might be helpful here, and Devora was quick to respond. "Everyday life in the school is filled with such examples, but you might find it useful to look at the transcript of a class that captures what I'm trying to say," and she reached for a document that included her notes on a sequence of classes she had taught. Then, excusing herself to run an errand, she suggested to Nurit and me that we take a short break, which would give me half an hour to review the material she had just handed over to me. This material included the following account:

> We read from 2:4 onwards [in Genesis]; the children know the tune pretty well and are regularly referring to the *te'amim*.[96] As I was about to go on to a new *pasuk*, Rafi raised a question concerning 2:9: "And from the ground the Lord God caused to grow every tree that was pleasing to the sight and good for food, with the tree of life in the middle of the garden [*b'tokh hagan*] and the

[96]As noted earlier, the biblical text is accompanied by musical notes called *te'amim*. Although chanting in accordance with musical notation is said to beautify the regular reading of the sacred text in religious services, the notation is also designed to emphasize the text's meaning. The children at Beit Rabban are taught the musical notation early on, and are generally expected to chant rather than simply read the Torah texts that they study.

tree of knowledge of good and bad." "Why," Rafi asked, "does it say that the tree of life is in the garden [betokh hagan], but not the tree of knowledge?"[97] Shmuel responded that he thought it did say that the tree of knowledge is betokh hagan, that betokh hagan refers to both trees. But Rafi said: "But then it should say it differently, like, 'I had bagels and coffee for lunch, and they were good', rather than, 'I had bagels for lunch and coffee.'" I said that, according to Shmuel, it's like: "I had bagels for lunch, as well as coffee," that is, "I had both of them for lunch." Rafi disagreed that this was how to construe the pasuk. Shmuel said that he would translate in accordance with his understanding; I suggested that he do that and then Rafi would translate in accordance with his. They both did this. Rafi translated the verse as follows: "God caused to grow from the ground every tree pleasant for seeing and good for eating and the tree of life inside the garden and the tree of knowledge of good and bad"; and Shmuel's translation conveyed "and the tree of life and the tree of knowledge inside the garden." I asked each of the other children what they thought. Then, I pointed out that, if you agree with Shmuel's reading, the question Rafi raised is no longer a question, since the verse is saying that both trees are inside the garden, but that, if you read the pasuk like Rafi, Rafi's question stands: that is, why does the text identify the tree of life as being inside the garden, but not the tree of knowledge? Then, I said that even if you take the passage, as Shmuel does, to mean that both trees are in the garden, you could still ask why things are phrased as they are. Why do we say, "I had bagels for lunch and coffee," rather than, "I had bagels and coffee for lunch"?

Then I raised the question of what betokh means, and the children had different opinions as to whether it means 'in the middle of' or just 'in'. I pointed out that, if you think it means 'in

---

[97]Note that, like a number of other translations, the just-cited Jewish Publication Society translation of the passage renders the Hebrew "b'tokh," which literally means "in," as "in the middle of." Had Rafi understood it as "in the middle of," a possibility that will soon be introduced into the conversation by Devora, the question he raised would have been, for reasons to be discussed below, moot. But at this stage in their inquiry, the youngsters have understood "b'tokh" to mean "in," which is what gives rise to Rafi's problem. Like the other children, he takes it for granted that the tree of knowledge of good and bad is also in the garden, but if this is the case, why does the text identify the tree of life as being in the garden, but not the tree of knowledge?

the middle of', the problem is not there, because it could be that the tree of life is *in the middle* but the tree of knowledge is just *in;* if, however, you think *betokh* means 'in', Rafi's question stands, because both trees are *in* the garden. Rafi wasn't happy about this possible solution, because he didn't think that *betokh* means 'in the middle'. Before going on, I suggested that we look at what Rashi says, and the children said "What about the Targum[98]?!" I was delighted and said we'd look at both. . . .

I found this incident—really just a snippet of a larger episode—a superb example of Devora's view that even texts that many adults might think unpromising educational material can, in the right educational setting, catalyze exciting discussion. And yet my recollection of most of the educational environments I participated in long ago as a child, in which we felt bored to tears by the material we were asked to study, gave me pause. I wondered whether in the absence of a gifted teacher like Steinmetz who sets the right tone, models a certain approach to the text and responds, as she did in this case, in thought-provoking ways to the issues that arise, it is really likely that such texts (for example, those filled with long genealogies or the details of sacrifices) would produce the kind of excitement that they seem to engender at Beit Rabban.

When Devora and Nurit reentered the room, I raised these concerns with Devora, and she readily agreed with the spirit of my comments. "I'm not saying that any random group of learners is likely to find any and all texts interesting. Beit Rabban's approach would be much less effective, if we hadn't helped the youngsters acquire strong Hebrew reading skills and the habit of reading very carefully, as they do in the episode just described. Without such a foundation, I'm not sure how many youngsters, or adults for that matter, would have noticed the problem in the text that led to Rafi's triggering question."

Devora thus seemed to acknowledge that certain conditions needed to be in place for the approach she was recommending to work; in addition to facility with Hebrew, it was necessary to have cultivated in the learners the disposition to read carefully and to be on the alert for problems that might spark their curiosity, and it was also necessary, at least at this early stage of education, for the teacher to be around to respond to and channel the questions that bubbled up from the kids. And this acknowledgement led me to somewhat greater sympathy for the approach she was encouraging. Yet I remained, and perhaps remain, doubtful. Over and above my continuing skepticism about the likelihood of finding teachers who could,

[98]The Targum is a classical Aramaic translation of the Bible.

in part by modeling, help youngsters acquire the right kinds of habits and skills, I still wasn't convinced that the raw, not preselected text was the best starting point for new learners of Torah. Might not an approach that strives to put learners in touch with texts that are more obviously interesting be a better bet for educators?

As these thoughts traveled through me, I realized that they were in part the product of having recently encountered an article on the teaching of Bible written by Moshe Greenberg, a professor of Bible at the Hebrew University in Jerusalem, in which he lays out a very different approach from Devora's. Agree or disagree with it, I think it's a great piece, Alice, and I would encourage you to take a look at it; but for now, let me share with you the relevant points of the article—the very ones I shared with Devora. According to Greenberg, the educator should seek out passages that he/she believes have the potential to be meaningful to the particular learners with whom he/she will be engaged. Writes Greenberg:

> The role of Jewish education is to transmit significant portions of these contents to the student, with "significant" having two connotations:
>
> 1. Meaningful, addressing matters of concern to students;
> 2. An amount and a selection representative of the source in question, providing an authentic taste of the original, so that the student may be impressed by its power.
>
>   If the student receives portions of the basic books, "significant" in both these senses, there is a prospect that he will recognize their moral and intellectual power and resort to them throughout the years.[99]

When I asked Devora about the difference between her view and Greenberg's, her initial response was to minimize it. She imagined, she commented, that he was thinking about a population of learners (say, in an after-school educational program, or adults coming together for a short-term program of learning) who would not have continuing opportunities to study Torah over many years. This is a very different situation from her own at Beit Rabban, where the children have the opportunity to study Torah every day over a number of years. Were she faced with the challenge to which she imagined Greenberg was responding, she, too, would probably focus on texts carefully selected for their ability to engage the learner and

[99]Greenberg articulates this view in "We Were As Those Who Dream," found in Fox, Scheffler, and Marom, eds. *Visions*, 122–132. The quotation can be found on 123–124.

to convey the text's power to address significant questions in profound ways.

Devora's comments substantially reduced the distance I had sensed between her view and that of Greenberg, but I'm not convinced that they would dissolve it. For what I'm not sure about is whether, presented with Devora's situation (a population of students that one can count on working with, beginning at a young age, over several years), Greenberg would abandon the approach he had articulated in favor of hers. To my mind, there may be some deeper differences between their views, ones that go well beyond differences in the educational contexts about which they may be thinking.[100]

Busy contemplating these matters, I was only marginally aware of the lull in our conversation, as the three of us, Devora, Nurit, and I, quietly mulled over the ground we had traveled. It was Nurit who finally broke the silence. "We've been talking a lot about what classroom life at our school is like, and I think there's an idea that's been right beneath the surface but that hasn't been mentioned. It's not just that we think of the classroom as a real community as opposed to a shell in which teaching and learning go on; our classroom strives to be a model of an *olam metukan,* literally, a repaired world, a world that's rightly balanced and just."

"Can you say a little more about this?" I asked. This time it was Nurit who looked over at Devora, who continued in the train of Nurit's comments. "Nurit is picking out a very important feature of our school. We're not educating for comfort and success in the world as it is. Our classrooms try to exemplify what a community ought to be. It's not just that better ideas and practices (for example, the development of more useful ways of helping the needy) come about through disciplined inquiry and through the contributions of very different people; it also has to do with the way people are expected to talk to each other. In a world where people do very little serious listening and responding, Beit Rabban takes these matters very seriously. We want to cultivate children who know how to talk with one another, people who believe that other people, including those who live differently from them, have ideas that are worth listening to seriously. Would that ideological subgroups in the larger Jewish community approached each other with the belief that each of them had something worthwhile to contribute to their shared conversation! If Beit Rabban is

---

[100]This discussion of approaches to the study of classical texts points to a few of the many interesting and important questions that bear on the way texts can and ought to be taught. For a very rich discussion of some of these matters, see Barry Holtz, *Textual Knowledge: Teaching the Bible in Theory and Practice* (New York: Jewish Theological Seminary Press, 2003).

successful, our students will approach people who have beliefs different from their own in this spirit."

As Nurit and Devora talked, I found myself recalling John Dewey's idea that "we may create in schools a projection in type of the society we should like to realize, and by forming minds in accord with it, gradually modify the larger and more recalcitrant features of adult society."[101] His notion was that the classroom as a community should resemble the kind of community we would hope to create in the larger society. The idea was that children who spent substantial stretches of time in such a community would acquire sensibilities that would render them eager to help build a world that looked like this kind of a community. I commented that the spirit of the Dewey quotation seemed very close to what Devora and Nurit had been talking about. They both nodded, and my sense was that the resonance between the school's outlook and Dewey's impressed them as much as it had me.

In the wake of the conversation, I found myself musing about the resemblances between Beit Rabban's philosophy and John Dewey's—not just the image of the classroom as a perfected community and the interest in moral education, but also the emphasis on problem solving and inquiry.[102] It's true that the Dewey School featured a much stronger emphasis on scientific method as exhibited in the practice of working scientists than would be found at Beit Rabban; but Beit Rabban shares Dewey's interest in cultivating people whose ideas about how to act are actively informed by their experience. Moreover, in the world of Beit Rabban as in the Dewey School, the message to youngsters is that our success in achieving our purposes depends heavily on the quality of our thinking, so we had better do everything we can to ensure that this thinking is careful and informed by relevant data. Put differently, my sense is that had Dewey been born into the Jewish world and taken Judaism seriously, he might have built a school that looked very much like Beit Rabban. Maybe his aura found its way into this school. It is, after all, only a few miles away from Columbia University, where Dewey taught for many years after leaving Chicago.

Having said all this, honesty compels me to add that the fit between Dewey and Beit Rabban is imperfect. For one thing, I think he would have been resistant to the idea of treating certain texts as foundational in the way that Beit Rabban and Jews across the centuries have treated books like the Bible and the Talmud. For another, though both Dewey and Beit Rabban emphasize the instrumental value of good thinking and learning, Beit

---

[101] John Dewey, *Democracy and Education* (New York: The Free Press, 1944), 317.

[102] Dewey discussed moral education in a variety of works. One of the texts identified in an earlier note, *Moral Principles in Education*, is particularly useful.

Rabban is carefully designed so that youngsters come to experience the activity of learning as constitutive of their identity, as an activity that is experienced as self-validating and in need of no justification.

There is also this difference. Whereas both Dewey and Beit Rabban emphasize that real and living problems—those problems that would engage us in our real lives outside of educational settings—have enormous potential to catalyze educationally fruitful thinking, there are in this area real differences in their views. If I read him correctly, Dewey believes that the educational process should be organized around real and living problems; Devora, on the other hand, is convinced that we can also be engaged by problems that may have no connection to our immediate concerns as human beings but that offer us intellectual challenges that admit of no obvious solution. Intellectually challenging puzzles are themselves, she thinks, engaging, and this is enough to get fruitful educational thinking off the ground.[103] Such is the case, for example, when the youngsters engage with puzzles that they encounter in the study of Torah. This is also true with the challenges posed by the light bulb activity: though the questions raised in this activity may be intellectually challenging, they are not real and living in the sense that something practical is really at stake for most of the kids. The reason is that for most of these youngsters, their Shabbat practices, whatever they may be, are ingrained and not a source of uncomfortable perplexity.

All of which is to say that, though intriguing, the fit between Beit Rabban's and Dewey's outlook is, as I began by saying, less than perfect. In any case, I will be on the lookout for other points of comparison and contrast.

That's it for now. Signing off.
Daniel

---

[103]Here Devora's views resemble psychologist Robert White's ideas concerning what he calls competence motivation. See in this connection Robert White, "Motivation Reconsidered: the Concept of Competence," *Psychological Review,* 66 (1959), 297–333. Also relevant are the ideas of Jerome Bruner, whom Devora often mentions in conversation. In *The Process of Education* (New York: Vintage Books, 1963), 50, Bruner writes: "One of the least discussed ways of carrying a student through a hard unit of material is to challenge him with a chance to use his full powers, so that he may discover the pleasure of full and effective functioning. Good teachers know the power of this lure. Students should know what it feels like to be completely absorbed in a problem. They seldom experience this feeling in school." See also Bruner's discussion of what he calls "the will to learn" in *Towards a Theory of Instruction* (New York: W. W. Norton, 1966).

LETTER 10
Probing Some Assumptions

The Power of Beginnings, the Pitfalls of Experience

As suggested in the general introduction, the larger educational vision at work in the practice of a vision-guided institution includes many ideas and values that go well beyond its existential vision, that is, its conception of the kind of individual and community it is striving to cultivate. We have already encountered a number of such beliefs, and additional ones will surface in the letters to come. The present letter draws attention to certain other significant ideas that give rise to the existence and design of Beit Rabban. More specifically, there is in this letter a strong emphasis on the ways in which Plato's dictum in The Republic that "In the development of anything, beginnings are all-important" is reflected in different aspects of the school. In relation to this theme, this letter returns to, and more fully examines, Devora's preference for inexperienced teachers, as compared with senior teachers who have been influenced by years of experience in more conventional schools. Reference to the desirability of finding teachers who are both well-trained and in sync with the school's unique integration of progressivism and seriousness about Jewish learning leads to a discussion of professional development schools as arenas in which neophyte educators can grow. This in turn leads to a discussion of Devora's hope that Beit Rabban would serve as a professional development school for a new Jewish educator preparation program ("HaSha'ar"), which she was instrumental in creating and which is organized around a conception of teaching and learning that is coherent with her own and the school's outlook.

Dear Alice:

Your question intrigued me: "Are there guiding ideas other than its understanding of the kinds of people it should be trying to cultivate that inform the development of Beit Rabban?" I think it's an important question, because although it is critical, a conception of the kinds of people you hope to cultivate is insufficient to give rise to a conception of the educational process. The move from vision in this sense—what I have sometimes been calling *existential vision*—to practice inevitably depends on a variety of other assumptions, including assumptions about human growth, learning and motivation, about the social milieu in which you're trying to actualize the existential vision, and about what the children bring with them from home.[104]

So the question should not be, "Are there ideas other than existential vision that inform the development of Beit Rabban?" but rather, "What are these ideas?" And the truth is that along the way we have already encountered a number of such ideas. But instead of revisiting them, what I would like to do now is to articulate certain additional ideas and motifs that seem to me to underlie Beit Rabban's existence and character. One of them, and perhaps the most important, might be captioned: "In the development of anything, beginnings are decisive!" I first encountered this view in Plato's *Republic*, in which he defends censoring the work of poets in order to control the stories children are exposed to. His reason is that early experience decisively shapes the character of human beings; save for a miracle, a bad start in life will forever contaminate a person's character.[105]

Everywhere I turn, I see traces of this view in Beit Rabban. Here are three examples. The first, and most obvious, is Devora's decision to start not a high school but a school for young children. Particularly given her strongly intellectual cast and interests, you might have thought that she would be more interested in adolescents; but her conviction that early childhood is the critical moment in the development of a human being, and that the habits of mind and heart then acquired will shape the future more surely than will later experiences, led her to start a school for younger children. (As an aside, I should add that when I tested this hypothesis on Devora, she laughed: "I certainly agree with what you're saying about the importance of early childhood experience and of elementary education; but you should tell Alice that the real reason I started a school for young children is that I had a little kid!" So much for my conjectures!)

---

[104]For a discussion of this point, see Seymour Fox's article on translation from vision to practice, "The Art of Translation," in Fox, Scheffler, and Marom, eds., *Visions*, 253–295.

[105]See *The Republic*, 66 ff. (Book III, 386–402).

Second, Devora's decision to start her own school, rather than engaging with an existing institution, also reflects her views on the power of beginnings. Which reminds me that I forgot to tell you about a conference I recently attended with Devora that focused on different approaches to the reform of educational institutions. Devora was very quiet most of the time, though clearly listening intently. In a private conversation in between sessions, she made a comment that explained her silence. "I don't really believe it's possible [or maybe she just said she thought it very unlikely!] for schools that already have a settled character to change in fundamental ways. They are, and will be, what they are!" And she went on to talk about the power of routines and about the ways in which institutional life has a tendency to keep the culture of institutions frozen in whatever equilibrium has somehow come into being.

"This is the reason," she added, "that I created Beit Rabban rather than trying to work for change in one of the existing institutions. True, starting your own school brings with it many problems; but the essential thing, establishing a pattern that mirrors your ideals, is at least a living possibility." I responded that I thought she had been very successful in this respect. The hint of a smile that she offered in response seemed appreciative but intimated an awareness of gaps between the reality and the ideal, and the look on her face made me flash for a moment on our earlier conversation concerning the difficulty of fully realizing the potentialities of the turning on electricity on Shabbat project. Though I want to pursue this question of gaps between ideal and reality more systematically, I have yet to do so; and I'll tell you more after she and I speak about this. But for now, let me come back to the third, and to my mind the most interesting, example of Devora's views concerning the power of beginnings. It has to do with the teachers.

You may recall my telling you something about Beit Rabban's teachers and about my initial conversation with her about them. Here's how I would characterize the teachers as a group: they are young (almost right out of college), warm and unassuming, and bright (well, *very* bright); many of them are products of Jewish day schools and have spent a year or more in Israel; and—this is the point I want to emphasize here—they tend to be *very* "green." As I may have mentioned some time back, most of them come to Beit Rabban without having studied to be educators and without significant teaching experience; in fact, most of them are not planning to become professional educators. When I first encountered them, I was greatly taken with how fresh and eager they were, but, to be honest, I was troubled by how little they brought with them in the way of background for their work as teachers.

As you may also recall, when I asked Devora about this, what she told me was this: she'd much rather have fresh, young teachers than so-called experienced teachers whose wisdom consisted of practices and ideas about successful teaching that supported an approach to education that was antithetical to Beit Rabban's philosophy. Experience, she intimated, is often just a measure of how thoroughly a teacher has been influenced by and has bought into conventional ideas about the nature and aims of the educational process.[106] I think it was actually in this connection that she related the story I reported to you earlier about the "more experienced" teacher who couldn't understand why Devora was unhappy with her having put up a big sign on the bulletin board that read *AVODAH METZUYENET.*

As I think about it, the episode with the teacher, or, in any case, Devora's understanding of it, is a great springboard to the topic I was planning to bring up in this letter. When I asked Devora how she responded to that teacher in this situation, she confessed that she did very little to try to change her outlook. "By that time, I had pretty much given up on her. Unfortunately, there had already been many similar episodes. One, in particular, remains vivid. Walking by her classroom, I heard her ask the children in the middle of a lesson, *'Mi hakham v'yode'ah et ha-milah?*[107] I remember trying to explain to her everything that I found troubling about this question. It's not just that I don't think that being smart is in itself a characteristic worthy of praise, but that in this instance knowing the meaning of the word has much more to do with having made a serious effort to review the material before class. Had she said something like, 'Who has reviewed the material and knows the answer?' I would have been entirely comfortable, since reviewing the material is not only the more pertinent attribute in this case but is, unlike raw smartness, something over which most children do have control."

I commented that it's precisely Devora's and the school's insistence that "little things" like this be in sync with the school's fundamental outlook that makes the school a wonderful example of a vision-guided institution.

"I don't think I would describe the language we use to describe what makes for worthy answers as a 'little thing.' In ways that may be very powerful, our language conveys our basic values and goals; so we have to be very careful about what we say."

"I agree completely," I responded. "What I was trying to say is that what distinguishes a vision-guided institution is that things that are conven-

---

[106]Here, Devora's view calls to mind that of Rousseau who writes at the beginning of *Emile* that what we call *wisdom* is often nothing more than the "slavish prejudice" into which we have been socialized. See *Emile*, 10.

[107]This means, "Who is smart and knows the meaning of the word?"

tionally regarded as 'little things' are treated as important bearers of the school's vision—a kind of 'God is in the details' perspective."

An almost pained smile accompanied Devora's next comment. "Well, I sure didn't succeed in convincing that teacher of this point. She just didn't get it. When I suggested to her that there is a gigantic difference between asking 'who is smart and knows the answer?' and 'who has *reviewed the material* and knows the answer?' she thought I was hair-splitting, rather than pointing to the details through which the core values of Beit Rabban get expressed. She couldn't accept the idea that what she was doing wasn't healthy. The funny thing is that I would not describe her as actually resistant to the school's educational beliefs. In a sense, the opposite was true. She didn't feel the need to change in any way because she was convinced that she was already happily aligned with the school's ideology."

"I guess," I commented, "it's a good illustration of how difficult it is to actually take hold of a new outlook and embody it in one's conduct. It's one thing to be able to 'talk the talk,' and quite another to live it out in one's actual work."

Devora nodded. "In her case, I think she was much too embedded in traditional ways of doing things and thinking. She brought with her ideas about teaching and learning, as well as about children, that were radically different from what Beit Rabban believes; and I don't think she ever really grasped the extent to which her approach did not align with Beit Rabban's outlook. At first, I was pretty optimistic about her. I thought that my working with her around these issues might make a difference; but the way she treated the kids didn't change, and by the time the *avodah metzuyenet* incident came around, I had given up."

By the way, this teacher didn't stay very long at Beit Rabban. It is inconceivable to Devora that the children should regularly meet up with teachers who communicate views and values that are so out of step with the school's fundamental commitments.

And this brings us back to the preference for "green" teachers. For all their inexperience, Devora explained, the young people she looks to hire are open to learning. True, when they arrive at Beit Rabban they don't yet have a settled identity as educators, but in at least one important respect this is a blessing. In educating them to the ideas and practices that define Beit Rabban, there is no need to overcome resistance born of years of thinking about education in a different way. True, the preference for such individuals makes it much harder to build a professional culture among the faculty; and it's also true that they often make elementary mistakes, and that the school (especially Devora) needs to commit an enormous amount of time to continuing teacher education. But paying this price, says Devora, beats the alternative.

I was impressed by the logic of Devora's position on this matter, but, when she voiced it, I felt discomfort welling up within me. I suspected (rightly, I think) that this was due to more than one concern, but, in the moment, only one of these concerns surfaced. "Isn't there," I commented, "a tension between, on the one hand, your belief in autonomy and your insistence that your teachers educate towards autonomy (as the school understands it), and, on the other hand, a deliberate effort to search for teachers who are inexperienced, fresh and open, and therefore capable of being shaped in the light of your ideas concerning the way educators should approach their work?" Put crudely (and I don't know that I put it this indelicately when I spoke with Devora), isn't there something at least morally odd about educating youngsters towards autonomy through the efforts of teachers whom Devora has molded in the image of *her* ideal of good teaching? What about *their* autonomy?

Even more generally, I found myself wondering whether there might be a "dark side" to vision-guided institutions: whatever their aspirations for their clients, they may be so directive towards their teachers that they stifle their autonomy.[108] After all, isn't it one of the marks of a vision-guided institution that it is animated by, and insistent about, a very clear conception of the process and aims of education?

I didn't raise this more general question with Devora, limiting myself to queries concerning the way this issue played out in her own school. And to her credit, though the question may have sounded harsh, Devora did not flinch from it. She immediately challenged the assumption at work in my comments that she sought out passive, malleable people whom she could shape according to her own requirements. Quite apart from the ethics of doing this, Devora was convinced that the training she offered the teachers could only be effective with young people whose general intellectual and social orientation and sensibilities were already congruent with the school's ethos. "I don't see myself as indoctrinating the teachers I hire in Beit Rabban's approach to teaching. Rather, I try to find people who are already pretty much in sync with the school's character, and then I help them develop and refine what they bring so that they can become more effective teachers."

I responded that I found this a very reasonable answer to my concern, but I added that at the level of practice the success of the school depended

.

---

[108]I owe the phrase "the dark side of vision" to Barry Holtz, who used it in the context of a discussion of the issue under consideration at a meeting organized by the Mandel Foundation in January 2005 around questions relating to the place of ideas relating to vision in teacher education. My own ideas about this issue benefited from this conversation.

heavily on her ability to find young people who had congenial sensibilities and predispositions. "Fortunately," she said, "I have been able to identify such people; but if I couldn't, that would be a very serious problem. The challenge I do face is helping young men and women that already find the Beit Rabban ideal exciting develop the pedagogical understandings and skills to do their work effectively. Fortunately, just spending a lot of time in the Beit Rabban culture is already a powerful vehicle of growth for them."

Hearing this, I commented that her ideas about teacher development (and especially her last remark) reminded me of the movement to establish what are called professional development schools for the internships of beginning teachers. The insight behind this movement is that we do a disservice to young teachers, and to American education, by immersing neophytes in educating environments that embody approaches to teaching and learning that aren't consonant with what we're trying to cultivate in them; the effect of such an immersion during this critical period in their professional development is that they acquire habits and beliefs that may be very hard to change down the road. What these young, developing educators need is to be immersed from the beginning in educational settings in which the role-models, the daily rhythms, and the practices embody our best ideas about education.

I didn't mention this to Devora at this time, but as I'm writing this, it strikes me that the insight concerning professional development that's shared by Devora and the professional development schools movement is reminiscent of the traditional Jewish view that the Israelites who had known slavery would not be allowed to cross the Jordan into the Promised Land because their personalities had been irreversibly and profoundly distorted by the experience of slavery. It's not that God and Moses did not try to help them overcome their slave mentality; but in the end neither repeated examples of God's power and beneficence nor instances and threats of God's wrath enabled them to transcend the personality traits they had developed in the course of being slaves. So, in the end, just as Devora decided that it's not going to do much good to try to change teachers whose years of experience have taught them that *avodah metzuyenet* (excellent work) should be singled out for rewards, or that mastery depends on being smart rather than on hard work, God too decides that it's better to invest in those whose outlooks have not been shaped and distorted by their long experience as slaves in Egypt.

Anyway, back to my conversation with Devora. As it turned out, she was already more than casually familiar with the professional development schools movement. In fact, in partnership with the Drisha Institute, an institute for advanced Jewish study for women, and with the help of a philanthropic foundation, Beit Rabban had recently designed and launched a graduate level educator preparation program in which Beit Rabban would function as a professional development school in which aspiring teachers would be immersed.

This new information suggested what was for me a whole new dimension of Devora's work. Over and above the awe at her energy that this new information inspired in me, I was also very curious to learn more about this project. Happy to oblige me, Devora began by informing me that although, as she had earlier told me, Beit Rabban had its origins in her search for a school that would meet the needs of her own children, she came to view it as one element in a more comprehensive effort to improve Jewish education. At a time like our own, when we are lacking dynamic conceptions of Jewish education, the role of Beit Rabban is to offer the field an image of what exemplary Jewish education might be. But since she also believed that the field is unlikely to improve without talented educators whose sensibilities, knowledge base, and skills equip them to work in the kinds of transformed schools that Beit Rabban represents, another critical element had to be a systematic effort to identify and educate such individuals. And this is how HaSha'ar was born. The idea was to identify promising individuals and to offer them a set of learning experiences which, in addition to introducing them to state-of-the-art ideas about teaching and learning, would have two other important features. First, these powerful ideas would be embedded in the design, in the very structure, of the learning experiences the students were to undergo in their program of study. Second, as I just mentioned, the program would include practicum experiences in Beit Rabban, an educational environment so different from what HaSha'ar students are familiar with from past experiences in schools that it challenges their preconceptions about teaching and learning and about what schools and kids can do.

"So," I commented, "through HaSha'ar you really do have the chance to influence the educational outlook of talented, open individuals before they have developed bad, difficult-to-break habits. It will be interesting to see what happens to the dispositions and the outlook which HaSha'ar cultivates in these people when they go into a school that's organized around a more conventional educational approach."

"Yes, it will," Devora nodded, "yes, it will."

In the silence that followed I found myself thinking further about the "freshness" of neophyte educators, and I then shared with her John Dewey's wonderful comment that it is not maturity but immaturity which is the great virtue in life! For whereas maturity signifies the attainment of characteristic and steady ways of dealing with life, it often also represents rigidity, the inability to attain new form in response to changing circumstances and understandings. Immaturity, on the other hand, can be viewed (and I think that this is the way Devora views it) not as a lack but as a positive capacity to take on new forms. While it is surely important to acquire ways of competently dealing with challenges, this should not come, as it often does, at the cost of becoming rigid and of losing the capacity to continue growing.[109]

Devora seemed interested in Dewey's view, but she quickly reminded me of an important aspect of her position that she had already voiced and wanted to reemphasize: she does not believe (nor does Dewey, by the way) that in their immature state human beings are simply blank slates, blobs of clay, that can be shaped in any form. At any given moment, native tendencies, as well as acquired habits, assumptions, and beliefs, are present which establish potentialities and limits. In searching for students for HaSha'ar and for educators for the school, therefore, it is not enough for her to identify individuals who are, in Dewey's sense, immature and open to growth; they also need to be the kinds of individuals whose inclinations, tendencies, and outlook are generally congruent with the school's conception of education.

This reminded me of a recent conversation I had with a representative of an extraordinary airline company that is based in the Midwest. Impressed by the fact that every person connected with this airline that I have ever dealt with has treated me with what feels like genuine respect and warmth, I asked this employee whether there was something unique about the company's training methods. She laughed and said that it had very little to do with training, and a lot to do with the company's ability to size up applicants. The company does work hard to cultivate the ways of dealing with customers that it wants to see in its employees, but the training only works with individuals who bring with them the right kind temperament and inclinations.[110]

As you might be able to tell, I have some sympathy for both the ideas I've been talking about: the idea that our capacity to grow into educators

---

[109]See Dewey's discussion of "growth" in *Democracy and Education*, especially 41–46.

[110]An almost identical point was made by William James, the foremost psychologist of his day, in his opening lecture to teachers concerning the contribution of knowing psychology to their work as educators. Coming to the end of his talk, James says: "To know psychology, therefore, is absolutely no guarantee that we shall be good teachers. To advance to that result, we must have an additional endowment altogether, a happy tact and ingenuity to tell us what definite things to say and do when the pupil is before us. That ingenuity in meeting and pursuing the pupil, that tact for the concrete situation, though they are the alpha and omega of the teacher's art, are things to which psychology cannot help us in the least." In William James, *Talks to Teachers* (New York: Henry Holt & Co., 1899), 9.

(or flight attendants) of a certain kind depends not just on training (however good it might be) but also on idiosyncratic individual characteristics like temperament and aptitude, and also the idea that the educational environments in which our primary development as educators takes place have a marked and often enduring impact on our educational outlook. At the same time, I am also very troubled by this view. There is a kind of pessimism written into it which is, to me, very disturbing: it's as though there is no overcoming bad beginnings. I don't know if you know the movies of the French filmmaker Francois Truffaut, films like *The Four Hundred Blows* and *Small Change.* In one of these films, *Small Change,* I think, we grimace in disbelief as a young child, maybe two years old, falls out of a tenth floor window, finally landing on and disappearing into a clump of bushes down below. A second later, with the audience still stunned by the horror of what we've witnessed, we see the boy crawl out from under the bushes; he stands up, brushes himself off, and runs along! Over and over again, Truffaut's movies offer us these kinds of images and stories, the message being that even though awful things may happen to us in the beginning, human beings are resilient enough to grow into healthy, life-affirming people.

I am moved by Truffaut's optimism, his faith that human beings have the capacity to move beyond the bad things that have happened to them. And I am troubled by a view that looks at children, at existing institutions, and at experienced teachers, and says, "I'm deeply pessimistic that you are capable of changing in fundamental ways, of growing beyond the values and orientations that you've acquired early on." Doesn't the idea of *teshu-vah*[111] point us in a very different direction? Doesn't this idea, which is at the core of Jewish thought and life, suggest that we have the capacity to change in fundamental ways? And if so, might this be true of us not just as individuals but also as professionals and institutions? The alternative is terribly bleak.

Sorry to leave you on such a depressing note, but I have to run.

All the best.
Daniel

---

[111]Literally, "returning" or "coming back"—the traditional Jewish term for *repentance.*

The Growth of Teachers

Potentialities, Obstacles, and Conditions

Building on themes sounded in Letter 10, this letter explores whether, contrary to the view Daniel has ascribed to Devora, experienced teachers are perhaps not so set in their ways that it is impossible for them to acquire radically different (and improved) approaches to their work through well-conceived professional development programs. This letter also explores why it might be that professional development programs for educators aren't more adequate, and it suggests reasons why it is premature to conclude that more effective programs couldn't be mounted. Along the way, distinctions are drawn between short-term and enduring changes, as well as between deep and more superficial (but not necessarily unimportant) changes in an educator's orientation.

Dear Alice,

Your recent letter brought me two surprises. First, based on what I've told you about her in the past, you expressed doubt that Devora would embrace the very strong view concerning the decisive power of beginnings that I ascribed to her. If, as you put it, she did hold this view, and most of her neophyte teachers had grown up in conventional schools, Devora (who is, after all, pretty savvy) wouldn't expect even them to approach the school environment in a fresh way. Here's why: although they may be new as teachers, their years of immersion in the conventional schools that Devora finds so troubling would, on the assumption that beginnings influence people decisively, have led them to absorb the ideas about teaching and learning and the rhythms of school life that these institutions embody and that Devora finds so pernicious. The fact that Devora believes that she can identify individuals who are the products of more conventional schools but who are not wedded to these ideas shows that she does not believe that beginnings are necessarily decisive—at least not as decisive as you imply.

It's a great point. Many of the teachers who come to Devora's school are survivors who have retained their freshness and openness despite having attended schools that might have been expected to eat away at these attitudes. Does this not show that early experience is not necessarily decisive, after all? And in hiring them in spite of their experience in conventional schools, doesn't Devora tacitly acknowledge this very point?

For what it's worth, here's what I think. First, it's probably not true that schools succeed in shaping all youngsters in their own image; there are always those who resist or rebel against the school's agenda,[112] and perhaps some of them, as adults, are attracted to schools like Beit Rabban that champion ideas that embody tacit, if not always explicit, critiques of conventional education. There are, in addition, at least two reasons why, even if in the course of growing up they have come to take for granted conventional understandings of what education is about, educators-in-training and neophyte educators may prove able to liberate themselves from the power of these old ideas and to see things afresh: not only has it been a long time since they have spent much time in schools, they are also entering them in new roles. I'm reminded of psychologist Erik Erikson's contention that, in adolescence, young people have the potential to come out from under the grip of ways of being and seeing things that have emerged in their earlier years of life and to redefine their basic psycho-social orientations.[113] Perhaps the same is true of adults who return to the world of schools as new educators or as educators-in-training; perhaps the reentry period offers a window of opportunity during which they may be able to re-imagine the nature and mission of these institutions and their own roles within them.

But even if these conjectures are true, it's an open question how long they will retain this kind of openness to new ways of thinking about what they are doing as teachers once they are submerged in the culture and the rhythms of a conventional educational environment. On this last point I think Devora would be more pessimistic than I am. Which brings me to the second surprise I experienced in reading your letter: your identification with Devora's views concerning the near impossibility of overcoming the effects of a teacher's early socialization in the school environment. Because of your own inservice education efforts with your staff and your par-

---

[112]There is an extensive literature about youngsters who *resist* the educational agendas of schools. The classic text which launched the conversation concerning resistance in education is Paul Willis's *Learning to Labor* (New York: Columbia University Press, 1981).

[113]See Erik Erikson, *Childhood and Society* (New York: W. W. Norton & Company, 1963); also, *Identity: Youth and Crisis* (New York: W. W. Norton & Company), 1968.

ticipation as a client in advanced leadership development activities, I expected you to react negatively, even angrily, to her apparently dismissive attitude towards such efforts. So I wasn't prepared for your comment that "Unfortunately, my own experiences with professional development efforts are pretty much at one with Devora's view."

I myself am not so sure. At any rate, I'm not ready to write off the challenge of helping working educators become, in more than marginal ways, stronger educators. It's not just, as I said at the end of my last letter, that Devora's perspective is too bleak to accept; after all, whether a view is bleak or depressing is not pertinent to an assessment of its truth.[114] The more important point is that we just don't know enough to render such a judgment. Most forms of advanced professional development in both Jewish and general education are so inadequate and so little influenced by everything we know about the conditions under which ingrained dispositions and attitudes undergo basic change that it seems to me premature to reject the idea of continuing education for educators as a tool of personal and professional (and ultimately, institutional) change. At a minimum, let's first create state-of-the-art professional development programs and track what happens to those who go through them.

Not that I'm wildly optimistic about the likely consequences of participating in such programs, assuming we were able to create them. Even great professional development programs that catalyze important insights and

---

[114]Although the idea that the bleakness of a view is not pertinent to an assessment of its truth seems reasonable across a variety of cases, there may well be, as Professor Michael Inbar has suggested to me, exceptions to this principle in the bald form in which it is articulated in the text. In particular, there are times when an assessment of the consequences of holding one view rather than another may actually be relevant to judging its merits. In his article, "The Will to Believe," William James defends the reasonableness of proceeding in this way under certain specifiable circumstances, and he illustrates what these circumstances are with attention to the case of the belief in the existence of a benign deity that oversees the cosmos. According to James, the relevant circumstances are the following: a) something of moment is at stake; b) the decision to believe or disbelieve is what he calls a forced option—that is, I can't escape make a choice among the competing options; c) the sciences will never conclusively decide the issue one way or the other; and, finally, d) what we believe is likely to have a strong influence, for better or for worse, on the tenor of our lives. Under these circumstances, James urges, it's entirely reasonable to adopt a belief based on the consequences of believing for the quality of our lives. See "The Will to Believe," in *Pragmatism and Other Essays* (New York: Washington Square Press, 1963), 193–213.

excitement about new ways of approaching teaching and learning do not guarantee any enduring benefits. As you said in your letter, "After the 'high' of the seminars I've attended, coming home is always a bath of cold water. The way the parents and most of the teachers think about the enterprise, the inertial pull of the school's customary way of doing things, and the limited resources (time and money, for instance) available for encouraging real change—all these things quickly whip me back into shape (the shape I was in before going off for my professional development experiences). I feel like the man who, having discovered the benefits of an afternoon nap while on a vacation, vows that he'll take such naps every day when back in his workaday world. But we all know what usually happens to such resolves."

All of which is to say that I understand Devora's and your own skepticism concerning the possibility that professional development programs will have a powerful and enduring effect. In particular, whether a change in the way I think about my work will endure when I return to a work environment that is organized around "the old way" of thinking and working is a serious and troubling question. But instead of making me cynical, this makes me raise a different kind of question: what would a program have to look like it if is to have a fighting chance of altering, in an enduring way, the way I approach my work? It's premature to dismiss this question, I think.

As you may have gathered, I myself have a measure of optimism concerning the ability of experienced educators to change, and my sense is that Devora has generalized too quickly from examples like the one about the incorrigible teacher who emphasized *avodah metzuyenet*. My concern is that she is paying a high price for this over-generalization. The price is that in opting for fresh, young people to serve as educators, she is forced to invest a lot of time in helping them develop rudimentary skills; and that she is missing out on a lot of experienced educators, people with savvy and with a long-term commitment to teaching, who might, over time, prove a lot more sympathetic to the school's ideals than she may think. Perhaps she could even find teachers who could make good on the aspirations embedded in the light bulb project I described way back!

Then again, these comments may betray some over-simplification. As I've continued to think about all of this, it strikes me that the question of hiring more experienced teachers may be more complicated than I've suggested. Here's why: I don't know if I've mentioned this already, but Devora strongly believes in maintaining very low teacher/student ratios; as far as she's concerned, this is one of the essential pre-conditions of quality education. The result is that whereas most schools feature much larger ratios, Devora aims for ratios of no more than 1:8, so that, not uncommonly, there will be two teachers with a group of 15 or so children. This, by the way, is one of the major reasons that Beit Rabban has the feel of being primitive in respect of equipment, desks, and so forth: she believes that from an educational point of view, it is much more sensible to plow limited financial resources into personnel than into creating a more comfortable or a more high-tech educational setting. (Here, by the way, is another example of an idea other than its guiding existential vision that informs the design of Beit Rabbán.)

So what does all this have to do with the question of hiring experienced or inexperienced faculty? Perhaps the answer is obvious: were Devora successful at identifying and attracting experienced faculty whose beliefs, dispositions, and sensibilities were (or could readily become) coherent with the school's culture, she would probably have to pay them a lot of more money than she needs to pay neophytes who are right out of school. If so, this might lower the number of teachers she could afford to hire, which in turn would adversely affect the desired teacher-student ratios. But these are just speculations, unconstrained by data or by input from Devora.

I'm afraid I've rambled on more than I should have. Truth is, I meant to say more about my disidentification with the pessimism exuded by Devora (and you) concerning the possibility of helping (at least some) old dogs learn new tricks; and I was then going to go on to the interesting question you asked concerning the place of evaluation at Beit Rabban; but now I fear that it's gotten so late that I will have to defer this question until later. Which is probably okay, because it will give me more of a chance to investigate this matter.

I hope all is well with you, and that the long midwestern winter will soon give way to spring. Be happy—it's Adar![115]

Daniel

Hi Alice! Treat this as a postscript to the letter you have just read. Just before dropping it in a mailbox, I bumped into Devora on the street and, since it was still on my mind, I shared with her our recent exchange concerning what seemed to me her undue pessimism about helping experienced teachers change. I found her response interesting and thought I'd pass it on to you while it's still fresh.

First, she said, though it may have sounded that way, she didn't mean to convey that experienced teachers can *never* change in fundamental ways; rather, she was suggesting that only under certain special circum-

---

[115]A traditional greeting for the Jewish month of Adar in which the festival of Purim falls.

stances was this a real possibility. She returned to my reference to *teshu-vah*, suggesting that it was very pertinent to her own view. "I do believe in the possibility of *teshuvah*," she said, "but keep in mind that *teshuvah* begins with *hakarat het*, with genuine, heartfelt acknowledgment of the way one's conduct has fallen short of the mark. Not that one needs to feel that 'I'm a sinner.' The important thing is to feel some dissonance, to experience some genuine doubt about how one's been proceeding and to recognize the need to do some rethinking. Without this, fundamental change is hard to imagine."

This reminded me, I told her, of the old light bulb joke. You know: Q: "How many psychiatrists does it take to change a light bulb?" A: "One; but only if the light bulb wants to change!" She liked this joke a lot, and said that it was very consistent with what she meant. "If that *avodah metzuyenet/Mi hakham* teacher were to come to the realization that her approach to the kids was or might be wrong-headed, this would not guarantee that her conduct would change; but at least we'd have a fighting chance."

This, I responded, sounds right to me, and it also suggests an important point about helping educators improve. Perhaps our efforts to help them acquire new ways of understanding and approaching their work need to begin with learning experiences that lead them to reflect critically on the way they are currently doing things. "Real and living doubt"—it doesn't have to be certainty—that the web of assumptions and practices that make up their approach is really sound may be a precondition of real growth.[116]

Devora identified with this point, adding that it would be wrong to think that, in having educators and visitors spend time in the Beit Rabban environment, she wants them to identify with the school's orientation. Rather, her hope is that encountering Beit Rabban's daily life will give them a chance to see an orientation so different from what they're familiar with that it will awaken the thought that their conventional understandings of good educational practice represent *choices* that may be worth revisiting in the light of other possible ways of thinking about education.

I nodded agreement, indicating that if immersion in a school like Beit Rabban can bring educators and others to call into question their conventional ways of thinking about education, that's already a big success. That said, I went on to say, I felt compelled to acknowledge (despite the rela-

---

[116]The emphasis on "real and living doubt" as a condition of serious inquiry and growth is central to John Dewey's approach to education. The phrase itself has its origins in the work of John Dewey's teacher Charles Sanders Peirce in "The Fixation of Belief," in *Charles S. Peirce: Selected Writings*, ed. Philip Wiener (New York: Dover Publications, 1958), 91–112.

tively optimistic stance I have been adopting in my conversations with her concerning the possibility of change) that even if adults can be brought to doubt their habitual ways of approaching things, it is likely to prove difficult to bring about enduring revolutions in the basic ways they understand their situation and their work.[117]

"So," Devora responded, "maybe we're not as far apart on this issue as it first seemed. I don't want to claim that there is absolutely nothing that would bring the teacher we keep discussing to a radically new perspective on the aims and effects of her work as an educator; but my guess is that I am more likely to be successful with an inexperienced teacher who isn't yet relatively set in her ways."

Although not uncomfortable with the view Devora had just articulated, I thought it needed to be fine-tuned; and I commented that even teachers who are very set in their ways are eager to change in some ways. "Look, for example, at the way they flock to CAJE [Coalition for the Advancement of Jewish Education] sessions that promise to offer them new ways of engaging students, new curricula, and new approaches to behavior management."

"This is very true," Devora said, "and perhaps it was too strong to say, as I did before, that teachers like the one we were talking about are incapable of *any* change. Maybe what we need to do is to distinguish between fundamental changes in the way educators think about what they do and more modest changes that take place within the framework of a relatively fixed orientation to their work. The *avodah metzuyenet* teacher was ready and eager for new 'tricks of the trade;' but she was far from ready to rethink her basic approach."[118]

Anyway, that's the substance of my last interaction with Devora about this matter. Though I think she's right that there is less disagreement between us than I had first thought, I still disagree significantly with her on the practical issue that's at stake. Meaning what? That I would not be as quick as she is to dismiss the effort to help experienced teachers undergo fundamental change; and I think that although some teachers, like the *avodah metzuyenet* teacher, may well be a lost cause, many teachers can and should be worked with.

---

[117]I have discussed this difficulty in "Socratic Teaching: A Critical Assessment," *Journal of Moral Education*, Vol. 23, No. 2, 1994, 119–134.

[118]It is noteworthy that a very similar point has been made at the institutional and system-wide levels by historians David Tyack and Larry Cuban in their book *Tinkering Towards Utopia* (Cambridge, MA: Harvard University Press, 1995). Their view is discussed more fully below (140–141).

Not that this is likely to be easy or that that we will be universally successful with experienced teachers. But the stakes are high here, so high that unless and until it is very clear that there aren't effective strategies for helping such teachers acquire new and more powerful ways of approaching their work, we shouldn't give up on finding these strategies. For if we could succeed in the effort to help these teachers *and* take advantage of the savvy they have gained from their substantial experience, we might be in a much better position to meet the challenges of Jewish education.

Let's be in touch soon.
Daniel

Student Assessment:
Educative and Miseducative[119]

Beginning with a discussion of the role of prizes and praise in educa-
tion, this letter explores the nature of and rationale for evaluation in the
life of Beit Rabban. It pays special attention to the school's beliefs con-
cerning the motivation for human learning and the effects of different
kinds of evaluation practices. The letter ends with a question, more fully
addressed later on: does Beit Rabban's apparent success as an educa-
tional institution depend on the fact that it attracts especially bright and
highly motivated youngsters?

Dear Alice:

I just got back from the annual Purim Carnival. My son, dressed as the
Yankees' old number 3 ("the Babe"), participated in the costume contest
(also annual). Along with scores of other children (many of them in the role
of Esther or Mordechai, with a Haman, a lamp-post, a butterfly, and a Bart

---

[119]The distinction between *educative* and *miseducative* experiences is articulated by
John Dewey in *Experience and Education* (New York: Collier Books, 1963). Dewey
introduces this distinction in developing an account of the differences between educationally desirable experiences and those that are destructive. The ideal of growth, as
he understands it, is central to his characterization of these differences, but one can
employ the distinction without being committed to this ideal. I have discussed this
distinction and the concept of growth in the following articles: "Dewey's Conception
of Growth Reconsidered," *Educational Theory* 40:3 (1990), 283–294, and "Dewey's
Groundwork" in Mordecai Nisan and Oded Schremer, eds., *Educational Delibera-*
tions (Jerusalem: Keter Publishing House and the Mandel Foundation, 2005),
119–139.

Simpson also in attendance), he walked across the stage, paused at a microphone to say his name and who/what he was, and then waited for the results from a panel of judges sitting below. Alas, he didn't win, but, fortunately, it didn't seem to dampen his spirits much.

I mention this because my inquiries into Beit Rabban have conferred on me, at least for now, different lenses through which I look at my day-to-day world. In this case, what struck me was the giving of prizes for costumes. While prizes and other extrinsic rewards, including praise, figure prominently in our culture and in our schools, one does not routinely encounter them at Beit Rabban; in fact, according to Devora, many of the parents believe that praise is too scarce a commodity in this school! But though she is aware of this perception, she is reluctant to change this aspect of Beit Rabban.

I mentioned some of the reasons for this reluctance when I spoke about the *avodah metzuyenet* teacher—you know, the one who would regularly single out for praise children who, in her judgment, had done excellent work.[120] At the time, I think I emphasized Devora's discomfort with the idea that, because of inborn or familial advantages for which they could claim no responsibility, some children should be regularly showered with praise, while others are left out. I think I also spoke about the school's commitment to autonomy, and Devora's concern that the kind of prize-giving that schools practice (grades, praise) breeds too great a dependence on the approval of others and unthinking acceptance of their standards of what is good and bad. These prize-giving practices have the effect of conveying to children that standards of appraisal are somehow "out there," rather than products of people like themselves.

But there are also some other points that need emphasis. One of them expands on the idea that children are harmed by a system that distributes praise based on some allegedly objective measure of achievement. That those who don't measure up may grow discouraged in ways that disastrously affect their learning is widely recognized among those who consider themselves progressive educators; less widely understood, Devora believes, is that so-called successful kids are also harmed by this system. In addition to the danger that they will become full of themselves, there is reason to worry that their ability to win praise for meeting preset standards will jeopardize their willingness to take intellectual risks in new directions; it may also, if they achieve the set standards with ease, undermine their developing habits of hard work.

I refer to all these points to distinguish them from additional reasons

[120]See Letter 3.

for being wary of prizes and other external messages signifying success or failure that have surfaced in my most recent conversations with Devora. Perhaps most important is her interest in encouraging her students to love learning and to engage in it for its own sake, rather than out of desire for any external reward. As you no doubt know, this idea has a long tradition within Judaism, as in this passage in the Talmud:

> Rabbi Elazar quoted this verse: "She opens her mouth with wisdom, and Torah of lovingkindness is on her tongue: [Prov 31:26]." What is the intent of this verse? Is there a Torah of lovingkindness and a Torah which is not of lovingkindness? Torah which is studied on its own merit is a Torah of lovingkindness, whereas Torah which is studied for an ulterior motive is not a Torah of lovingkindness. . . .[121]

But traditional though it may be in Jewish thought and, at least sometimes, in Jewish practice, the attitude towards learning that this passage articulates is far from what children growing up in America learn. In a world in which prizes and penalties surround the activities of learning in which children engage, they are quickly socialized to learn for the sake of rewards and in order to avoid penalties. The way grading works in American schools is a prime example of this phenomenon. Beit Rabban is very concerned not to encourage this attitude towards learning.

As I am writing this, I can think of another reason why Beit Rabban may stay away from conventional grading systems and other practices that establish hierarchies of success among the children. I have already described to you how impressively conversations flow in Beit Rabban classrooms; it is, as we have discussed, a school that wants to nurture a learning community that features sharing and building on one another's ideas. But this is, I think, much less likely to happen in the way it regularly does at Beit Rabban if the children are—as is typically the case in most schools—in competition with one another for prizes of one kind or another, including the teacher's approval of their ideas. And here I hope I am being responsive to a question you raised a while back about the place of evaluation at Beit Rabban.

The important point is that for reasons that are intimately connected to its larger educational aspirations, Beit Rabban is very reluctant to dish out prizes and praise. I hasten to add, though, that this reluctance should not be taken to mean that it is cavalier about, or indifferent to, evaluation. Nothing could be further from the truth. Here's a story Devora told me:

[121]Talmud Bavli, Succah, 49b.

"Once, when my son (about nine at the time and a student at Beit Rabban) was at the eye doctor, the eye doctor asked him to read the chart. Sensing what he thought was hesitation (actually, I think my son was trying to see whether he could remember the sequences of letters from having looked at the chart before removing his glasses!), the eye doctor told my son not to worry: it's not like a test at school, he explained; he's just trying to help my son see better! This struck my son as a ridiculous distinction; it had never occurred to him that anything that happened at school was designed just to test you rather than to help you learn better. How scary—that we are supposed to assume that the tests which doctors administer are to help you, but that the tests which teachers give are to . . . to what? I think that the belief embedded in the doctor's comment is common; despite the generally good intentions of teachers, standardized assessment activities and assigned tasks more often than not convey to kids that the teacher's goal is to trick them, or to allow them to show how smart (or stupid) they are relative to the other children; they do not convey that the teacher is trying to help you find out what you need to learn and how you can more effectively learn. Which, of course, is why cheating in many conventional schools makes sense. But why would you ever cheat on an eye exam? You'll end up with glasses which don't help you see well!

"Which brings out one of the big differences between Beit Rabban and many conventional schools. Instead of rewarding children for 'being good' at the likely cost of encouraging a smug, self-satisfied attitude in those who are adept at getting good grades, at Beit Rabban we approach evaluation in a way that will lead the children to view it as a tool that can help them become better learners."

Devora's comment reminded me of two very different things. One of them was the research of Carol Dweck—I don't know if you're familiar with her work—who argues, with strong empirical evidence to back her up, that children whose orientation towards learning focuses on becoming better learners tend to become much more effective learners than do learners who are preoccupied with "looking smart."[122] The second thing her comment reminded me of was an incident, described to me a few days earlier by a teacher working with the first/second graders, which provides some impressionistic evidence that the kids are actually influenced by the Beit Rabban approach. In this class, the children have a regular "spelling challenge." Every week, each child chooses ten words he/she doesn't know how to spell and wants to learn, with the words coming from the youngster's own writing, reading, or studies. The idea, as the teacher ex-

---

[122]See Carol Dweck, *Self-Theories: Their Role in Motivation, Personality, and Development* (Philadelphia: Psychology Press, Taylor & Francis, 2000).

plained it to me, is to challenge each child to increase the number of words he/she knows how to spell, and, more importantly, to begin to focus the children on attending to conventional spelling in their writing. The way it works is that, on a certain day, the children exchange lists, ask each other to write down the words on their lists, and then go over the words to see which ones they have succeeded in learning and which ones they need to study more (which they then mark to so indicate). Anyway, on this particular occasion, at the conclusion of the day's spelling challenge, one little girl came up to the teacher to ask whether she could put a mark next to a word she had spelled correctly. She explained that, when asked the word, she hadn't actually been sure how to spell it; she had ended up guessing correctly, but she felt she needed to study it more.

When I described the incident to Devora, she smiled appreciatively, adding that such behavior would be unlikely in a child who hadn't been nurtured in the Beit Rabban community. She illustrated the differences between the children in her school and the products of more typical schools with an anecdote from her own experience in the school:

> I was teaching Torah in the fall to a class of first and second graders. One of the children, a second grader, had just transferred to Beit Rabban after kindergarten and first grade at a traditional day school. All of the other children had been at Beit Rabban since kindergarten. Ze'ev, a second grader whose parents know little Hebrew, asked one day why we use an edition of the Torah that has only Hebrew, rather than one with an English translation. I asked the children what they thought about why we do that. Efrat, the child who had recently transferred to Beit Rabban, responded that if we had an English translation the teacher wouldn't be able to "to trick us," the idea being that teachers test children with the goal of tripping them up and finding out what they don't know. This correlated with all sorts of other behaviors which Efrat exhibited (which I think are typical of children in traditional schools) which were aimed at demonstrating how smart (or fast) she was at something, often at the expense of thinking things through. Ephraim, a first grader who had begun Beit Rabban in kindergarten, gave a very different answer than did Efrat: "Because if we had an English translation, we would just look at it rather than working hard at figuring out the Hebrew, and then we wouldn't learn it so well."

Though personally sympathetic to Devora's approach to evaluation, I wanted to know how she would respond to a common challenge to this perspective: by de-emphasizing the reward/penalty, approval/disapproval, features of evaluation, I asked, aren't you depriving yourself of a powerful motivational tool? Devora responded quickly: "Only if you believe that external goads are necessary to motivate children to learn. And the truth is, goads like approval/disapproval, prizes and competition are necessary, but only when educators have failed in their fundamental job, which is to offer children opportunities and a social environment that make for meaningful learning. And though the educator who uses evaluation as a stick or carrot to stimulate or reinforce the impulse to learn may succeed in spurring particular learnings, this may be at a high price: for the children may be and, I think, are acquiring very undesirable dispositions and attitudes along the way."

I commented that this point reminded me of the observation, which I associate with John Dewey, that the tools we use in our efforts to facilitate learning—and surely our approaches to evaluation are prime examples—are not just neutral vehicles but are themselves, for better or worse, interventions that affect children in powerful ways.[123] As Marshall McLuhan put it: "The medium is the message." Which means that we need to assess our evaluation practices based not just on their immediate motivational impact and on whether they help us identify what the learners have learned but also on the way these practices affect the children's attitudes towards what they are learning and towards themselves as learners.

Devora nodded appreciatively in response to my characterization of Dewey's ideas, murmured something about wanting to reread him, and then underscored her own view: if a teacher is true to his or her job, then (unless children have been socialized in their homes or in other schools to need external rewards) you will find them working hard and productively without them.

"But," I asked, "do you really think that everything can be learned 'for its own sake?' I mean, aren't there a lot of important things that are unlikely to be learned for intrinsic reasons?"[124]

---

[123]Dewey writes: "Collateral learning in the way of formation of enduring attitudes, of likes and dislikes, may be and often is much more important than the spelling lesson or lesson in geography or history that is learned [and evaluated.] For these attitudes are fundamentally what count in the future. The most important attitude that can be formed is that of desire to go on learning. If impetus in this direction is weakened, [the price is necessarily too high]." *Experience and Education*, 48.

[124]Reference to intrinsic (as opposed to extrinsic) reasons for learning is an occasion to take note of the fact that some unclarity surrounds this notion. Jerome Bruner makes a useful attempt to address this matter in *Towards a Theory of Instruction*, 114: "Almost all children possess what have come to be known as 'intrinsic' motives for learning. An intrinsic motive is one that does not depend upon reward that lies outside the activity it impels. Reward inheres in the successful termination of the activity or even in the activity itself. Curiosity is almost a prototype of the intrinsic motive."

"Of course there are times at Beit Rabban when children learn things that aren't immediately exciting to them, and there are many times when the teacher's job is to get the children to do this kind of learning when they would rather not; but in these situations, we try to organize the activity in a way that will be interesting to them, and we help them, when it is not already obvious, to understand how knowing or knowing how to do certain things, for example, mastering Hebrew vocabulary needed to read the text of the Torah, makes it possible to more meaningfully engage in activities that they do find rewarding. And this makes a world of difference! Practicing the piano may not be fun for the child, and the music teacher may have to use his or her influence to keep the child from abandoning the activity; but if the child recognizes that this kind of practice contributes to effective performance and feels that effective performance is something he or she aspires to because of the pleasure it gives, or because it gives one a meaningful role in the community, or for other reasons, the activity turns into something very different from rote learning."

Devora paused, and then added, "So you're right to suggest that there are any number of occasions when our children are less than fully voluntary learners; but this is a far cry from organizing the experience around competition, rewards or fear of punishment, or turning evaluation into a goad. And let's not lose sight of what to my mind is the most important point: though there is something to the view that not everything can be learned out of curiosity or interest, a lot more can be learned this way than most people think. And Beit Rabban is living proof of this."

This last point hit home. I immediately thought about the little girl who asked to make a mark signifying "Needs More Study" on her spelling test because she didn't feel she really knew the word, and about the exciting mathematical games Beit Rabban children regularly play (I'll send one of them along to you, Alice), games through which they learn mathematical thinking and properties. I've tried some of these games with my own son and have been amazed by how quickly he took to them. But, perhaps just to hear how she would respond, I registered some skepticism.

"How do you know the school is 'living proof?' Is there a basis for believing this beyond the kind of anecdotal and impressionistic evidence we've been pointing to?" I interjected. "I mean, as long as we're talking about evaluation, how do you go about evaluating your own efforts, and judging them, as you now seem to be doing, to be successful? I certainly haven't seen the kids taking the kinds of tests that my grade school teachers used to assess our progress and the school's success!"

"I would have been surprised had you said you did see such tests, since we don't rely on them at Beit Rabban. The kind of separation between learning and evaluation that is found in most schools is simply not present here. At Beit Rabban, every task, game, or activity is an opportunity for the teacher to gauge the children's strengths and weaknesses, the skills, attitudes, and habits they are acquiring, and the kind of knowledge base they are able to call on to think about the problem at hand. Partly this is so because of the kinds of activities our teachers prepare for the kids, activities which, while engaging, require the children to draw on their skills and knowledge; but it's also because the teachers here are 'down on the ground' with the children, themselves participants in the process of learning and therefore able to watch them up close. Of course, another reason these activities can provide us with the kind of index we need of the children's progress is that our teacher-student ratio allows the teachers to follow the growth of each child in great detail in an ongoing way."

Though I found Devora's answers very illuminating, something had been gnawing at me as she was speaking, and now, as it came into shape, I put it into words. Proceeding delicately, for fear that I might offend her, I commented: "All of this is very interesting, and I'm reasonably confident that the kids who go to Beit Rabban love learning for its own sake. But can you really generalize from this to the idea that the school has the power to nurture this attitude?"

Now it was Devora's turn to be uncertain about what I had in mind, and in response to her quizzical look I continued. "What I mean is this. My impression is that the children at Beit Rabban are not 'run-of-the-mill' children. They strike me as exceptionally bright, intellectually curious and self-motivated. Now it is, of course, possible that these are garden variety children who have been favorably influenced by the culture of the school, and in fact I have little doubt that the school culture *does* positively affect the way the kids approach learning; but I have a feeling that's not the whole story. More pointedly, have you considered the possibility that Beit Rabban attracts a self-selected subgroup that finds the school's ethos and approach to learning particularly congenial, and that other children might find it a hard environment in which to thrive?"

"It's an interesting question," Devora responded. "Let's come back to it the next time we talk." Which I am very eager to do. More on this soon, I hope.

In the meantime, I wish you the very best.
Belated Happy Purim!
Daniel

LETTER 13
Problems, Real and Alleged, Including:

Finding Teachers; Money;
the Non-intellectual Dimensions of Education

Though it is briefly addressed, the question raised at the end of the preceding letter concerning the school's interest in very bright children is largely deferred until the next one. In response to a question raised by Alice, this letter focuses attention on some of Beit Rabban's real and alleged problems. These problems range from the difficulty of finding the right kind of teachers, to financial woes, to the school's inadequate physical plant and the alleged connection between this problem and the school's difficulty in attracting a sizeable clientele. This discussion also explores the idea that scarcity of financial resources, though a serious problem, may help an institution keep focused on its essential priorities.

Also discussed in this letter are questions relating to the amount of heterogeneity a school should include and to whether Beit Rabban is insufficiently attuned to non-intellectual dimensions of learning and children. The case is made that Beit Rabban does not disregard the children's creative and imaginative capacities, which are given room for expression and development in problem-solving activities.

Dear Alice,

Fair enough! It does, as you say, seem "too good to be true" and maybe it's time to search out the soft underbelly of this school. What are the problems? Where does it fall short of the ideal? What is it really like? Let me begin by confessing that, as I gave thought to your questions, I found myself wondering whether, because of my excitement, I, and perhaps Devora as well, have been guilty of embellishing the reality in describing the school to you. It's common knowledge that when a person has grown strongly wedded to a particular perspective or interpretation, there may be a tendency to neglect or interpret away features of the world that

123

don't cohere with this interpretation, as well as to overemphasize those that do.[125] In any case, I decided to raise this matter with Devora herself.

Yesterday, over lunch at a kosher restaurant not far from the school, I put the question to her. "I've been meaning to say something to you about this," was her first comment. "As I've read a couple of the letters describing the school that you've sent your friend Alice (yikes! I never did ask permission to show them to her, and I hope you won't object), I have had a very mixed reaction. On the one hand, I've felt pleased because your letters are pretty true to the life of this school; but I too have wondered whether a reader would respond that this sounds 'too good to be true.' More to the point, I myself have wondered whether you have painted an overly flattering picture of Beit Rabban."

"Have I?" I asked.

"Perhaps not overall," she responded, "but in some ways you have. For example, nobody would guess from your descriptions that the children at Beit Rabban are sometimes less than models of good behavior. They are, after all, kids!"

We both laughed, and we traded a few stories about kids "cutting up" and pulling pranks. Then, in a more serious vein, Devora commented that although the classroom communities that I have been painting in some of my letters are not uncommon in the school, there have been groups that have fallen appallingly short of the ideal. And she went on to describe a situation in which a group of eight- to ten-year-olds was exhibiting all sorts of antisocial patterns of conduct and interaction that were not conducive to learning. Much teacher time and energy focused on trying to remedy these difficulties.

After we discussed this very hard situation for some time, I asked Devora if she could say something about other kinds of problems that seemed to her particularly daunting. Devora thought for a minute, and responded. "One of the most serious problems I already shared with you. It's very hard to find teachers who combine a strong Jewish knowledge base, educational competence, and the kind of attitude towards children and education that is at the heart of Beit Rabban. My solution—finding smart, young, but inexperienced teachers and educating them as teachers myself—is far from optimal. For all their good intentions, the pedagogical instincts of

[125]For an older but still excellent discussion of this phenomenon in relation to the possibility of objectivity in the sciences (and, by extension, in other domains), see the chapter entitled "Observation and Objectivity," in Israel Scheffler's *Science and Subjectivity* (New York: Bobbs-Merrill, 1967), 21–44. I return, in a somewhat different vein, to the question of whether I have painted a true-to-life portrait of Beit Rabban in Letter 16.

these young people are not always sound, and, as I have already mentioned, fostering their growth as educators takes up an awful lot of my time. To top it off, for many of them, Beit Rabban is a way station on a journey to further schooling or to a different career. Though, on balance, I prefer this situation to hiring more conventional teachers, it would be much better if we had a pool of educators to choose from who, in addition to being sympathetic to the school's educational outlook, came to us with a lot of educational sophistication and viewed teaching as their career rather than as an interesting interlude."

"I am guessing," I responded, "that finding such teachers would be very hard. I mean, not only are they rare, but I wonder whether, should you succeed in identifying and recruiting them, you would be able to pay them enough to hold on to them very long. I'm thinking not just about the fact that you don't have the strongest financial base, but also about your insistence on a 1:8 teacher/student ratio."

"Well, I myself am not convinced that, if we could find such teachers, we would lose them to other institutions. But you're certainly right that Beit Rabban has a fragile financial base, and this is a very serious problem."

"Wouldn't it help if you took in more students?"

"It would," Devora smiled a little sadly, "especially if they included some who come from very well-to-do families with the capacity to help us out. But as of today, Beit Rabban has not yet been able to attract a sufficiently large or wealthy population of families to get us 'over the top.'"

When I asked Devora why she thinks that is, she began by pointing to the school's physical plant. As I've mentioned to you, Beit Rabban is located in a pretty primitive physical environment; and although I personally have been charmed by the juxtaposition of the primitive surroundings and the rich inquiries and conversations that are going on (it reminds me of ill-clad, gawky-looking Socrates soaring with his interlocutors through an intellectual paradise in the streets of ancient Athens), I can see why many potential clients for the school might, as Devora suspects, be turned off by the physical environment.

It sounds like a kind of chicken-and-egg problem, I said. "The school doesn't have the financial wherewithal to have a building of its own because it doesn't have a large, well-heeled school population; and it can't get this school population because the physical environment is a turn-off. This is where a generous donor who is committed to the school's vision would come in handy."

Devora smiled. "From your mouth to God's ears!"

We sat quietly for a minute or so, and then I commented that the school's weak financial base makes having a guiding vision that articulates its key educational aspirations all the more important.

Devora waited for me to explain.

"What I mean is this. I've heard some people say that talk about vision is pretty useless if you don't have the resources to realize that vision; but it seems to me that when you don't have much money, having a vision is especially important because the vision gives you a basis for deciding what expenditures, among the many that might be made, are really essential from the standpoint of what you're about."

Devora nodded.

"In fact," I continued, "if you wanted to look on the bright side, you could even say that your scarce resources problem, worrisome as it is, at least has a silver lining."

Devora looked at me with a bewildered expression, again waiting for me to continue.

"Here's what I was thinking. When you have little money (and analogous considerations apply to time) each expenditure must be weighed very carefully. You constantly have to ask yourself: 'Since I have limited resources, what's the most effective way to use them?' And here your vision, your underlying conception of what you're really after as a school, is of the utmost importance in determining how to proceed. So, in a way, having little money may help to keep the school's core aspirations in focus. If, on the other hand, suddenly you had all the money in the world, there would be a greater danger of losing focus, since even things peripheral to the central vision would be affordable."

"I see what you mean, and I suppose it's true that having ample financial resources carries its own dangers. All the same, I would happily accept the risks that come with having a stable financial base. There's an awful lot we could do to help Beit Rabban become a better and more stable school, as well as to extend its reach and influence."

I was pretty sure that getting a better building would be high on her wish list, but I wanted to hear more about how Devora would spend additional resources, were they forthcoming. But my thinking was interrupted by Devora, whose thoughts had returned to the school's failure to attract a more sizeable clientele.

"To be honest, though the building factor is significant, there is also another reason the school may not be attracting more families," she commented, and she then revisited a theme that had emerged earlier in our conversations. "As I have mentioned in the past, my sense is that people get uncomfortable because Beit Rabban doesn't neatly fit into their preconceived categories. The Orthodox community views us as tref[126] because we don't use the 'Orthodox' label, and 'Conservative' or 'Reform' Jews see a curriculum with a strong emphasis on Jewish texts and conclude that we

---

[126]Tref here means "not Kosher" or "off limits".

are 'too Orthodox.' And then there are others who look at the way the school encourages rich intellectual engagement in even young kids and conclude that Beit Rabban is 'too intellectual' or 'too intense' an environment. Some even feel that in its emphasis on the intellect, the school does not sufficiently cultivate the emotions and the imagination of the children. The result is that many people whose children might in fact thrive at Beit Rabban are reluctant to send them to us."

"This means, I take it, that you don't think these perceptions of the school are well-founded."

"No, I don't think they're at all well-founded. Whether it is Orthodox or liberal, as long as a family believes in intellectual openness, intellectual challenge and engagement with Jewish learning, ideas, and practices, they should not find the school a threat; and were they to give it a chance, I suspect that many from both these worlds would find it a more compelling educational environment than the alternatives they now gravitate towards. And in the case of the liberal community, although they often seem disturbed by the school's seriousness about text study, my own feeling, as you probably realize by now, is that the kind of autonomy they say they value itself requires the kind of deep knowledge of Jewish texts that Beit Rabban encourages."

"Yes," I nodded in agreement. "Many of the people I know feel that they are exercising autonomy when they decide what to believe or how to live as a Jew based on how this coheres with political and social commitments that have their origins outside of Jewish culture. Not that I don't also use the lenses that belong to me as a citizen of the modern world to better understand the meaning and consequences of adopting a particular Jewish outlook or set of practices. But, that said, the idea of deciding for ourselves what it means to be a Jew or how to live as a Jew, or whether to take on or let go of a Jewish observance, translates into something pretty superficial if we don't also have an understanding of, or know how to access, the ideas and debates within Jewish tradition that address these matters."

There was now a lull in the conversation, until I continued. "So I agree with you about this point. But right now, I'm more interested in the other criticism of the school you just identified: the idea that Beit Rabban is too intellectual an environment. To be honest, I've heard this concern voiced by more than one person, and it has two parts to it. One of them I alluded to the other day when I wondered out loud whether the school succeeds because its student body consists of a small group of exceptionally smart kids. As I'm sure you know, some people describe Beit Rabban as elitist. The other concern, and it's the one you just alluded to, is that the school focuses on the children's minds at the expense of their hearts and imagination. Is there in your opinion truth to these concerns?"

"Well, I certainly hear them often enough."

"And?"

"Well, let's start with the first one. It's true that Beit Rabban is aimed at, and does best with, bright, motivated children. Though not everybody in the school is gifted (the school is actually more heterogeneous than we had hoped it would be), we are very concerned to meet the needs of gifted children. But I don't make any apology for this . . ."

"Hold on. Why do you say that it's more heterogeneous than you had hoped? What's wrong with heterogeneity?"

"I'm not at all against heterogeneity. On the contrary, my concern is that we are usually insufficiently attuned to the extent of heterogeneity among learners: kids, like adults, bring very different constellations of strengths and weaknesses to the activity of learning. It's part of the school's philosophy that because all kids have special needs, there's got to be a lot of individualization in any educational program; and if the range of differences among the children is too great, this is going to be very hard to accomplish. Put differently, it's our very belief in heterogeneity, combined with an appreciation of what it takes to genuinely meet the needs of very different kids that sets limits to the range of heterogeneity that we try to encompass."

"And the range of kids that you're interested in is, in respect of ability, on the upper end of the spectrum."

"Yes," she nodded, "because I believe that these children also have the right to a good education and that their needs are not well attended to in most other schools; too often they are patted on the back, but not seriously taught in a way that's responsive to their capabilities and needs. As for the other criticism, my feeling is that to say that Beit Rabban emphasizes the mind at the expense of the heart or the imagination betrays a complete failure to understand the school."

Devora paused and then turned to me. "Look, I could explain to you why I think this; but if you don't mind, I'd find it much more interesting to hear what you think. You have been observing the life of this school for some time now. Do *you* think this is a fair perception of Beit Rabban?"

Though caught by surprise, I was not uncomfortable with the question. Truth be told, I had been giving it some thought while observing the school, particularly since I kept hearing this kind of criticism. As I thought about how to frame my response, I thought back to some of the activities I had heard about or witnessed—to the project organized around deciding whether light bulbs can be turned on over Shabbat, to the deliberations about how to respond to needy street people, and, on a more day-to-day level, to the way activities like Torah study or math are approached in the life of the school. These all involve various species of problem-solving activities, and how well these problems are solved clearly depends on good thinking informed by good ideas. But nothing could be further from the truth than the suggestion that this emphasis on problem solving and serious inquiry comes at the price of not nurturing the children's creativity, or their imagination, or their feelings. The idea that these intellectual emphases are incompatible with nurturing these qualities reminds me of the equally wrongheaded but popular idea that scientific inquiry is cold and devoid of feeling. Think for a moment about the young children struggling to figure out how to use their tzedakah money and how to help the homeless guy around the corner. The children didn't mechanically deduce a solution to the problems they faced. They had to create solutions to these problems. Similarly, in trying to make sense of tensions or anomalous phrases in the text of the Torah, it takes creative ingenuity to transcend the problem at hand in a meaningful way. I very much like the idea that the kids are encouraged to be creative in relation to real problems that they're trying to solve. This approach sends out two important messages. One of them is that creativity need not be confined to the arts; there is room, even a need, for creativity in meeting the challenges of everyday life. The other is that it's not sufficient for a solution to be "creative;" it's also essential that it be subjected to hard thinking in order to judge whether it effectively solves the problem which it claims to be addressing.

When I conveyed these ideas to Devora, she added that what I had said about creativity is also true of imagination. "Think about Joe again. If the children are serious about helping Joe, they have to exercise their imagination in a serious way. They have to put themselves in his shoes. 'What is it like to be Joe, and how is it going to feel to be the recipient of money or sandwiches, or clothes from young children?' If they don't use their imaginations well, they are much less likely to be successful in their efforts to help."

"This is not just a feat of imagination," I added. "Though imagination may well enter into it, what you're really talking about here, and asking the kids to try, is an act of empathy; and thinking about the way empathy enters into the children's efforts to respond to Joe actually strengthens my sense that the school is more interested in social and emotional development than outsiders may sometimes think."

Reflecting further on this matter, I shared my developing impression that Beit Rabban shares John Dewey's idea that traits like good thinking, creativity, imagination, empathy and action hang together organically, and that it is a mistake to think that you can do any of them well without the others. This point, I said, has important implications for pedagogy.

"I like this idea," Devora commented, "and I want to give you an example from a very different realm, from Torah study. Some time back the six- and seven-year-old children in the first-year Torah class were studying the Creation story, an activity that included working on watercolors illustrating each day of Creation. This particular year it also included looking at and talking about some of Michelangelo's Sistine Chapel paintings. Anyway, on the day I'm thinking of, we were studying the verse in chapter 2 which describes God's creation of the human being: 'Vayitzer hashem elohim et ha'adam afar min ha'adama vayipakh be'apav nishmat hayim vayehi ha'adam lenefesh haya.' [Then the Lord God formed man of the dust of the ground, and breathed into his nostrils the breath of life; and man became a living soul.] Suddenly, Jeffrey, a first grader with quite a literary bent, says: 'This is how I imagine it. The ru'ah elohim[127] from Perek Aleph [Chapter 1] comes in a gust—no, I mean a breeze—and swirls up the dust and, as the dust comes down, shapes it into the form of a human being.' This was followed by other children explaining the way they visualized this idea. For me, it was a very powerful moment. It wouldn't have happened without careful attention to the text, but it was a gigantic imaginative leap beyond the words themselves."

"This must have been a very moving experience. Can you explain how it's an instance of imagination in the service of problem solving?"

"I think I can," Devora responded. "In this instance, the children were struggling to understand the passage in the second chapter of Genesis in which God shapes the human being out of the dust of the earth and breathes into his nostrils the breath, or spirit, of life—and so animates him. Jeffrey, who was working his way towards an understanding of what this might have been like, recalled and made use of the reference to ru'ah Elohim in the first chapter to make sense of this description. His imagination, which took both visual artistic and literary form (because you could see him seeing it and he said it in a beautiful way), was working in tandem with critical thinking to make sense of, to give meaning to, the text."

I too loved the example and found myself tracing the image that Jeffrey had described in my own mind's eye. By now we had finished lunch, and we started walking back in the direction of the school. We moved along quietly for a while, taking in the sights and sounds of the city, and, at least in my case, thinking about the conversation we had been having. As I did so, I realized that there was something more I wanted to say.

"You asked me," I said, "whether I thought there was any truth to the perception that Beit Rabban underemphasizes the non-intellectual dimensions of life. There's one more thing I need to say about this. Some people think of 'intellectual activity' as intense and serious in a way that precludes being relaxed or having fun. But when I watch the kids at Beit Rabban struggling to find solutions to the problems they're encountering in texts or in other arenas, they seem to be not just intellectually but emotionally en-

---

[127]Ru'ah Elohim is often translated as "the spirit of God" but it's also translatable, as it is here, as "the wind of God."

gaged, and having a great time! Whether this would be true of children who felt unable to keep up with the flow of the work or conversation is another question; but for those who can, it seems to me that it's not just the children's minds that are involved in their school-work but their hearts as well. And that's pretty impressive."

"Yes," Devora was nodding. "People regularly think that being intellectually serious and having fun are incompatible, and, as you just said, they couldn't be more wrong. You're reminding me of one of my favorite incidents—I guess I have a lot of favorite incidents! One day, a parent of a prospective student was visiting the school and was observing the five- and six-year-olds during what we now would call *Explorations* but used to describe as *choice time*. One child, Marty, was working with some others on constructing a city in the block area. The kids were deeply engaged in the activity, terrifically serious about what they were doing. When the prospective parent came by, Marty looked up and said, 'I'm the mayor of this city, and it's my job to fix the lights.' If you knew that Marty's Hebrew name was Meir, you might have picked up the double pun in what he said to the visitor. The name Meir sounds like "Mayor," and the word 'meir' in Hebrew means 'one who illuminates.' To me this was a very funny comment, and a great example of intellectual playfulness coming from a boy busily engaged in building with blocks. But the parent seemed to miss all of this and commented on her way out that she hadn't seen the children having fun. I think she failed to see that engaged play can be very, very serious—and still be fun!"

We were now at the end of our time together, and I realized that the rest of our conversation concerning Beit Rabban's real and imagined problems would not take place today. Oh, well. I bid you adieu.

Daniel

Differences, Individualization, and Inclusivity

Is it wrong to segregate children not just on the basis of religion but also on the basis of ability? Building on Devora's comment, mentioned in Letter 13, that it's legitimate to organize a school around children who are exceptionally bright, in this letter Daniel passes on to Alice Devora's explanation for her conviction that such a focus is neither elitist nor unwise. The plight of "gifted children" in both conventional schools and at Beit Rabban is given attention in this letter, as is inclusivity, an ideal that has occupied a prominent place in recent discussions of American education.

Dear Alice:

Thanks for not letting the "Is this just a school for exceptionally bright children?" issue get by without more attention. As you suggested, maybe it's not sufficient to say, "Yes, it is," and to move along. Maybe, as you urge, we need to ask, "Is this desirable?" In your words, "To me, it smacks of elitism, this idea of separating out particularly able children and giving them a separate education. This is a time when a large part of the educational community in America is moving towards inclusivity, towards educating different kinds of children together; and it's doing so because of a conviction that when children of different abilities, races, and cultural backgrounds are educated together, they are more likely to develop mutual understanding and respect.[128] Now I'm not complaining about parochial

---

[128]The conviction that Alice articulates here has been central to public discourse on education in the United States since *Brown v. Board of Education*, the 1954 Supreme Court decision that overturned the doctrine of "Separate but Equal," thereby ending *de jure* racial segregation in public schools and giving rise to the movement to integrate the schools.

school education per se, though I certainly have plenty of friends who worry that this in itself is a threat to the well-being of a democratic polity made up of many different groups that must learn to get along with each other. But when you couple this kind of segregation by religion with segregation by ability, I too begin to worry. Isn't Beit Rabban going to produce a bunch of smart-ass intellectuals who think they're better than everyone else? I'd like to hear what Devora would say about this."

When I put your questions to Devora, she said that she appreciated the legitimate concern that stood behind your objection to the school; and she agreed that it is important that children blessed with special abilities not come to think themselves superior to children who don't have these abilities. But she expressed strong disagreement with you, and, by extension, with the mainstream of contemporary educational thinking, about the way to accomplish this. As she sees things, children at Beit Rabban are far less likely to develop an inflated view of themselves than are children attending so-called inclusive schools where everyone, regardless of ability, is lumped together.

When I asked her to explain why she thought this, here's how she responded. "Gifted children who attend regular schools," she began, "constantly find themselves knowing answers that other children don't. Without any effort at all, they're ahead of the pack, bored out of their minds and, at least initially, reaping the best of grades. I say, 'at least initially,' because, as is well known, in the end the failure of regular schools to give these children adequate intellectual challenges leaves many of them frustrated and demoralized. It's simply not true that rubbing shoulders day in, day out, with less able children can be counted on to give rise to egalitarian sentiments, any more than spending time in a racially mixed classroom necessarily gives to rise to racial tolerance and respect. Too often, the opposite is the result: these gifted kids learn less than they might, while developing an inflated view of themselves and a disparaging view of their peers.

"All of this also produces some other pretty terrible outcomes. It's not just that the children aren't challenged and don't work hard. Worse than that, they don't develop the expectation that they will be challenged—or rather, they develop the expectation that they *won't* be challenged!—and, as I mentioned in an earlier conversation, they learn not to work hard or take intellectual risks. I believe that all of us, children included, need to feel challenged, and that feeling good about ourselves is connected to success in meeting real challenges. All too often, gifted children are deprived of this opportunity. These are children whose needs go unmet.

"Now I'm not claiming that attending a school for so-called gifted children is necessarily a solution to these problems; actually, I suspect that some of these schools cause as many problems as they solve. But attending the right kind of school, a school like Beit Rabban, may well address the principal needs of these children. No matter how bright these children are or what their level of achievement is at any moment in time, our teachers believe that the school's job is to provide them with genuine intellectual challenges. When they do this job well, the children become acquainted not just with their abilities but also with their limitations. The reason for this is that they regularly encounter challenges that are, at least for now, beyond them; also, they are surrounded by other children who are sometimes quicker, more imaginative, or more penetrating than they are when it comes to interpreting and addressing a question. Far from becoming full of themselves, they develop, along with a love of learning, a measure of humility and the expectation that their peers will say worthwhile things.

"Couple this," she continued, "with what we discussed in connection with the teacher who thought that praise should focus on *avodah met-zuyenet*. If you'll recall what we said at the time: Beit Rabban does not believe that children should be praised and rewarded for the gifts that they have, because their possession is just a matter of good luck. And so achievements that flow easily from the possession of these gifts are not necessarily worthy of praise either. What *is* worthy of acknowledgement is serious effort to make use of whatever gifts we do have, the effort to set meaningful goals based on our interests and potentialities and to evaluate ourselves in relation to them. If we're successful, Beit Rabban kids learn to value themselves and others based on these things, not on the basis of any objective level of achievement. All in all, they're much less likely to be full of themselves than are gifted children who have gone through conventional classrooms, regular or gifted."

I don't know what you'll make of this response, Alice, but, agree or not, it is certainly thoughtful. As for me, I'm not sure if I agree with all aspects of her view, but I would identify myself with Devora's claim that educators' noble purposes in creating inclusive classrooms that mix children of widely different levels of ability are rarely achieved. Too often the teachers just don't seem up to the challenge of adequately responding to the range of needs found in the classroom. And when this happens, it may be that all the youngsters, gifted and non-gifted alike, are worse off. To my mind, by the way, the problem isn't that there is something wrong with these teachers. Rather, and this is something Devora also implied, I think we tend to be troublingly naïve about what it takes to meet the needs of children who are very different from each other, especially in one classroom.

> Gotta run. Take care.
> Daniel

Is Basic Institutional Change
a Realistic Hope?

Is it possible to develop vision-guided institutions out of existing institutions, or need one start from scratch? Beit Rabban's founding was grounded in the belief that it is not promising to begin with existing institutions that have a settled culture and a membership representing a wide variety of beliefs and values. To Daniel's surprise, it turns out that Alice shares this view. In response, Daniel tries to make the case that it may be possible to make more than a little headway with existing institutions. The letter ends with a description of a hypothetical intra-Jewish voucher system designed to increase the number of vision-guided institutions. This letter also includes a short discussion of visionary leadership, a theme that is picked up again in Letter 17 and in the Postscript.

Dear Alice:

For a long time now you have patiently, and sometimes enthusiastically, responded to Devora's ideas (and my own) about the importance of vision in education. And now, finally, you give voice to the pessimism and cynicism that accompany your excitement. I found your comments so interesting that I decided—and I hope you won't object—to share the passage that most intrigued me with Devora. Here's the section I shared:

> It's fine and good for you and Devora to extol the benefits of having a guiding vision; but you're talking about something that's more easily talked about than done. In schools and synagogues I have been involved with, we've engaged in "visioning" activities *ad nauseam* with virtually nothing to show for it. A group of us, you know, the usual suspects called *the critical stakeholders,* is convened and under the guidance of some kind of visioning guru or facilitator, we spend a few sessions trying to develop what's called a mission or vision for our institution. If we're lucky, some-

one is able to dig up from out of some pile the results of our last visioning activity, and we then use that as a starting point for our discussions. Then, through a series of guided exercises, each of us is encouraged to voice what we take to be the core values and aspirations around which our school or synagogue is to be organized. Needless to say, because our institution is made up of very different kinds of people who have joined for different kinds of reasons, what we are looking for tends to be very different; and so our facilitator guides us in a search for common ground among our disparate views; and what results—PRESTO!—is our vision. The only problem is this: what we agree on are a bunch of platitudes that nobody would dissent from and that we probably would have agreed on before the conversation: *Torah, Avodah, Gemilut hesed*—Study, Prayer, and the Doing of Good Deeds. Don't get me wrong: there's nothing wrong with these ideals; but they're so vague and abstract that they offer very little concrete guidance. This, of course, is not an accident: because if we formulated anything more concrete, disagreements would surface that are avoided by keeping things at a very high level of generality. And so, when all is said and done, the vision statement is completed, possibly trotted out before the community as would be a figurehead leader, and then put to bed, with no real change to show for all this effort. So, as for me, though you're beginning to convince me of the power of what you're calling vision-guided institutions, I'm pessimistic about the possibility of turning the school I have been associated with, or others that I know, into such institutions. We harbor way too much diversity among our constituencies to make it possible to come up with a clear vision that would engender passion and guide practice.

Devora's response is not hard to reconstruct. "I think she's right," she said, "about the difficulty of transforming existing institutions into ones that are vision-guided. There are at least two big reasons why this is so, and Alice has pointed to one of them very well in saying that the attempt to build a compelling guiding vision by achieving consensus among people with different values will give rise to something that is pretty vacuous and insufficiently exciting to inspire changes at the level of practice. This is one of the reasons why I haven't wasted my energy trying to change existing institutions, but have sought to develop my own. And, as you well know, I haven't done so by bringing together a variety of people and inviting them to enter with me into a visioning process. Instead, I decided to create an institution designed to achieve my own deepest educational aspirations, aspirations that form a coherent whole; and I worked hard to fashion an institution that would be true to these hopes. And then I invited interested families to join me not in fashioning the vision but in developing a community, a culture, that is organized around it. I had—I still do have—deep faith in this vision, as well as a hope that a sufficient number of families would be attracted to a school that was striving in intelligent ways to turn it into a reality."

"I take it, then, that, as you see it, leaders do far more than clarify, articulate, and serve the will of the community. They play a very active role in shaping institutional purpose and identity."

"Let's just say," Devora responded, "that I don't think Beit Rabban would have developed into the rich and coherent institution that it is if I hadn't actively shaped it in light of a vision in which I passionately believe of what learning is and Jewish life should be."

As she spoke, Devora reminded me of the kind of politician, not necessarily of a particularly long-lived variety, who says, "I refuse to be all things to all people. I will support and vote for what I genuinely believe in; if enough of you identify with these commitments, so be it; if not, I will step down." I have great admiration for the principled way she approaches her work as an educator, but I need to tell you, Alice, that I myself do not fully identify with certain aspects of her (and, now I realize, your own) view. For one thing, I wouldn't disparage the significance of finding agreement in a community about "*torah, avodah,* and *gemilut hesed.*" Truth is, if the constituents of an educating community were to take any one of these seriously, if they were to say, "Okay, let's systematically organize our educational initiative around, say, *torah* or *gemilut hesed,*" they would be a whole lot further along than most schools are today.

To show this, let me play out one of these possibilities. Let's assume that your "critical stakeholders" (say, you, your rabbi, your president, and the head of your Education Committee) were willing to agree that *gemilut hesed* should be central to your congregation's and school's identity. As you implied, it would probably not be hard to generate this agreement; after all, the idea seems almost platitudinous. And yet, taken seriously, consider the implications!

First off, you would probably need to get a little clearer about what you mean by *gemilut hesed,* as well as to think through what a person who possessed the qualities associated with this virtue would look like: what sensibilities, motivations, hopes, beliefs, dispositions, and skills would inform his or her behavior? This could be explored in a more or less in-depth way; but I suspect that it could be done meaningfully without unduly testing the patience of already busy individuals. And in fact, if it's done in the right way, you and the other stakeholders are likely to find such an inquiry immensely rewarding and a rich contribution to your own growth as Jewish human beings.

But let's go further. Let's assume that you have succeeded in getting a measure of clarity and agreement about these matters. See what a wonderful position you are suddenly in, in relation to your educational institution. As examples: you now have a pretty good basis for deciding what kinds of learning experiences it's important for the children to undergo, or at least you know what questions to ask. For example: if we're really serious about our children growing into adults with the disposition to help people who are suffering or in need, how important is it for them to come face to face with profound human need early on, or to see in palpable ways the effects of the acts of tzedakah which they perform? And so forth.

Similarly, a decision to nurture the dispositions associated with *gemilut hesed* provides a basis for deciding which stories, figures and debates to highlight in the curriculum (be it the Torah curriculum, Jewish history, or Rabbinic literature). Not only that: this decision also gives you guidance in figuring out how to approach these materials. That is, your awareness that in teaching these materials you're not just trying to transmit information about the place of *gemilut hesed* in Jewish civilization, but are trying to encourage certain kinds of sensibilities, impulses, and forms of conduct will, if taken seriously, powerfully guide your pedagogy. (As an aside, I just want to say that I get impatient with people who say that if you opt for tzedakah or *gemilut hesed,* this means giving short shrift to the study of Jewish texts. I don't believe this at all. As I just tried to indicate, what identifying *gemilut hesed* as important does do, is to give you a sense of direction in deciding what texts to teach and how to approach them.) And at another level, clarity about the importance of *gemilut hesed* in your school would also be invaluable in helping you figure out the kinds of teachers that are best for your school, not to mention the things to focus on in inservice education.

Having said all this, I need to add that I have voiced this optimistic-sounding view without having acknowledged, much less responded to, the second reason why Devora identified with your pessimistic assessment of the possibility of bringing about deep change in existing institutions. I alluded to this second reason some time back when I referred to the skepticism concerning deep institutional change that Devora expressed to me during a conference organized around the need to reform existing educational institutions. Her basic point was simple but important: institutions embody cultures, and cultures tend to resist changes that challenge the basic assumptions around which they are organized. Since it's hard to imagine vision-guided change that doesn't challenge the basics of the existing culture, the likelihood of transforming an ordinary educating institution into one that is vision-guided is not at all high.

As I think about her point now, it strikes me that it's very close in spirit to, and receives empirical support from, a view espoused by David Tyack and Larry Cuban in a book entitled *Tinkering Towards Utopia*. Having pondered the course of American educational history, here's what they conclude. Though reformers have long sought the radical transformation of American educating institutions, efforts to change the fundamental character of American educational institutions (what they call the "grammar of schooling") have generally been very unsuccessful. The only changes that seem capable of taking root are changes in specific practices (what they call "second-order" changes) that don't challenge this grammar of schooling.

I have to acknowledge that this is a very serious challenge to the idea that it's possible to transform existing institutions into ones that are meaningfully vision-guided. That said, I'm not ready to write off the possibility of significantly improving them.[129]

Not that I'm naive about the difficulties; some very painful experiences have made me vividly aware of them. But I don't think they warrant despair. If the right constellation of professional and lay leaders come around to the idea that their institution will be more successful if they seriously attend to their guiding vision and if they approach the challenge of institutional change with patience, energy, and good thinking, I suspect that much more can be accomplished than some skeptics believe. If Beit Rabban is a kind of existence proof that a seriously vision-guided school can come into being and survive, perhaps what we also need are existence proofs that demonstrate that it is possible under some conditions for existing institutions to change for the better in deep and enduring ways.

Anyway, all of this is a long way from saying that I am much more optimistic than is Devora about the possibility of turning existing educating

---

[129]It is noteworthy that, although they are skeptical of change efforts that challenge the grammar of schooling, Tyack and Cuban are not pessimistic about the possibility of substantially improving schools. Rather, their research leads them to highlight the potentialities of second-order changes that don't challenge the deepest assumptions around which the institution of schooling is organized. In their view, even what may seem like modest transformations (for example, changes in some of the practices of teachers) may reverberate through the educational environment in ways that give rise to significant improvement. Hence, the title of their book, *Tinkering Towards Utopia*. Whatever the merits of their view regarding the impossibility of deep change at institutional and system-wide levels in the public school arena, my own view about Jewish educating institutions is more upbeat than is theirs (and Devora's) concerning the possibility of fundamental change. In any case, it's premature to abandon efforts guided by this aspiration. That said, there is much to be learned from their analysis that may be relevant to Jewish educational settings.

institutions, made up of a fairly diverse clientele, into significantly more vision-guided institutions. I do, though, think it's well worth a serious effort; and in pursuing this agenda, it may be helpful to remember the old adage, "The perfect is the enemy of the good." If we judge ourselves based on an institution that is vision-guided down to its very details, we may well get demoralized; but if we remember that even a little clarity of vision, reasonably carefully brought to bear on our practice, has the potential to take us light-years beyond where we now are, we may approach this challenge with a measure of enthusiasm.

That said, a confession. Years back, I was much closer to Devora's position than I now am. Daunted by the extent of diversity harbored in so many contemporary Jewish educating institutions, I came close to the kind of view that you and Devora expressed. Doubting that the diverse constituencies that make up typical existing institutions, especially congregations, could ever come together around a vision grounded in Jewish ideas that was more than empty rhetoric (because anything more powerful would necessarily leave some members happy and others feeling marginalized) I arrived at the idea, which I've now also heard elsewhere, that perhaps Jewish communities should experiment with the kinds of voucher/ choice plans being debated in the world of public education.[130]

Here's the idea: instead of assuming, as we usually do, that children who go to Hebrew school should attend the educational program run by their congregation, the organized Jewish community would provide congregations and other institutions that want to offer educational programs with incentives to develop very distinctive educational programs, each with a different emphasis, and the community would provide all members with a listing of all these programs which accents their distinctive agendas. Membership in any of the community's congregations (or Jewish Community Centers), or perhaps just a contribution to the Jewish community's annual fund-raising campaign, would entitle a family to a voucher repre-

---

[130]An idea that was once associated with libertarian and conservative groups, school choice has in more recent times sometimes been embraced by subgroups in other segments of the general community that are interested in school reform. Much has been written about this subject in the last twenty-five years. The earliest and most influential discussion of choice plans for American education, at least in the latter part of the twentieth century can be found in Milton Friedman's "The Role of Government in Education," in his *Capitalism and Freedom* (Chicago: University of Chicago Press, 1962), 85–107. For more recent discussions, see, for example, Myron Lieberman, *Privatization and Educational Choice* (New York: St. Martin's Press, 1989) and Peter W. Cookson, *School Choice* (New Haven: Yale University Press, 1994).

senting the cost of an education in any one of these educational programs, and it would be the job of families to then select a school whose aspirations cohered with their own. In some cases, the best program would turn out to be the one offered by the family's congregation, in others not. In this way, families might, for purposes of education, self-select into schools and parent communities that are congruent with their own aspirations, with the result that there would be a much better fit between each school and the community it served.

Even when I was most excited about this idea, I was mindful of at least some of its problems. For example, breaking up the close relationship that now obtains between a synagogue's membership and its educational program may have various negative repercussions. And certainly it would be a difficult challenge to get local institutions to create schools that really are organized around distinctive visions. There are also other problems on which I won't dwell right now, for example, those that arise because geographical proximity does not necessarily walk hand in hand with ideological affinity; or the fact that adopting the kind of system I have described may require abandoning the idea that a congregation's school is but one element in a comprehensive congregational educational program that includes and integrates the youth group, religious services, and social action activities. Still, the idea seemed pretty interesting to me, at least in the context of communities with sizeable Jewish populations. Truth is, it still does, and it might be interesting to see it tried some place; certainly I'd like to see the idea debated.[131] What do you think?

That's it for now. Looking forward to hearing from you.

Daniel

---

[131]Accompanied by references to some literature that may be of interest, this theme is again discussed below, in the *Postscript*, 159–160.

Is this Portrait Accurate
(and Does It Matter?)
and
Vision-Guided Practice Redefined

In this letter, Daniel again examines, this time from a different angle, a question addressed earlier on: Is Daniel's and Devora's portrayal of Beit Rabban as a vision-guided institution true to life, or is it biased by their preconceptions about the school? After wrestling with this question, Daniel explains why, even if his account turned out not to be true to life, it would be worth presenting, as a vehicle of explaining what a vision-guided institution is. But he goes on to argue that his account is true to life; and this, he suggests, is important to establish, given people's skepticism concerning the possibility of building vision-guided institutions in the real world. Near the end of the letter, Daniel notes that both he and Devora recognize that Beit Rabban is far from fully congruent with its guiding existential and educational vision. And reflection on this point leads him to let go of the earlier definition of a vision-guided institution as one that is "down to its details" suffused with the guiding vision in favor of a definition that emphasizes the role of the vision as a tool of educational improvement.

Dear Alice:

I'm not sure I really know the best response to the problem that you asked me to address. I've already told you that it's at least conceivable to me that because of my enthusiasm for Beit Rabban I may be missing or not properly interpreting features of the school that don't cohere with my conception of it. You know the old saying, "Believing is seeing;" sometimes, it's not what we see that determines what we believe, but what we believe that determines what we see or how we interpret it.

Put differently, though I do have a reasonable degree of confidence in my perceptions, I wouldn't be shocked to get a very different take on the school from someone else, for example, someone who may have had a bad experience teaching in the school or as a parent. In truth, I would be surprised if an account of any vision-guided school, be it the Dewey School, A.S. Neill's Summerhill, or one of Steiner's Waldorf Schools, would go completely uncontested. There will always be someone, and sometimes clusters of someones, who will challenge the master narrative of the school's vision and reality and who will paint a very different picture of the school than would those who really believe in it.[132] But these more abstract considerations should not distract us from the immediate question pertaining to Beit Rabban: where, in this particular case, does reality lie? Is the school as Devora paints it, or is that painting something which largely exists in her mind (and possibly my own) rather than in the world?

How would I answer these questions? I ask myself. I'm not entirely sure, so forgive me if I fumble around a little in responding. Certainly I think that the complex reality of any social institution is unlikely to be fully or adequately captured by any single perspective on it, and to that extent, seeing the school primarily through the lens of its vision gives rise to a measure of distortion. But—and this is a significant "but"—I really do believe that Beit Rabban is shaped by a thoughtfully conceived vision that

---

[132]Not surprisingly, other domains also exhibit a tendency to revisit, sometimes very critically, the organizing principles that give rise to conventional perspectives on a social phenomenon. Consider, for example, the academic study of American educational history. Many mainstream accounts we're familiar with were written by "believers," by people who were convinced that American public schools have functioned as a powerful instrument in the service of human good, helping to create a society featuring individual well-being, social justice and technological progress. This one might call "the master narrative" of American educational history; and it is this story that, over many years, Americans have told themselves, their children and the world about their educational system. But as it turns out, not everybody sees American educational history in this benign way: along come the so-called revisionist historians who paint a very different, much less flattering picture of the role that schools have played in American life, a picture that highlights class, race, and gender bias and that suggests that schools have served to promote the interests of America's dominant cultural and economic groups at the expense of others. The writings of Diane Ravitch and Arthur Schlesinger exemplify the more traditional, mainstream approaches to American educational history; the writings of Michael B. Katz and Colin Greer exemplify revisionist accounts. It is noteworthy that there are today a number of superb historians, including Carl Kaestle, William Reese, and David Tyack who strive to achieve balance among these sometimes bipolar perspectives on American educational history. See the bibliography for specific references.

actually guides decision-making; and in this respect it's very different from most of the educational institutions I'm familiar with.

In saying this, by the way, I am not denying that many more conventional schools, those we don't normally think of as vision-guided, are sometimes, unawares, guided by implicit visions, and that they are therefore much more than a conglomeration of miscellaneous practices. It's entirely possible that through immersion in such an institution a gifted social anthropologist or qualitative sociologist would discover certain values and principles at work in its practices, values and principles that the members of this educational community have not articulated to themselves.[133] But this is a long way from having a vision that you have subjected to careful examination and that you really do employ systematically as a guide to your work. It is this that distinguishes Beit Rabban from so many other institutions.

Let me also add this: though I readily concede that the reality of life at Beit Rabban is more complex than what emerges from any account of the school that emphasizes, as does my own, the coherence between vision and practice, I am beginning to realize that this does not particularly bother me. The reason is to be found in the way our correspondence began and got its sense of direction, that is, in your asking me to provide you with a "for instance" that could communicate what I mean by a vision-guided institution. My intention is not so much to offer a factual account of Beit Rabban, as it is to paint, for you and for me, and for anyone else who might be interested, a portrait that can serve educators like you and myself as a "something to shoot for." The fact that most people, including many educators, have no sense at all of what it means for an educating institution to be deeply suffused with a guiding vision is, as far as I'm concerned, sufficient reason to offer this kind of a portrait. Which is to say that even if it were true that I have painted "Beit Rabban shel mala" rather than "Beit Rabban shel mata"[134]—Beit Rabban as it is at its best and in its aspiration rather than a "real" Beit Rabban that is only partially in harmony with its guiding vision—I would not be dissatisfied.

---

[133]For examples of research that reveals a school's implicit values, see Jules Henry, "Golden Rule Days," in *Culture Against Man* (New York: Vintage Books, 1965), 286–305, and Philip Cusick, *The Egalitarian Ideal and the American High School* (New York: Longman, 1983).

[134]*Yerushalayim shel mala* and *Yerusalayim shel mata* refer, respectively, to the heavenly Jerusalem (Jerusalem as it exists in our image of the ideal) and to the earthly Jerusalem (a place which, though it may sometimes intimate and point us towards the ideal Jerusalem, is very far from perfect).

But, as I've said, I *don't* think my portrait of Beit Rabban is untrue to the reality; and for what may be an obvious reason this makes me happy. If it were largely fantasy, my account might succeed in illustrating what a vision-guided educating institution is, but it would not satisfy skeptics who might say, "Sure, you can paint a beautiful picture of such an institution, but that's different from actually creating and maintaining one under real-world conditions." The fact that a living institution like Beit Rabban is to a substantial degree vision-guided offers an existence proof to the skeptics: "You say a vision-guided school can't exist in the real world; but the surest evidence that you're wrong is that there are such institutions."

Does the likelihood that the school falls short of its aspirations in many respects bother me? As I have thought about this question, I have come to the, for me, unexpected conclusion that it doesn't. There are two reasons for this. One of them is that it's important, especially for others who may seek to develop vision-guided institutions, to realize that perfection may be beyond us, and that any living institution, even the very best, will in various ways fall short of its highest aspirations. If we don't accept this, we're likely to grow demoralized pretty quickly. A look at the heroes of Jewish history—King David is perhaps a perfect example—helps make this point: our heroes embody greatness in some respects, but they typically have big flaws as well. Adolescents may have a powerful need to reject feet-of-clay heroes, but Jewish tradition invites us to respond to them in a more complex way: not to sweep their flaws under the rug (as Plato might have recommended) but to honor them for their greatness and to emulate their virtues, while yet acknowledging their imperfections. Such a response allows us to use what is best in these heroes as guides to our own lives, but it also allows us to be at least a little charitable with ourselves when we fall short of being the people we would like to be. Analogous considerations apply at the institutional level, I think.

There is, as I mentioned, also a second reason, one that's related to the first, why I'm not troubled by the fact that a school like Beit Rabban isn't fully animated by the vision it aspires to embody. And articulating this reason involves revising something I said early in our correspondence. If I remember correctly, I described a vision-guided institution as one that is "informed down to its very details" by its vision. Well, as we've been discussing, in the real world, a definition that is this stringent may leave us with no vision-guided institutions standing. So it may be that we need a somewhat less demanding set of requirements if real institutions, institutions that will inevitably be imperfect, are to qualify as vision-guided.

Were I disposed to defend the original "informed down to its details" definition, I might respond that it is a mistake to compromise the integrity of the ideal: "Continue," I might say, "to define a vision-guided institution as one that is fully coherent with its ideal but recognize that living institutions will at best be imperfect examples of such institutions." This would be an acceptable defense, I think; but I'm coming around to the idea that it's preferable not to define a vision-guided institution as one that has achieved full coherence between vision and practice, and that a definition that acknowledges that there may be gaps might be better. The reason is this: one of the critical roles that a vision can play in the life of even a very good institution is that of critic of existing practices; it offers a basis for scanning what we are doing and deciding what needs to be changed. A definition that insists on full coherence doesn't point us to this critical role of vision. So perhaps we're better off defining a vision-guided institution as one that is actively and seriously using its vision to guide and improve its educational practices, without the suggestion that it has achieved anything resembling perfection.

I guess I had some intimation of this before our correspondence, but the point is much clearer to me now than it was when we started. So I thank you for this. By the way, when I shared some of these thoughts with Devora, she strongly identified with them. For one thing, she very much liked the idea of characterizing a vision-guided institution as one in which the vision is an active tool in shaping what goes on, rather than as an institution that has succeeded in fully realizing the vision. Certainly, she added, it's only in this sense that Beit Rabban is vision-guided: she has always been aware of, and profoundly troubled by, what seemed to her significant gaps between what the vision called for and what the school embodied.

"But," I responded when she said this, "at least the vision gave you something which most other schools don't have: a principled perspective from which to evaluate your present circumstances and to determine changes to strive for."

"That's true," she said. "And though I'm really anguished by some of the school's shortcomings, this image of the school as struggling as best it can—and not always successfully—to improve itself through its identification of and response to new problems is wholly consistent with what we hope to convey to the children about the way they should approach their own learning and lives." Though these weren't her words, the gist seemed to be that, as institutions or as individuals, perfection will always elude us. What is possible for serious but imperfect human beings (and institutions) with limited control over their situation is to keep identifying and, in a thoughtful and determined way, interpreting and addressing the problems that need attention if things are to improve; and the presence of a guiding ideal in which we believe is an invaluable tool in this effort.

I was about to respond to Devora that her comment embodied what seems to me a healthy perspective for idealistic but fallible human beings to carry around with them, when Devora added, "But, then again, there are times when the gap between vision and reality seems to me so great, that I begin to feel like the vision of this school only exists in my head. Those are hard moments!" As I've said before, she's a thoughtful person, who mixes idealism and candor in a way that I find very refreshing.

Looking forward to hearing from you.

Daniel

LETTER 17
Visionary Leadership

Occasioned by Devora's announcement that she is resigning, this letter examines the role of the visionary leader in the life of an educating institution and whether a vision-guided institution can remain faithful to its vision when its founding visionary leader leaves. At the end of this letter, Daniel responds enthusiastically to Alice's announcement that she has taken a job with a new transdenominational school, and he applauds her comment that the development of a serious vision needs to be one of her highest priorities. He urges her to begin by clarifying her own conception of an educated Jewish person and an exemplary Jewish community, paying attention along the way to the ideas of other thoughtful individuals who have wrestled with this question. And with this their correspondence ends—at least for now.

Dear Alice:

It really is a small world—and also a surprising one! That you should find out in a casual conversation with a near-stranger from Manhattan that Devora is planning to leave Beit Rabban is surprising enough; it's all the more amazing that you should find this out before I did. But, sure enough, when, after receiving your letter, I called her, she confirmed the news. When she started the school some eight years ago, she had never imagined that she would be running it forever; and for a few years now, she has been thinking about taking on some new challenges and trying to figure out how to orchestrate a smooth transition. Because of Beit Rabban's unconventional character, finding someone to take her place may prove a particularly daunting problem.

What it will mean for Beit Rabban, I really don't know, and I'm sure a lot will depend on the character of her successor. It will be interesting to see what happens! In the meantime, her imminent departure offers an opportunity to think about the role that leaders, particularly founding leaders, play in the life of vision-guided institutions. There is no doubt in my mind that a visionary leader is of the utmost importance to the development of such institutions, so much so that it's hard for me to imagine them emerging without such leaders.

But, you may be thinking, "What does he mean by *visionary leaders?*" Fair enough. Roughly this: leaders who have a clear and strong sense of what they are after, educationally; who have an almost visceral sense of the kinds of practices and curricula that are coherent with their aspirations; and who have the ability to approach all decisions through the lens of the vision that inspires them, coupled with an insistence that the vision not be seriously compromised in the name of political considerations, numbers or dollars. And not only this: it's also the ability to represent and communicate the vision in compelling ways in dealing with teachers, parents, youngsters, and other internal and external constituencies. There's a Hebrew phrase, "*meshuga la'davar,*" which, as you know, roughly means "single-mindedly crazy about the thing/idea," which is critical here. The visionary leader is not someone who "just talks" the vision but who also embodies it in word and deed and is passionate about it. There is a kind of wholeheartedness here that is very impressive; but it's got to be coupled with the good judgment, savvy and flexibility that allow you to be guided by the vision under circumstances that are not just difficult but ever-changing.[135] And, of course, the ability of visionary leaders to move from the realm of aspirations to educational practice also requires that they have at their command a body of reasonable ideas about human learning and growth that will guide them in developing a credible approach to education that is appropriate for their particular clienteles. Plato had the luxury of imagining, or rather, willing into being through an act of imagination, a vision-guided educational system from which all the obstacles to success had been removed: there was a perfect testing system to assess the abilities and character of the children, a perfect curriculum, and no question of scarce resources. Not so for mortals who live in the real world, and for whom bringing into being and sustaining environments that resemble their guiding ideas is inevitably a continuing and complex challenge.

---

[135]For a thought-provoking discussion of vision-guided leadership that is grounded in Jewish texts and concerns, see Ahad Ha-Am, "Moses," in his *Selected Essays*, trans. Leon Simon (Philadelphia, Jewish Publication Society, 1912), 307–329. Building his discussion on an interpretation of the roles played by Moses and Aaron in taking the Israelites out of slavery in Egypt and through the desert, Ahad Ha-Am raises the possibility in this article that it may be impossible for a single individual to embody all of the traits that are needed to be an effective visionary leader.

Speaking of Plato, there is also another respect in which his idea of a visionary leader differs from what I have in mind. Plato's leader has an unwavering conception of the good that is to be achieved through education, the truth of which is guaranteed by an act of rational intuition which is immune to error. But as I see things, our conceptions are never immune to error, and we should therefore embrace them with something short of certitude. For this reason, the kind of visionary leader that I'm thinking of combines thoughtful commitment to a guiding conception along with a willingness to rethink and revise it in response to new insights occasioned by experience and reflection. For me, this willingness marks the principal difference between a visionary leader and a fanatic.

In any case, I think Devora exemplifies what I mean by "a visionary leader," and in thinking about the role she has played in the life of Beit Rabban, I am reminded of Yeats' line in "Among School Children:" "Who can distinguish the dancer from the dance?" The connection between her, the vision, and the school is so organic, almost symbiotic, that it's sometimes hard to imagine that they could exist apart from one another. But, fortunately, I think, this inability to imagine does not signify anything important. Many schools do outlive their visionary leaders in meaningful ways. True, the transitions may be fraught with difficulties of various kinds; there may be anxieties that the school will collapse or will "never be the same;" and the new leadership may in subtle or not so subtle ways alter the institution's character. But all of this does not necessarily signify the death of the institution as a vital entity. There are, after all, in various domains of human activity institutions that have continued to thrive after enduring the departure of their founding visionary leaders. In fact, there are times when a new leader, bringing different skills and the sometimes salutary perspective of an outsider, has the power to recognize and address important issues in the life of the institution that were unrecognized or unaddressed in earlier days.

Many people will be quick to remind me, though, that this doesn't always happen; some institutions do "go downhill," losing their sense of direction, when their founding leader departs. And this is certainly true. But this "going downhill" stuff is more complicated than you might initially think. In some cases, it's just a short-term phenomenon after which the institution, as it were, regroups around its new leadership. In other cases, what is called "going downhill" is really no more than change in a new direction; and though this change may not, everything considered, be bad, it may be viewed as bad by those associated with "the old ways." We frequently see this phenomenon in the arts, in music, in politics, and certainly in education.

So, while it may be sad, the departure of a founding leader is not necessarily a reason for despair. That said, there is no denying that it is a critical moment in an institution's life. And as I said before, what happens will depend heavily on the availability of a quality leader to take the founding

leader's place; by this I mean a person who, while at home with and committed to the school's culture and vision, has the particular skills that the school needs at this moment in its development, rather than someone with certain generic leadership abilities (although this person may have and need these as well). Whether this kind of leadership is available is a matter that is to some extent beyond the control of the institution and we all know that in Jewish education in particular there is a dearth of adequately prepared educational leaders.

But let's assume for the moment that an institution succeeds in identifying an appropriate individual to replace the founding leader. This may not be enough to assure that it will survive and thrive with its guiding vision intact. This outcome may also depend on another important variable. Has the founding leader succeeded in institutionalizing the school's vision by establishing hospitable norms, policies and practices and by creating a community of parents, educators, and children who understand and genuinely share the vision, so that the culture of the school is substantially self-sustaining?

Here's what I have in mind when I say this: we know of "bad schools" that seem incapable of substantially improving despite the introduction of new, high quality leaders and teachers; these are schools in which a self-sustaining dysfunctional culture has established itself. But perhaps this phenomenon does not apply exclusively to dysfunctional institutions and cultures; maybe it's possible to institutionalize the ethos and vision of a thriving school in a similar way, so that it too survives, possibly with differences in accent and changes in senior personnel. Just as in dysfunctional schools, initially idealistic and enthusiastic personnel eventually come to share in the norms and attitudes associated with this dysfunctionality, so too it may be that in a thriving school, educators who may initially not be fully identified with its character will eventually come to share enthusiastically in its vision as embodied in the life of the school. I want to be careful not to minimize the difficulties here: it is no doubt very hard to institutionalize a vision in such a way that it is capable of surviving changes in leadership. And this may be especially difficult, as Devora herself pointed out to me one day, when the institution's vision and practices are significantly out of sync with the way most people, educators included, think about education; but my sense is that this is one of the critical challenges of a visionary leader who is intent on seeing his or her school continue to be vital after he or she has moved on.

So it will be interesting to see what happens, but that's another story. So, too, is the journey that you (also a departing educational leader!) are about to embark on. I was excited to hear that you have accepted a position as the educational director of a small, transdenominational, pluralistic school in your community. Given what you've said about yourself in the

course of our correspondence, it sounds like you're well suited to this institution. And I was delighted to hear that you've come to see the development of a serious vision for the school as a high priority as you set about your work. As you yourself observed, the fact that the school calls itself "transdenominational" and "pluralistic" doesn't really tell us much about its actual educational aspirations. It doesn't sound like the school has a very developed vision at this point, which makes this an important challenge for you to take on.

In response to your query concerning how best to approach this challenge, I'd suggest that a useful starting point may be a serious effort to achieve greater clarity concerning your own conception of the kind of individual and community you would hope to encourage through the educational process. And if you undertake this challenge, I hope that along the way you search out the views of other thoughtful individuals who have wrestled with these matters, especially those who have thought about them somewhat systematically.

Not that if you clarify your views on these matters, you will—or would even want to—impose them unilaterally on your new school. But in working with the school to develop a compelling vision that will inform its practice, it will be invaluable if you can offer, in a way that invites thoughtful discussion, a credible perspective of your own on larger questions of educational purpose. My hope is that you succeed in guiding your new community towards a shared vision of the kinds of Jewish human beings and the kind of community you want to cultivate; and if you succeed in doing so, I also hope that you'll take the next step of thinking very carefully about the practical implications that flow from this vision, making sure to draw on the best available research in thinking through the challenge of educational design. Having a conception of what you want to achieve is great, but it's not enough; too often institutions that achieve this fall seriously short of their aspirations because they don't address this second challenge seriously. The result is that, despite having thought about their aspirations, they end up allowing all sorts of conventional, faddish, and idiosyncratic practices to shape the character of their practice. Put differently, a vision-guided school in the best sense has an educational stance that includes not just inspiring guiding hopes but also thoughtfully developed ideas about the way to try to actualize these hopes in the real world. One last piece of advice: if, as I hope, your new institution succeeds in clarifying a set of educational aspirations that you and the other stakeholders find inspiring and in developing an approach to education that promises to help you achieve these aspirations, I hope you remain open to the possibility that your guiding ideas about means *and* ends may need to be revisited and revised in the light of what you learn in the course of your work.

In any case, if I can be helpful to you in this new venture, let me know. In the meantime, I want to thank you for the opportunity afforded by our correspondence to think through a bunch of educational issues. I look forward to continuing our conversations about Beit Rabban, your new school, and other matters. I wish you the very best.

Daniel

The Significance of Vision-Guided Schools Revisited

Challenges and Affirmations

Dear Devora:

It's been a while since we have been in touch, and I hope that your year in Jerusalem, far from the responsibilities of leading Beit Rabban, has been going well . . . or as well as things can go in the midst of the difficulties in which Israel is presently embroiled. As you know, with your own and Alice's permission, I have been sharing my correspondence with her concerning the school with a number of people; and I thought you would be interested in the response of one of them, a friend and colleague, who is an exceptionally thoughtful philosopher of education. Let me begin by saying that, like me, he was very enthusiastic about Beit Rabban and impressed by your own talents. But at the same time he wondered whether there is much to be learned from Beit Rabban that will improve education beyond its walls. He was, for example, skeptical that Alice will be able to make much use of what she had learned through her encounter with Beit Rabban in developing her own school. Let me quote what he says directly. After expressing great admiration for the school, he adds:

> But when we ask what relevance this has for Alice, it turns out that like Plato's Republic creating a Beit Rabban depends on the coming together of the most unlikely circumstances—a philosopher queen, a city with enough kids of the right kind to have cohorts with necessary prereqs, enough, even if not abundant, financial resources to get something going that is truly a **creation.** And, even that institution is probably ephemeral.
>
> At the end we come down to earth and you still have some faith that "we" presumably diverse Jews, many like myself with the shallowest understandings of Judaism, can develop our vision of Jewish education and somehow turn that into a better school for our kids.

> In a way, Beit Rabban reminds me of Summerhill, the Dewey
> School, Dennison's First Street School[136] and others like that, the
> shadows of individual geniuses. Here's my somewhat cynical
> judgment—institutions like that can inspire, but they are largely
> irrelevant to what more or less democratic, more or less hierar-
> chical institutions need to enhance what they do.[137]

Both very high praise for you and the school and, if he is correct, devastat-
ing criticism for anyone who thinks it will have an impact beyond its four
walls! Now that I have been pondering his comments for a while, I thought
I would share with you, as I have with him, my reactions.

He is right that Beit Rabban was made possible by the unlikely convergence of a number of circumstances, some of which are individually
unlikely. The most important of these (I hope I am not embarrassing you) is
you yourself. The admirable combination you embody of vision grounded
in deep understanding *and* the capacity to make substantial headway in
actualizing it under real-world conditions is rare. Isn't it, as my friend al-
leges, naïve to think that the example of Beit Rabban will have much impact on schools, in general, or on educators like Alice, who do not have
your passion, depth of Jewish knowledge, educational sophistication, and
practical savvy?

My own sense is that although his concerns are legitimate, his assessment is too pessimistic. For one thing, even if it's true that the existence of
a school like Beit Rabban depends on the unlikely convergence of a number of these critical circumstances, it's important for all of us to remember
that here and there such schools do come into being and that there is
therefore good reason to strive to create them. It sure beats the alternative
of giving up before we try and falling victim to a self-fulfilling prophecy.

Equally important, at least some of the circumstances that make such
schools possible *can* sometimes be counted on. Here Beit Rabban is illus-
trative: although the presence of a sufficient clientele with the right profile
and sufficient financial resources to enable the school to function may
count as "unlikely circumstances" in a place like Madison, Wisconsin, they
are not, as the case of Beit Rabban shows, so unlikely in a big metropolitan
area like Manhattan. As with many other businesses, location is a key to
success.

---

[136]George Dennison, *The Lives of Children* (New York: Random House, 1969).
[137]This is a verbatim excerpt from the helpful response that a reading of the Beit Rabban manuscript elicited from my friend and colleague Professor Francis Schrag of the
University of Wisconsin.

This is not to deny that some of the critical circumstances cannot be readily engineered, the most important one being the identification and recruitment of effective and truly visionary leaders; for such people are not, and never will be, a dime a dozen. But even in this arena, we need not be entirely passive. If we genuinely believe in the need for visionary leaders, we can act in such a way as to make this "unlikely circumstance" much more likely than it would otherwise be. This was essentially what Plato recommended: having determined that visionary leadership is essential to the maintenance of a community that is, in the deepest sense, thriving, he insisted on the importance of developing social and educational practices that would facilitate identifying appropriate individuals and offering them the kind of education that would fit them for their vocation of leadership. Analogous considerations apply to our own situation: our community (general or Jewish) is unlikely to produce exceptional educational institutions organized around powerful visions if it does not insistently and thoughtfully address the need to identify and attract potentially strong leaders and to educate them in such a way that their capacity for vision-guided leadership is nurtured.

But we are only likely to approach this challenge in a serious way if we are convinced that we need to be creating vision-guided schools. This is one of the reasons why it is important to disseminate portraits of institutions like Beit Rabban. If successful, such portraits will inspire those who make educational policy to seek out and adopt strategies for the cultivation of visionary leaders; they will inspire educators to develop or to seek employment in congenial vision-guided educational environments; and they will inspire parents to demand and search for such schools for their children.

Now perhaps it's true that there is little likelihood of transforming public schools that are trapped in the tentacles of numerous, and often mutually conflicting, bureaucracies and constituencies into vision-guided schools (though, again, we should not forget that this does sometimes happen).[138] But the fact (if it's a fact) that most public schools are thus trapped by no means establishes the impossibility of creating more than a very few vision-guided schools. It could just as well, and more aptly, be used to establish the need to dismantle the existing system of education and to re-

---

[138]Deborah Meier's experience with Central Park East in New York powerfully illustrates what can be achieved in a public school setting if a passionate, intelligent, visionary leader is put in charge and is freed from some of the normal bureaucratic constraints that hem in most schools. See *The Power of Their Ideas* (Boston: Beacon Press, 1995).

place it with organizational practices and structures that would encourage the emergence of such schools. Whether, as I mentioned in an earlier letter to Alice, voucher plans are a good idea is not something I want to comment on right now; but it seems to me that one argument for voucher plans is precisely that they may be more conducive to the growth of schools that are organized around powerful visions.

And what about people like Alice? I don't know her well enough to speak about her potential to exercise visionary leadership; but let's assume for the moment that she doesn't have the capacity, the genius, to use my friend's word, to become a visionary leader like you or A.S. Neill. And let's also assume (something which I think is true) that she lacks the depth of Jewish knowledge that you possess. Is it unrealistic to hope that, if she comes to appreciate what you have achieved in your school, she will be better off? I don't think so, and here's why.

Even if Alice lacks the clarity and depth that inform your vision of the aims of education, the encounter with Beit Rabban has given her an understanding and appreciation for the way in which a conception of the aims of education can seriously inform the design of an educational institution in matters as different as physical organization, hiring, curriculum, pedagogy, and evaluation. Whereas, before, she might well have felt—and I actually think she did!—that there was little to be gained by giving thought to one's guiding educational priorities (that is, to questions of vision), now she understands that it is essential for her to identify a set of educational aspirations and to think systematically about how they might be expressed in the life of her school. I'll grant that the guiding vision she comes up with, alone or in the company of her parent community, may not be terribly sophisticated or even enjoy universal support; but I am guessing that even a little clarity in this area can go a long way in helping to give coherence to a school.[139] I tried to make this point to Alice by showing how even a crudely developed, but serious, commitment to foster *gemilut hesed* could help give significant direction to an educating institution.

---

[139]The point is analogous to one made by Dewey concerning the place of foresight in human affairs. Dewey says that even under the best of circumstances, our ability to predict the future is slight, and for this and other reasons he warns against making control of the future the principal focus and aim of present deliberation; but, he adds, "control of the future is indeed precious in exact proportion to its difficulty, its moderate degree of attainment." However slight it may be, the control over the future that may be achievable through the exercise of intelligent foresight is significant and ought not to be undervalued. See John Dewey, *Human Nature and Conduct* (New York: Modern Library, 1950), 266.

And this brings me to my friend's comment about inspiration. He makes it sound as if inspiration is nice but ineffectual. I'm not convinced that that is true. If, as I believe, Alice has been genuinely inspired by Beit Rabban and by the role that you played in sustaining it, there is a good chance that this will energize, guide, and actually improve her own efforts in significant ways. Not in all arenas perhaps, but in ways that are more than marginal.

That said, as I reflected on my friend's comments, I became uncomfortable with my failure to advise Alice to engage in some sustained and serious study of sources, both Jewish and general, that will deepen her deliberations concerning the kind of people and community her school should be trying to cultivate. Just as someone who wants to create a "learning community" is likely to approach the challenge more thoughtfully after encountering, comparing, and developing a personal stance towards different conceptions of what a learning community is, so too in the case of people deliberating about the kinds of human beings their school should try to cultivate: they too will benefit from a serious encounter with different views that address this matter. True, I urged her in this direction, but I think I may have underplayed the amount of study and reflection she should undertake. Alice would, I think, benefit from a serious program of study that helps her think systematically about the kinds of people Jewish education should be striving to cultivate, accompanied by the opportunity to think carefully about educational strategies, policies, and practices that might advance this agenda.

So these were my reactions to my friend's response to our correspondence. As you can see, I remain optimistic—though I confess to moments of doubt—about the potential of schools like Beit Rabban, if well-publicized, to have a positive effect on education. Which is why I would like to make public my correspondence with Alice and with you.

All the best.
Daniel

APPENDIX
Family Chumash Learning

A s mentioned in the main body of the text, family learning added an important dimension to the education that Beit Rabban offered its students at the time of this study. Though my intention here is to illuminate the family Torah learning that the school encouraged all families to participate in each weekend, it is noteworthy that the challenges were by no means limited to specifically *Jewish* learning; indeed, the families often received "family math challenges," which would regularly appear in the *Beit Rabban Newsletter*.

Family Torah learning was not understood as an opportunity for the parents to review class material with their child or to test his or her learning; rather, it seemed designed to catalyze genuine conversations among members of the family concerning a text in the Torah that the child had been studying—shared inquiries in which the child could function as an integral participant. In the case of the kindergarten/first grade class, the questions brought home by the children were questions they themselves generated in the course of their study of the *parshat hashavua* [the weekly Torah portion]. Below are some representative questions voiced by the youngsters in the course of one year and brought home by them for family discussion:[140]

- Why did God give the land of Canaan to Avraham [Abraham]? (Genesis 12)
- Why did God test Avraham? (Genesis 22)

---

[140]These questions are drawn from the *Beit Rabban Newsletter*, Vol. 5, No. 1, Fall, 1995—Setav, 5756, 2–3.

- Why did Avraham want to pay for the land where he was going to bury Sara? (Genesis 23)
- Why did Rivka [Rebecca] want Yaakov [Jacob] to get the blessing instead of Esav [Esau]? (Genesis 27)
- Why was Yaakov surprised to find that God was in the place where Yaakov slept? (Genesis 28)
- Why did Yosef [Joseph] want Binyamin [Benjamin] to come to Mitzrayim [Egypt]? (Genesis 42)
- What made Yosef finally decide to say who he was? (Genesis 45)
- Why did Yaakov [the grandfather] bless Menashe and Ephraim, instead of Yosef blessing them? Why didn't Yaakov bless his other grandsons? (Genesis 48)

In the case of older children, the questions brought home for discussion related to topics the children were currently studying in the course of their ongoing study of Torah. In Letter 3, the reader encounters one example of such questions. Below I include a few others.

- Discuss with your family what it is that causes God to decide to confuse the languages of the human beings. (Note: You might be interested in comparing 11:6 [Genesis] to 3:22, both of which have the following structure: *vayo'mer hashem . . . hen . . . v'ata . . .*)
- *Bereishit Rabba* (a collection of *midrashim* from about fifteen hundred years ago) includes a disagreement between two sages as to whether God was pleased or displeased with Avram [Abraham's given name] after Lot and Avram separated. How do you evaluate Avram's behavior in this story? Make sure to review chapter 13 [in *Genesis*] before discussing this question. Please write down your family's ideas below. *Shabbat Shalom.*
- As we studied chapter 15 [Genesis], a lot of questions came up about the ritual of the covenant between God and Avram—*brit bein habetarim*. Here are a few of the questions which the children raised: Why did Avram need to take animals, and why these specific animals? Do these animals symbolize something and, if so, what? Why does Avram cut the animals but not the birds? Some children wondered, if these are symbols of the covenant, why doesn't God explain this, as God explained to Noach [Noah] that the rainbow is a symbol of the covenant (chapter 9); this led to consideration of similarities and differences between Noach and Avram and between God's covenants with Noach and Avram.

This weekend, please read over chapter 15 as a family. Please discuss the elements of the ritual and how you think they might be connected to what God is telling Avram. Please write down your family's ideas below. Shabbat Shalom.

.

Bibliography

Ahad Ha-Am. "Moses." In *Selected Essays*. Philadelphia: Jewish Publication Society, 1912, 307–329.

Aristotle. *Nicomachean Ethics*. Indianapolis: The Bobbs-Merrill Company, 1962.

Beit Rabban Newsletter, Vol. 5, No. 1, Fall, 1995—Setav, 5756, 2–3.

Beit Rabban Newsletter, Vol. 5, No. 2, Spring 1996—Aviv, 5756.

Beit Rabban Newsletter, Vol. 7, No. 1, Winter 1998—Choref, 5758.

Bettelheim, Bruno. *The Children of the Dream: Communal Child-Rearing and American Education*. London: McMillan Company, 1969.

Boyd, William Lowe, and Herbert J. Walberg, eds. *Choice in Education: Potential and Problems*. Berkeley: McCutchan Publishing Corporation, 1990.

Blumberg, Ilana. "Learning Chesed: Community Service in a Kindergarten Classroom." In *Kerem: Creative Explorations in Judaism*. Spring 1995, 53–56.

Bruner, Jerome. *The Process of Education*. New York: Vintage Books, 1963.

_____. *Toward a Theory of Instruction*. Cambridge, MA: Belknap Press of Harvard University Press, 1966.

Bryk, Anthony S., Valerie E. Lee, and Peter B. Holland. *Catholic Schools and the Common Good*. Cambridge, MA: Harvard University Press, 1993.

Coleman, James. *Equality and Educational Opportunity*. Washington, D.C.: U.S. Government Printing Office, 1966.

Commission on Jewish Education in North America. *A Time to Act*. Lanham: University Press of America, 1991.

Cookson, Peter W. *School Choice: The Struggle for the Soul of American Education*. New Haven: Yale University Press, 1994.

Counts, George S. *Dare the School Build A New Social Order?* New York: Arno Press & The New York Times, 1969.

Cusick, Philip. *The Egalitarian Ideal and the American High School*. New York: Longman, 1983.

George Dennison. *The Lives of Children*. New York: Random House, 1969.

Dewey, John. *The Child and the Curriculum/The School and Society*. Chicago: Phoenix Books, 1956.

_____. *Democracy and Education*. New York: The Free Press, 1944.

_____. *Experience and Education*. New York: Touchstone, 1997.

_____. *Human Nature and Conduct: An Introduction to Social Psychology*. New York: The Modern Library, 1950.

_____. "Interpretation of the Savage Mind." In *Philosophy, Psychology, and Social Practice*, edited by Joseph Ratner. New York: Capricorn Books, 1965, 281–294.

_____. *Moral Principles in Education*. Carbondale and Edwardsville: Southern Illinois University Press, 1975.

Dorff, Elliot. "Pluralism." In *Frontiers of Jewish Thought*, edited by Stephen T. Katz. Washington, D.C.: B'nai Brith Books, 1992, 213–233.

Dweck, Carol S. *Self-Theories: Their Role in Motivation, Personality, and Development*. Philadelphia: Psychology Press, Taylor & Francis, 2000.

Dworkin, Gerald. *The Theory and Practice of Autonomy*. Edited by Sydney Shoemaker, *Cambridge Studies in Philosophy*. Cambridge: Cambridge University Press, 1988.

Erikson, Erik H. *Childhood and Society*. 2nd ed. New York: W.W. Norton & Company, 1963.

_____. *Identity: Youth and Crisis*. New York: W.W. Norton & Company, 1968.

Fox, Seymour. "Towards a General Theory of Jewish Education," in *The Future of the American Jewish Community*, edited by David Sidorsky. Philadelphia: Jewish Publication Society, 1973, 260–271.

_____ and William Novak. *Vision at the Heart: Lessons from Camp Ramah on the Power of Ideas in Shaping Educational Institutions*. Jerusalem & New York: The Mandel Institute and The Council for Initiatives in Jewish Education, 1997.

_____, Israel Scheffler, and Daniel Marom, eds. *Visions of Jewish Education*. Cambridge: Cambridge University Press, 2003.

Friedman, Milton. *Capitalism and Freedom*. Chicago: University of Chicago Press, 1962.

Goldberg, Myla. *Bee Season*. New York: Anchor Books, 2000.

Greer, Colin. *The Great School Legend: A Revisionist Interpretation of American Public Education*. New York: The Viking Press, 1972.

Halbertal, Moshe. *People of the Book: Canon, Meaning, and Authority*. Cambridge: Harvard University Press, 1997.

_____ and Tova Hartman Halbertal. "Yeshiva," in *Philosophers on Education*, edited by Amelia Oksenberg Rorty. London: Routledge, 1998, 458–469.

Heilman, Samuel. *Defenders of the Faith*. New York: Schocken Books, 1992.

Henry, Jules. *Culture Against Man*. New York: Vintage Books, 1965.

Holtz, Barry, ed. *Back to the Sources: Reading the Classic Jewish Texts*. New York: Simon and Schuster, 1984.

_____. *Textual Knowledge: Teaching the Bible in Theory and Practice*. New York: Jewish Theological Seminary Press, 2003.

Huxley, Aldous. *Island*. New York: Bantam Books, 1962.

James, William. *Talks to Teachers*. New York: Henry Holt & Co., 1899.

_____. "The Will to Believe," in *Pragmatism and Other Essays*. New York: Washington Square Press, 1963, 193–213.

Jencks, Christopher. *Inequality*. New York: Basic Books, 1972.

Kaestle, Carl. *Pillars of the Republic*. New York: Hill and Wang, 1983.

Kant, Immanuel. *Groundwork of the Metaphysic of Morals*. Translated by H.J. Paton. New York: Harper & Row, 1964.

Katz, Michael B. *Class, Bureaucracy, & Schools: The Illusion of Educational Change in America*. New York: Praeger, 1975.

Kohn, Alfie. *Punished by Rewards: The Trouble with Gold Stars, Incentive Plans, A's, Praise, and Other Bribes*. Boston: Houghton Mifflin, 1999.

Lampert, Magdalene. "The Teacher's Role in Reinventing Mathematical Knowing in the Classroom." Institute for Research on Teaching, College of Education, Michigan State University, 1988.

Lawrence-Lightfoot, Sara. *The Good High School: Portraits of Character and Culture*: Basic Books, 1983.

_____, and Jessica Hoffman Davis. *The Art and Science of Portraiture*. San Francisco: Jossey-Bass, 1997.

Lieberman, Myron. *Privatization and Educational Choice*. New York: St. Martin's Press, 1989.

Mann, Horace. *The Republic and the School*. New York: Teachers College Press, 1957.

Mayhew, Katherine and Anna Camp Edwards. *The Dewey School*. New York: Atherton Press, 1966.

Meier, Deborah. *The Power of Their Ideas: Lessons for America from a Small School in Harlem*. Boston: Beacon Press, 1995.

Metz, Mary. "Desegregation as Necessity and Challenge." *Journal of Negro Education*. Vol. 63, No. 1, 1994, 64–75.

Neill, A.S. *Summerhill School: A New View of Childhood*. New York: St. Martin's Press, 1992.

Nisan, Mordecai. *"Educational Identity" as a Primary Factor in the Development of Educational Leadership*. Jerusalem: Mandel Institute, 1997.

Peirce, C. S. "The Fixation of Belief." In *Charles Sanders Peirce: Selected Writings*, edited by Philip P. Wiener. New York: Dover Books, 1966, 91–112.

Pekarsky, Daniel. "Dewey's Conception of Growth Reconsidered." *Educational Theory*, 40(03) (Summer), 283–294.

_____. "Dewey's Groundwork." In *Educational Deliberations*, edited by Mordecai Nisan and Oded Schremer. Jerusalem: Keter Publishing House and the Mandel Foundation, 2005, 119–139.

_____."Education and Manipulation." *Philosophy of Education* (1977), 354–62.

_____. "Guiding Visions and Educational Planning." In *Curriculum and Consequence*, edited by B. Franklin. New York: Teachers College Press, 2000, 15–29.

_____. "The Place of Vision in Jewish Educational Reform." *Journal of Jewish Education* 63, no. 1–2 (1997), 31–40.

_____. "Socratic Teaching: A Critical Assessment." In *Journal of Moral Education.* Vol. 23, No. 2, 1994, 119–134.

_____. "Vision and Education." In *Judaism & Education: Essays in Honor of Walter I. Ackerman,* edited by Haim Marantz. Beer-Sheva, Israel: Ben Gurion University of the Negev Press, 1998, 277–292.

Peters, Richard. "Reason and Habit: the Paradox of Moral Education." In *Philosophy of Education,* edited by Israel Scheffler. Boston: Allyn and Bacon, 1966, 245–262.

Plato. *Republic.* Translated by G.M.A. Grube. Indianapolis: Hackett Publishing Company, 1992.

Powell, Arthur G., Eleanor Farrar, and David K. Cohen. *The Shopping Mall High School: Winners and Losers in the Educational Marketplace.* Boston: Houghton Mifflin Company, 1985.

Ravitch, Diane. *The Troubled Crusade: American Education, 1940–1980.* New York: Basic Books, 1983.

Rawls, John. *A Theory of Justice.* Cambridge, MA: Belknap Press of Harvard University, 1971.

Reese, William. *The Origins of the American High School.* New Haven, Conn.: Yale University Press, 1995.

Rosenzweig, Franz. *On Jewish Learning.* Edited by Nahum Glatzer. New York: Schocken Books, 1955.

Roth, Philip. *Goodbye Columbus and Five Short Stories.* New York: Bantam Books, 1959.

Rousseau, Jean-Jacque. *Emile.* London: J.M. Dent & Sons Ltd., 1969.

_____. *The Social Contract.* Translated by Maurice Cranston. Middlesex, England: Penguin Books, 1968.

Scheffler, Israel. *In Praise of Cognitive Emotions and Other Essays in the Philosophy of Education.* New York: Routledge, Chapman, and Hall, 1991.

_____. "Observation and Subjectivity." In *Science and Subjectivity.* New York: Bobbs-Merrill, 1967.

Schlesinger, Arthur. *The Disuniting of America.* New York: W. W. Norton, 1998.

Schoem, David. "Jewish Schooling and Jewish Survival in the Suburban American Community." In *Studies in Jewish Education: Volume 2,* edited by Michael Rosenak. Jerusalem: Magnes Press, 1984, 52–64.

Silberman, Charles E. *Crisis in the Classroom: The Remaking of American Education.* New York: Random House, 1970.

Skinner, B.F. *Walden Two.* New York: MacMillan, 1948.

Smith, Marshall and Jennifer O'Day. "Systemic School Reform." In *The Politics of Curriculum and Testing: 1990 Yearbook of the Politics of Education Society,* edited by S. H. Fuhrman and Malen B. Philadelphia: Falmer, 1991, 233–267.

Snook, I.A., ed. *Concepts of Indoctrination: Philosophical Essays.* London & Boston: Routledge & Kegan Paul, 1972.

_____. *Indoctrination and Education.* London & Boston: Routledge & Kegan Paul, 1972.

Steinmetz, Devora. "A Curriculum for Developing Life-Long Learners of Text." *Jewish Education News.* Summer 1993, 14–16.

_____. "Vineyard, Farm, and Garden: The Drunkenness of Noah in the Context of Primeval History." *Journal of Biblical Literature* 113/2 (1994), 193–207.

Strauss, Leo. "What is Liberal Education?" In *An Introduction to Political Philosophy.* Edited by Hilail Gildin. Detroit: Wayne State University Press, 1989, 311–320.

Tyack, David B. *The One Best System: A History of American Urban Education.* Cambridge: Harvard University Press, 1974.

_____ and Larry Cuban. *Tinkering Towards Utopia.* Cambridge, MA: Harvard University Press, 1995.

White, Robert W. "Motivation Reconsidered: The Concept of Competence." *Psychological Review* 66 (1959), 297–333.

Willis, Paul E. *Learning to Labour.* New York: Columbia University Press, 1981.

Wirth, Louis. *John Dewey as Educator.* Huntington, NY: R. E. Krieger, 1979.

Index

Numbers followed by a colon indicate the Letter number followed by the page number.